Transnational Crime, Crime Control and Security

Series Editors
James Sheptycki
Social Science
York University
Toronto, ON, Canada

Anastassia Tsoukala
Sport Sciences
University of Paris XI Sport Sciences
Orsay, France

Transnational crime and security are key modalities of governance in a globalizing world. World-wide, there is a tendency to treat every imaginable source of harm as a potential source of insecurity, and therefore as a crime. The catastrophic imagination is fueled by the precautionary logics of a world system troubled by systemic risk. As these logics become pervasive, security measures are invoked in an effort to control the imagined sources of harm, and the consequences are not always clear-cut. Further, the terminology of transnational crime, threat, risk and (in)security (and the phenomena to which they refer) is substantively deterritorialized, raising further theoretical and practical difficulties. Research and scholarship concerning these issues touches upon crucial features of the world system. This series offers wide inter-disciplinary scope for scholarship exploring these central aspects of global governance and governance globally.

David Sausdal

Globalizing Local Policing

An Ethnography of Change and Concern Among Danish Detectives

David Sausdal
Department of Sociology
Lund University
Lund, Sweden

ISSN 2947-4264　　　　　　ISSN 2947-4272　(electronic)
Transnational Crime, Crime Control and Security
ISBN 978-3-031-18918-0　　　ISBN 978-3-031-18919-7　(eBook)
https://doi.org/10.1007/978-3-031-18919-7

© The Editor(s) (if applicable) and The Author(s), under exclusive licence to Springer Nature Switzerland AG 2023

This work is subject to copyright. All rights are solely and exclusively licensed by the Publisher, whether the whole or part of the material is concerned, specifically the rights of translation, reprinting, reuse of illustrations, recitation, broadcasting, reproduction on microfilms or in any other physical way, and transmission or information storage and retrieval, electronic adaptation, computer software, or by similar or dissimilar methodology now known or hereafter developed.

The use of general descriptive names, registered names, trademarks, service marks, etc. in this publication does not imply, even in the absence of a specific statement, that such names are exempt from the relevant protective laws and regulations and therefore free for general use.

The publisher, the authors, and the editors are safe to assume that the advice and information in this book are believed to be true and accurate at the date of publication. Neither the publisher nor the authors or the editors give a warranty, expressed or implied, with respect to the material contained herein or for any errors or omissions that may have been made. The publisher remains neutral with regard to jurisdictional claims in published maps and institutional affiliations.

This Palgrave Macmillan imprint is published by the registered company Springer Nature Switzerland AG.
The registered company address is: Gewerbestrasse 11, 6330 Cham, Switzerland

For my mormor,
*who wouldn't have understood much of this,
but who would've loved it anyway.*

Acknowledgments

Ten years ago, what you are about to read was a fleeting idea that would eventually turn into my doctoral work and thesis. A lot of time has passed. A lot of things have happened. And now the idea has come to life as an academic book in its own right. It is unfortunately impossible to mention all the people and places that have made the book possible, not to mention all the work, fun and frustration that has gone into it. I nevertheless want to give a special mention to the following friends, family and colleagues—people without whom this book would have remained a mere thought, and people without whom I would probably be doing something much different than doing fieldwork, teaching, reading, as well as writing books, papers and, yes, endless emails:

First of all, I want to thank my family for being there for me—and for allowing me the time and space that an ethnographic study necessitates. Thank you, mum, dads, brothers, sisters, Nynne and Siv. Family is important, friends too, and I am grateful for the many old and new friends I have who have always been both encouraging and overbearing. As this book is predominantly shaped and molded in academic circles, I of course also feel a great need to thank the colleagues/mentors/friends who have helped me along the way. A big thank you to all of the clever and good-hearted people at the Department of Criminology at Stockholm University, the Department of Anthropology at the University of Copenhagen, the Centre for Global Criminology (CGC) at the University of Copenhagen, the Faculty of Law at the University of Copenhagen, the Department of Criminology and Sociology of Law at the University of Oslo, the Department of Anthropology at Princeton University, ISCTE - University Institute of Lisbon and the Centre for Research in Anthropology (CRIA), as well as the Department of Sociology at Lund University. While these are the academic milieus that overall have shaped my thinking and writing, there are of course specific persons who have had a greater impact than others. Here I have to mention Henrik Vigh, Magnus Hörnqvist, Katja Franko, James Sheptycki, Helene Gundhus, Lars Holmberg, Micael Björk, Vanessa Barker, Keith Hayward, John Borneman, Paul Mutsaers, Kevin Karpiak, Thomas Bierschenk, Leanne Weber, Didier Fassin, Kjersti Lohne, Jan Beek, Hege Leivestad, Ana Aliverti, Catarina Frois and António Castelo.

One thing is the support of family, friends and colleagues. Another thing is the necessary endorsement from the people and places you as an ethnographer want to study. In my case, my study of a group of Danish detectives would of course not have been possible without the support of the Danish police and the detectives more specifically. Thanks for putting your trust in me, taking the time and allowing me to get the chance to get an insight into your workaday lives—and indeed into your various worries, which has ended up being the main focus of the book. I truly appreciate it. A special mention goes out to chief consultant Charlotte Bergen Skov and Police Inspector Jørn Kjer who, more than most, pulled the strings, not to forget about all of the individual detectives whose names have here become pseudonyms but whom I very much remember. Thank you!

Lastly, I should also remember to thank the European Research Council (ERC) under the European Union's Horizon 2020 research and innovation program (grant agreement CRIMTANG—#725194) and its generous funding, which has granted me the possibility to further explore my research into the global and transnational aspect of police work.

Copenhagen, October 2022 David Sausdal
Sincerely

Contents

1	Introduction	1
2	Xenophobia	25
3	Orwellianism	61
4	Terrorism	95
5	Cynicism	125
6	Politics	155
7	Nostalgia	193
8	Conclusion: A Policing Puzzle	217
	Bibliography	225
	Index	249

1

Introduction

> **Vignette 1**
>
> "That's globalization for you, right?", a Danish police detective assertively concludes. "With open borders and people moving around so easily and undetected it's hard to keep track. Seriously, sometimes it feels like we're trying to empty the Baltic Sea using a teaspoon. That's our job. We are the teaspoon police!" "Yeah, well put, that's exactly our job", a colleague smiles and joins in. "And we do it. Of course, we do. [Pausing for a moment]. But it also seems like these days there is not much left of what police work used to be, right? It's obvious that the world around us is changing and that policing must change with it. That's the name of the game, isn't it? However, with all these changes and all the things we now have to do and, not least, what we cannot do, I sometimes doubt whether this is something worth doing". "Hear, hear!" a third detective colleague responds, almost shouting, "It sometimes feels like we are the last real policemen! A rare and dying breed. Cheers to that!"

The above vignette and the conversation included occurred on a sunny summer day in 2015. A larger group of Danish police detectives and I, the ethnographer, were enjoying an afterhours drink on of the balconies of Copenhagen's downtown police station. Though moods were high, having just clocked off and with a weekend to look forward to, the detectives' chatter eventually turned toward the negative. While smiling and having some laughs, they also gave off a more concerned vibe. The detectives were still putting in an effort at work, yet many if not most of them also seemed to think that something was off—that something about their work was changing for the worse. On the one hand, they knew that something had to change. Trends in crime and policing were demanding this of them. On the other hand, they also seemed to feel that some of these changes were not bettering but weakening their profession. As they contemplated, could these changes mean that they were about to be the last of their kind, "the last real policemen"? Of course, the detectives were being melodramatic. They were making fun. But as I sat there, and as I had sat and been with them for many months already, I nevertheless got the sense that there were some real feelings of vocational loss hiding behind the fun-making façade.

Before going further into what the Danish detectives' concerned words might mean—and why I have chosen to kickstart the book with this exact example—I should probably introduce the study's wider context. In essence, this book and the ethnographic study that it builds on started out, like most research does, with a question. The question was the following: What does it mean to local police forces that their daily work is increasingly becoming a part of a more global world order? Or, as I have sometimes rephrased the question when talking to family and friends, how is it affecting police work in Denmark that the criminals they are chasing are no longer just Danish Kasper from around the corner, but, growingly so, individuals from countries outside of Denmark?

In the pages that make up this book, I will provide some answers to the above questions, showing how a group of Danish detectives responded to the new and more internationally oriented work tasks that they are increasingly asked to do. Put in a more disciplinary vernacular, this book and its chapters may therefore be seen as an attempt to respond to a recurring call for further research into what Bowling has discussed as "the globalization of *local* policing" (Bowling, 2009). Though Bowling already pointed to this specific globalizing process and the need to know more about it more than a decade ago (and although many other criminologists and policing scholars alike have similarly called for more detailed and preferably ethnographic insights into not just the globalization of conventional public policing but local criminal justice more broadly (cf. Sheptycki, 2005; Bowling & Sheptycki, 2012; Pakes, 2012; Lemieux, 2013; Sheptycki, 2018; Franko, 2019; Vigh & Sausdal, 2021), few studies have come to light (see however Bowling & Kopf, 2017; Feldman, 2019; Olwig et al., 2019; Aliverti, 2021). This is a shame. Because even though it remains valuable to focus on the growth of various international and transnational policing collaborations such as Europol (Deflem, 2006; Den Boer & Bruggeman, 2007; De Bolle, 2020; Safjański & James, 2020), Interpol (Anderson, 1989; Sheptycki, 2004; Stalcup, 2013; San, 2022), UNODC (Blaustein et al., 2020; Blaustein et al., 2021) or Frontex (Andersson, 2014; Aas & Gundhus, 2015; Franko, 2021), much police work, be it more globally or locally oriented, is at the end of the day carried out by individual countries' police forces. Though causes and consequences may be discussed and sought countered in many an international forum, it is still very much up to the Danish, Dutch, United States, Indian, South African police, and so on, to deal with the actual crimes and criminals. According to Bowling and Sheptycki, this is why there is a need for a broader "social-spatial typology of transnational policing", which doesn't only encompass the more obvious global, transnational and otherwise international examples, but which also examines how "local policing agencies and units [become] transnationally linked" (2012, p. 25).

The Field, Methods and Study

To help fill the above-described knowledge gap, I set out to do an in-depth ethnographic study on the matter, hoping to use the Danish police as a telling case study. The main part of the study was carried out in 2015 from February through August, while also including lots of follow-up observations and interviews. Choosing the Danish police as a specific case in point was a matter of relevance but also convenience. I am myself Danish and, from prior studies and engagements (see Sausdal, 2014), I already had some valuable contacts within the both lower and higher echelons of the Danish police who would help me gain access and make the project feasible. Moreover, the Danish police were, and still are, of particular relevance in wanting to understand how local policing is affected by globalizing trends. Like many countries worldwide, Denmark has experienced a significant increase in the number of crimes carried out by foreign nationals (Kruize, 2016; Kruize & Sorensen, 2017). In addition to this, the Danish police often think of and present themselves as a police force especially willing and able to contribute to the growth and advancement of international-cum-global policing efforts (Hestehave, 2017; Dansk_Politi, 2018; Christensen, 2021). The influx of cross-border crime coupled with their pronounced self-interest in becoming more global made the Danish police a worthwhile study object.

After some prolonged negotiations with the Danish National Police management, I was eventually granted access. Such negotiations are never easy and straightforward (cf. Punch, 1979; Reiner & Newburn, 2007; Björk, 2018). As a notoriously skeptical and self-protective organization, the police are rarely thrilled about the prospect of allowing in outsiders. This was also true in my case. As Danish policing researcher and ethnographer, Holmberg (2014, 2015), has rightly pointed to, the Danish police, following what he sees as an international trend, have arguably become increasingly disinclined to allow external researchers to look them over their shoulders. This, Holmberg argues (2015), has to do with a combination of an amplified focus on organizational control and appearance as well as the fact that the police themselves have increasingly been employing academics. The police's growing employment of and otherwise contracting with academics to conduct the exact analyses the police find fitting have potentially lessened their interest in working with external and impartial university researchers.

Given that the (Danish) police don't feel compelled to automatically allow an outside eye to study their daily work and given how they themselves have a certain research capacity, the externally based researcher, like myself, has to be able to point to the potential worth of his/her study, not just in scholarly terms but in terms of how it may also benefit the police. I was in luck however. In wanting to research how the Danish police were transitioning into a more global order, I had chosen a subject of great interest to them. As already mentioned, the Danish police do acknowledge the challenge of transnational, cross-border crimes as well as the subsequent need for them to develop new and fitting means of countering these. At the time of my study, the police also acknowledged how this was a transformation not easily implemented—problems of implementation still spoken about today and of particular interest to this book. Therefore, in my suggesting to ethnographically study the types of investigative work mostly affected by the transition, I was offering the police management a potential insight to the problems it was causing as well as its potential solutions. The management accepted. We signed a contract. And after some more meetings and email-correspondences, two specific field sites were chosen that would allow me to examine the workday of globalized local policing.

The first designated field site was a detective unit named Task Force Burglary (TFB). TFB was established and commenced its work in 2012 as a special investigation unit specifically tasked with combatting a massive increase in burglaries in Denmark primarily thought to be caused by international thieves (Kruize, 2016; Kruize & Sorensen, 2017). The task force was strategically placed in the affluent suburbs north of Copenhagen as part of the police station, *Station South*, which is one of the North Zealand Police District's four major police stations. The North Copenhagen suburbs with their many mansions and villas were (and still are) among the places that are most often targeted by burglars, which was also why it was decided to place a committed burglary police task force in the vicinity. What made TFB special was that it, unlike other traditional police units organized under one of Denmark's 12 regional police districts (14 if including Greenland and the Faroe Islands), were mandated to work and operate across district lines. And not just that. It was expected of TFB and its detectives to increasingly collaborate with relevant international partners in their daily efforts to locate and convict cross-border criminals. Furthermore, the task force had been granted state-of-the art surveillance and information technologies alongside its own covert stakeout unit, all this to up its chances of success. As the national management itself put it: "TFB is in this way a kind of pilot—a pilot project of future police work better focused on global more than just local issues".

TFB doesn't exist anymore but has instead become a part of a larger national unit with a similar focus on particularly complex and cross-border crimes. At the time of my observations, however, TFB consisted of around 20 police detectives, all selected for their prowess in investigating cross-border crimes. The detectives were organized into smaller investigation teams, with each team usually working its own cases. In addition to the employment of police detectives, three criminal prosecutors were stationed at TFB to work exclusively with TFB cases. This everyday involvement of prosecutors is not common in a Danish policing context given, among other things, by the fact that the Danish police themselves, and not the prosecutor's office, are mandated to run and lead criminal investigations—a discretionary power which the Danish police prides itself on and which is a rarity when looking at the division of labor between the police and prosecutors in many other countries. Besides the detectives and the prosecutors, TFB was also the home of a crime and data analyst, a liaison officer from Romania, as well as for the occasional interpreters who were assisting the detectives with their many cases involving foreign nationals. The entire TFB personnel was headed by three senior officers, who comprised the TFB management. In terms of demography, the personnel employed at TFB were predominantly male, ethnic Danes, in-between 35 and 65 years-old, and most of them, the detectives particularly, from a middle or lower middle-class background.

The second field site chosen for my fieldwork was that of Task Force Pickpocketing (TFP), a task force which, comparable to TFB, had been established on the back of significantly increasing crime numbers and political pressures (Kruize, 2016). TFP was however not an actual task force in the same sense as TFB. Instead, TFP was a smaller group of specialized and highly experienced detectives who were organized under the Copenhagen Police's Theft and Robbery Section. When I first visited them in early 2013, during a pilot study (Sausdal, 2014, their office were located at Copenhagen Central Station. Later, when I began my larger ethnographic fieldwork in 2015, they had been given a corner office on the 5th floor at Copenhagen Police's *Station City*—Copenhagen's most well-known police station located in downtown Copenhagen, not far from the central station and just next to the meat-packing district. This is a part of Copenhagen (in)famous for accommodating an urban mix of street criminals, prostitutes, pimps, drug dealers, users, tramps, tourists and, signalling its ongoing gentrification, many young and hip Copenhageners.

The TFP mandate, the TFP organization as well as its workday were both similar and different from that of TFB. One major similarity was that a considerable amount of time at TFP was also spent investigating and apprehending cross-border criminal suspects—foreign nationals who however were not suspected of burglary but, as the task force's name communicates, pickpocketing. Although "pickpocketing" sounds like a petty crime in the style of Oliver Twist, and although it in legal terms is a petty crime, pickpocketing in the case of the TFP-detectives' daily work involved a wide range of criminal acts, many of which are more serious and complex. Though they did investigate the occasional stealing of a mobile phone or a wallet, the TFP detectives mostly worked with the kinds of organized pickpocketing and fraud known as "shoulder surfing". "Shoulder surfing" is when a criminal observes a person's credit card pin, for example by looking over the person's shoulder, and then steals the card and uses it to take out a large sum of cash. In addition, TFB also worked other cases of credit card fraught, for example investigating cases of "skimming" where a device is mounted top of a cash machine in order to scan, copy and possibly sell-off the credit card data. And they also investigated suspects posing as police officers to scam and steal from gullible tourists. During my time with them, TFP consisted of five to six detectives, though, when running bigger cases or larger operations, often aided by colleagues from the Eastern Foreigner Control Section (EFCS). The TFP detectives were all male. Most were between 30 and 40 years old, although one of them was significantly older, with 30 years of experience working with pickpocket policing. The detectives were all ethnic Danes. And like the detectives at TFB, they all came from a middle-class or lower-middle-class background.

All in all, I ended up spending more than 1000 hours observing the task forces' detectives' daily work. I was with them day and night, making an effort to report for (field)work when they did. My time with the Danish detectives also included several interviews with close colleagues of theirs as well as national and international experts. I interviewed representatives from the Danish National Police, Europol, Eurojust, Interpol, Frontex and UNODC in order to get an understanding of the (dis)connections between the detectives' local work and the larger global policing network they were part of—or to study how the Danish detectives were indeed "transnationally linked" (Bowling & Sheptycki 2012, p. 25). In terms of the detectives' day-to-day work, I got to follow, observe and listen to them as they sat in front of their computers, writing up cases, using various computer programs to locate, disseminate and analyze cross-border criminal activity, as well as checking up on the different kinds of surveillance they had running. At TFB especially, the detectives had a range of surveillance technologies at their disposal such as wiretaps, hidden cameras, bugs, GPS trackers and, more recently, license plate scanners. During my fieldwork, I also participated in the task forces' many daily briefings and meetings as well as in the occasional kitchen, canteen and off-work chatters. And I of course was also together with the detectives when they left their offices. I was there when there went on stake-outs, when they went to check up on or install surveillance equipment, to conduct searches, to make arrests, to interview suspects, witnesses or victims or to visit colleagues, and often got to accompany them for their obligatory days in court or when they occasionally had to transport suspects to and from jailhouses.

Unfortunately, due to contract clauses, I am not allowed to go into too much detail, especially when it comes the particularities of the task forces' surveillance technologies and practices as the police see these as "secrets of the trade". As the National Police Management reasoned: "We can't have the criminals know exactly what we can and cannot do. They are already way ahead of us in this global day and age, so there is no reason us giving away the few advantages we do have". Though understanding the police's reasoning, it is admittedly a limitation of the study that I won't be able to offer more precise details as to their surveillance practices. There is no denying the great scholarly as well as public interest in charting the finer and often clandestine details of (cross-border/transnational) detective work (see also Ericson, 1981; Hobbs, 1988; Marx, 1988; Gill & Hart, 1997; Innes, 2003; Loftus & Goold, 2012; Loftus et al., 2015; Bacon, 2017; Hartmann et al., 2018; Feldman, 2019; Loftus, 2019). Yet, as this book is more concerned with the detectives' various appreciations of their (globalized) work more than its detailed application (something I will soon return to), a lack of information into the minutiae of the detectives' surveillances is possibly less of an issue.

Observing the task forces' detectives weren't easy. Being granted official access by the police management, for example, is often not enough to have actual full and undisclosed access (Reiner & Newburn, 2007; Hunt, 1984; Punch, 1989). Although frontline officers may formally accept management orders, thus allowing the ethnographer to show up, this doesn't mean that they accept the ethnographer per se. Mutual rapport has to established. Frontline officers will measure up the ethnographer, trying to gauge whether s/he can be trusted or not. This was also very much the case in my studies of the two task forces. As I also discuss in a newly published paper, the detectives constantly trying to figure out whether I was a good or bad "collaborator" (Sausdal, 2023). Keeping in mind the contronymic meaning of the word, they often aired their thoughts on whether I was there to help *or* spy, as a friend *or* foe, collaborating with them *or* with believed enemies such as the media or liberal-minded academics. By and large, their questions remained unanswered. I told them that I was interested in understanding how their work was affected by being more oriented toward global issues, and that I was hoping to be able provide some useful suggestions. But I also kept reminding them that it was important for me to remain impartial. While usually accepting my explanation, the vagueness of my response didn't make their apprehensions go away. As others have also highlighted, most if not all police ethnography consists of such constant apprehension toward the ethnographer (cf. Punch 1989, Reiner & Newburn 2007). While the ethnographer over time may become increasingly accepted and trusted by frontline officers, doubts remain. Doubts become endemic more than episodic to police ethnography, something to be constantly dealt with (cf. Sausdal, 2023).

Though I am perfectly aware of how we as police ethnographers can never be sure that we will become privy to every last aspect of the people and lives we study, I did however never experience the Danish detectives refusing to talk to me or not allowing me to be present. I can't of course with any certainty say that they didn't steer me away from certain aspects of their work or that their conversations weren't moderated because of my presence. Nevertheless, as this book and its various empirical examples are a testament to, the detectives didn't seem to shy away from speaking about a range of controversial issues. More than once was I told that "this better not be on the frontpage tomorrow", signaling that the detectives knew that what they were about to say wasn't (at all) politically correct or, for that matter, fully within the confines of their work regulations (see also Reiner & Newburn 2007). What eventually gave me such privileged insight into what I believe to be very close to their actual practices and perceptions—this backstage look behind the "smokescreen" often laid out by the police in relation to the public (Van Maanen, 1973)—might have something to do with who I am and how I was perceived. Being an at the time 30-year-old, white, heterosexual, Danish "bloke" from the countryside, who is fond of football, beers and banter, and who has family members in the Danish police force, I probably had a comparatively easier time making the detectives trust and relate to me. Recalling the demographic layout of the task forces (or the entire Danish police for that matter), my background was quite similar. Besides being skeptical of my academic intentions, there is therefore the chance that detectives felt more at ease as I they had an easier time seeing themselves in me than they would have had had I strayed more from the average police demographic. "David's alright". "He's okay". "He can be trusted, can't you?", "He's allowed to be here", were estimations I often encountered as the detectives would tell new colleagues about me, signaling their believed yet also fragile confidence in my trustworthiness.

Everyday Dissatisfactions

Speaking of "being there"—of the ethnographer being allowed to be present and observe what the police *actually* do and say in their daily work (see Bacon et al., 2020)—I was there when the disillusioned conversation mentioned in the introduction's very beginning occurred. Returning to the detectives' peculiar chinwag, the question remains why I have chosen to start the book by recounting these words and not others? During the time I spent with the task forces, I filled my moleskins and portable recorder with numerous examples of their work, dialogues and viewpoints. Looking over my notes and recordings, I could have chosen to focus on many different aspects of how believed globalizing processes were affecting the detectives' workday. Nevertheless, one aspect quickly came into focus. Though the Danish detectives carried out their work in what to me seemed as a professional and committed way, and although the detectives had many different thoughts on the matter, one central sentiment kept resurfacing: They were frustrated. The task forces' detectives—and many of their colleagues whom I also encountered—continuously complained about the current state of their work. And, of specific interest to my research focus, very often their complaining was framed in relation to the Danish police dealing with what they interchangeably spoke of as "a more global world", "globalization", "international developments", "outside changes" or "foreign issues"—issues they believed to overshadow more conventional, local interests. Among the detectives, globalization, and the globalizing of local policing in particular, were not met with much enthusiasm.

This is perhaps not that surprising. As many studies have already shown (cf. Chan, 1997; Holmberg, 2003; Manning, 2006; Loftus, 2009; Westmarland, 2015; Martin, 2018; Cockcroft, 2020), police officers are known to be quite conservative and skeptical toward developments that threaten the(ir) status quo, and perhaps even more so when developments involve foreign issues, thus conflicting with the police's often-described tendencies toward xenophobia (cf. Bowling et al., 2004; Holdaway and O'Neill, 2006; Sollund, 2007; Chan, 2011; Mutsaers, 2019). That police detectives do not like changes brought upon them—them not liking the global, the foreign, the outside(r), and so on does indeed seem to fit an old and well-established story about the orthodox if not timeworn practices and perceptions of police officers. This much is true.

Still, a central belief of this book is that there were more to the detectives' complaining and concerns than what for example the clichéd concept of "police culture" (cf. Loftus 2009) usually implies—that is that their petulance was not simply a matter of conventional conservative police grumpiness and parochialism. As the introductory quote also hints at, the Danish detectives' disillusions were not only a matter of them not liking suspects with international passports. True. The detectives were not great fans of foreigners. Still, the detectives' disillusionments seemed less centered on their instinctive dislike of foreign nationals and were instead directed toward the many daily, vocational changes they were experiencing—changes and developments which the detectives saw as part of the globalizing policing tale. Indeed, as one of the detectives affectedly put it: "with all these changes and all the things we now have to do and, not least, what we cannot do, I sometimes doubt whether this is something worth doing".

What some of these believed "changes" and "things they now have to do" are will be covered in much more detail in the book's different chapters. As of now, to lay a foundation, the simple but important thing I wish to convey is that a day very rarely went by without the detectives seemingly carping about what their job was becoming. They detectives were complaining about how many of the things they otherwise liked about their jobs were "going down the drain". They were romanticizing about "the good old days". And they were speaking about how they believed that "these days there is not much left of what police work used to be". Some even openly contemplated leaving the police. And some did, thus adding to the international trend of police resignations (Charman & Bennett, 2022).

At first, I remember feeling mystified when hearing the detectives speak about their feelings of vocational loss, including the dramatized depiction of themselves as "the last real policemen". (Being the reason why I selected this exact example and emic epithet to launch the story I will be trying to tell here). Because, even though it may be true that many police forces are the home of a conservative-cum-traditionalist work culture, and that it is therefore expectable to find complaining and concerned police in the face of change, I was still surprised by the level of police aggravation if not apathy I encountered. Yes. Police officers are known to complain a lot. Skepticism is not just a part of their work culture but integral to police jargon and their daily bantering and storytelling (Fielding, 1994; Sollund, 2007; Waddington, 1999; cf. Kingshott and Prinsloo, 2004; van Hulst, 2013; Sausdal, 2020b). One may even say that the police like to complain, to present themselves as utter pessimists. But police speaking about themselves as the last of their kind seems to be a different story. Looking for example at the sheer expenditure on law enforcement in recent times (Farrell & Clark, 2004; Robinson, 2020), with international and transnational policing being an especially costly post, it seems ludicrous to be talking about a dying profession. Coupled with the significant not only monetary but also political and public support many police forces (still) enjoy, which is especially true of the Danish police (Justitsministeriet, 2016), one should perhaps rather speak of a rise of policing rather than a downfall—a potentially new "golden (and global) age of policing", not a gloomy one.

Golden or not, the Danish detectives did not feel particular glad. Though the specific police detective who framed them as being on the brink of extinction was guilty of embroidering, and although his detective colleagues saluted him in an openly sarcastic manner, the numerous hours I spent with the detectives did reveal that their nostalgia wasn't just fun and games. One could of course think that this particular detective's yearning for yesteryear had something to do with him being an old-timer, him simply reminiscing about the glories of the past like veteran people and professionals tend to do. But this wasn't the case. In fact, the detective who uttered the wistful words was only around 30 years old. In truth, many concerns about current developments I observed during my study were largely shared by the old as well as the young, men as well as women, white and non-white, heterosexual and otherwise. In their complaining, they stood united.

The detectives were concerned. They were frustrated. Yet, as the introductory example also shows, and thus adding to the perplexity of it all, while the detectives found the globalizing of local policing problematic, they also often found it necessary. "It's obvious that the world around us is changing and that policing must change with it", they said—a type of statement I often encountered. Put differently, the Danish detectives, and many of their colleagues, *did* understand that their old, conventional ways of working (and thinking) were not always of much use in a world of more complex and growing cross-border crime—not always of much worth in an era where criminal activities are becoming more multifaceted, digitalized and increasingly moving across borders (UNODC, 2010; Von Lampe, 2012; Siegel, 2014; Ruggiero, 2013; Bruinsma, 2015; Sheptycki, 2017; Vigh & Sausdal, 2021). Indeed, as all of the book's chapters also illustrate, the detectives' frustrations about change often came with the puzzling acceptance of the need of change. For example, as one of them told me in one of our last conversations before I eventually had to finish up my fieldwork and return to my university desk: "It's kinda like knowing that you need the medication, but also knowing that it'll probably end up killing you". Surely, this an overly crude and morbid way of seeing things—a perspective which again says a lot about the police's hankering for gallows humor and expertise in unpolished language (Sausdal, 2020b). Still, it finely emphasizes the Danish detectives' displeasure with the current state—a vocational displeasure put forth with an added splash of hopelessness.

The Structure and Content

The structure and content of the book can best be described as a theoretical smorgasbord, borrowing from and adding to an array of policing studies, yet with a keen eye on the global/transnational policing literature (cf. Anderson, 1989; Anderson et al., 1996; Sheptycki, 2000, 2002; Deflem, 2002; Andreas and Nadelmann, 2006; Nadelmann, 2010; Bowling & Sheptycki, 2012; Lemieux, 2013; Bradford et al., 2016; Feldman, 2019). Phrased differently, rather than introducing a chronological narrative or a comprehensive conceptual framework, I will be describing several different ways in which the Danish police in general, and some Danish detectives in particular, experienced and expressed concerns in the face of globalizing changes—different ways in which they found it harder and harder to do the kind of work they appreciate as both "real" and rewarding police work. While first and foremost being a contribution to existing knowledge about the globalization of (local) policing, this also means that the book includes a variety of theoretical perspectives and discussions of relevance to policing research more broadly. Importantly, an eclectic smorgasbord-approach is not chosen to confuse the reader, nor because of a lack of interest in providing a grander and more coherent narrative. It is chosen because of how it is simply the most effective and empirically sound way of illustrating the variety of ways in which global policing developments affect conventional, local policing practices and perception in Denmark and maybe even beyond. If I had chosen to only look at the gathered empirical material through one theoretical prism, I would have risked muffling the many voices and worries raised. Speaking of said voices and worries, in order to exactly allow the detectives' sentiments to be heard, the book and its chapters are built around 37 empirical vignettes combined with telling quotes and observations. The use of empirical vignettes is inspired by Emerson et al.'s (2011) advice on how to structure and write ethnography, recommending the use of ethnographic "excerpt-commentary units" (ibid., chapter 7). It should also be seen as tribute to one of the founding fathers of Danish police ethnography, Lars Holmberg, who used a similar approach in his now almost 25-year-old work on Danish patrolling officers' discretionary powers (Holmberg, 1999).

With the above in mind, I hope that the reader will appreciate how each of the vignettes and chapters tell their own unique story about the globalization of local policing while also, in combining the stories, offering up a larger perspective. Applying a musical metaphor, the book may be understood as consisting of individual chords that by themselves resonate, but which also, when piled together, form a meaningful, yet from the detectives' point of view, disharmonious melody. To start off with one of the most-debated issues in not just the global policing literature but policing research altogether, Chap. 2 delves into the issue of xenophobia. As local police officers, like Danish detectives, are increasingly introduced to a world beyond their beats, they inevitably encounter people and phenomena more foreign to them. The chapter describes and discusses this development, offering up examples that confirm but also add to existing perspectives on police xenophobia. Essentially, it is shown how many of the Danish detectives' work frustrations are related to the fact that they often find it less gratifying to police foreign nationals—a sense of loss which both frustrates and infuriates them, occasionally making the detectives direct their work frustrations and anger outward at the foreign suspects.

Chapter 3 looks in another direction. Rather than observing the police's encounters with and thoughts about their new "foreign" suspect pool, it looks at how police work is (supposed) to be carried out in an era of growing cross-border criminality. As criminal activity has become more peripatetic (traversing analogue as well digital borders), the central idea of modern-day policing is that it too should become more peripatetic. The Danish detectives and the Danish police management agree, repeatedly stressing the utmost importance thereof. They need, the say, better and more extensive collaborations with internal, external and especially international policing partners. Even more so, the police point to the necessity of a greater use, implementation and integration of various information and surveillance technologies. Yet, as the chapter illustrates, even though the task forces' detectives all agreed that they need to cooperate more with people outside their units, districts and country and, more so, make use of various new policing technologies, they remain surprisingly reluctant to do so.

Whereas Chap. 3 examines the vocational paradoxes and apprehensions that many new means of policing and monitoring criminal activities introduce, Chap. 4 touches upon another apparent enigma. A budding number of studies have during the last ten or twenty years pointed to a problematic "militarization" of public police forces (cf. Kraska, 2007). There have even been talks about the making of a "blue army" (McCulloch, 2001). In a Danish policing context, there is much truth to this. The Danish police have been increasingly mobilized and armed in attempts to counter terrorism and other external frights and crimes. Yet, as the chapter also illuminates, contrary to ruling ideas about how public police forces and conventional cops enjoy the added martial tendencies in police work, the Danish detectives I spent time with largely saw it as a depressing obstruction. More than feeling mobilized, they felt mired—feeling unhappy and often unable to take proper care of the work they are actually supposed to.

Chapter 5 goes to the heart of a heated debate within not only global policing studies but policing and criminology more broadly. Reading the available literature, a great contemporary concern is that a globalizing of policing will introduce a troubling distance between law enforcers and those at the receiving end of their powers. Be it in the form of information or surveillance technologies or added bureaucratic measures, a central idea/worry is that such "policing at a distance" (Guild & Bigo, 2017) not only comes with a decrease in human rights, transparency and accountability but also further police cynicism if not violence. As for example micro-sociological studies have also shown (Collins, 2008), it is seemingly easier for people to carry out inconsiderate and violent acts when the addressee is further removed and not physically present. In my studies of the Danish detectives' everyday work, the problems of a growing amount of policing at a distance were apparent as the detectives often just "met" their suspects as data, voice recordings or as photos on a computer screen. This development did seem to produce more cynicism and indifference among them. Nevertheless, differing from what several policing at a distance studies are arguing, I did not experience the Danish detectives appreciating being growingly removed from their suspects' everyday lives. Rather than appreciating more detached kinds of police work, the detectives were largely disliking it.

Now, it is easy to think that a police force and its officers would enjoy a day and age defined by many a criminologist and policing scholar as consisting of a "punitive turn" or "penal populism". Indeed, why wouldn't a group of Danish law enforces be relishing the fact that Danish politicians increasingly look toward stricter and more pervasive forms of law enforcement as well as harsher punishments as a productive way to deal with a range of societal fears and issues? The detectives I spent time with were certainly all strong believers in the necessary introduction of more punitive and pervasive measures (often introduced by politicians with a look toward global crimes and dangers). Yet, as Chap. 6 dissects, in their daily work, the detectives often came to the realization that the perpetual political introduction of laws and regulations were, paradoxically, often more of hindrance than help.

Chapter 7 sums up and discusses the Danish detectives' different concerns and frustration. It does so by relating them to other existing discussions on local (public) police loss and nostalgia found in the literature. As Bayley and Shearing (1996) for example pointed out more than 20 years ago, many of the changes and transformations that conventional public police forces undergo may be the cause of an "identity crisis". The chapter discusses the genesis and consequences of such a potential crisis, doing so in relation to the many examples offered throughout the book's prior chapters. In the end, the chapter includes a call for taking the issue of vocational loss and police nostalgia seriously as something more than a mere and negligeable reflection of a forever wistful, conservative and even aggressive police culture.

Following its seven chapters, the book reaches its conclusion. Though the chapters go into different territories, they also touch upon many central debates within contemporary policing research. Be it questions of police xenophobia, surveillance, technology, militarization, counterterrorism, cynicism, violence, law and order politics or nostalgia, these all rank among some of the things most-discussed in and beyond present-day studies of policing. Simultaneously, these are also essential issues in global policing literature (which is surely also why I came across these very issues). What the conclusion ultimately argues is that a growing globalizing of local policing comes with the risk of local police dissatisfaction and detachment. Though by all means understanding that their work need to change to better mirror a more globalized society, Danish detectives simultaneously feel that these changes are making for a less interesting and engaging kind of work. In a time of unparalleled policing reach and weight, a group of Danish detectives' paradoxically feel increasingly disillusioned and disoriented.

This, in essence, is the book's central finding. And though I initially argued that the book didn't really have an overarching theoretical framework, one could perhaps say that its conclusion says otherwise. Though not comprising a grander theoretical but more of an overall methodological perspective, all the chapters demonstrate the importance of (also) studying the everyday, emotive and even existential perspectives of police work (Fassin, 2017; Sausdal, 2020a). Even when dealing with big issues such as the globalizing of policing, the book serves as a reminder of the continuous worth of looking at how "globalization [is] an artefact manufactured and received in the local" (Burawoy, 2001, p. 148). In order to fully understand the various effects of (police) globalization, we have to consider its daily, quotidian practices instead of assuming its discourse. This is what Burawoy and many other ethnographers of globalization have repeatedly been arguing for over 30 years now—an argument yet again echoed throughout the following policing-related pages.

Bibliography

Aas, K. F., & Gundhus, H. O. (2015). Policing humanitarian borderlands: Frontex, human rights and the precariousness of life. *British Journal of Criminology, 55*(1), 1–18.

Aliverti, A. (2021). *Policing the borders within*. Oxford University Press.

Anderson, M. (1989). *Policing the world: Interpol and the politics of international police co-operation*. Clarendon Press.
Anderson, M., Den Boer, M., Den, M., et al. (1996). *Policing the European Union 'theory, law, and practice'*. Oxford University Press.
Andersson, R. (2014). *Illegality, Inc.: Clandestine migration and the business of bordering Europe*. University of California Press.
Andreas, P., & Nadelmann, E. (2006). *Policing the globe: Criminalization and crime control in international relations*. Oxford University Press.
Bacon, M. (2017). *Taking care of business: Police detectives, drug law enforcement and proactive investigation*. Oxford University Press.
Bacon, M., Loftus, B., & Rowe, M. (2020). Ethnography and the evocative world of policing (part I). *Policing and Society, 30*, 1–10.
Bayley, D. H., & Shearing, C. D. (1996). The future of policing. *Law and Society Review*, 585–606.
Björk, M. (2018). Politistudier—Metodologiske problemer og praktiske råd. In M. H. Jacobsen (Ed.), *Kriminologi: Metoder I* (pp. 453–481). Hans Reitzels Forlag.
Blaustein, J., Chodor, T., & Pino, N. W. (2020). Making crime a sustainable development issue: From 'drugs and thugs' to 'peaceful and inclusive societies'. *The British Journal of Criminology, 60*(1), 50–73.
Blaustein, J., Chodor, T., & Pino, N. W. (2021). Development as a historical component of the United Nations' crime policy agenda: From social defence to the millennium development goals. *Criminology & Criminal Justice, 21*(4), 435–454.
Bowling, B. (2009). Transnational policing: The globalization thesis, a typology and a research agenda. *Policing, 3*(2), 149–160.
Bowling, B., & Kopf, C. (2017). Transnational policing in Europe and its local effects. *European Law Enforcement Research Bulletin., 3*, 47–57.
Bowling, B., Phillips, C., Campbell, A., et al. (2004). Policing and human rights: Eliminating discrimination, xenophobia, intolerance and the abuse of power from police work. *Identities, Conflict and Cohesion (2000–2005), United Nations Research Institute for Social Development, 3–5 September 2001, Durban, South Africa*. 3–26.
Bowling, B., & Sheptycki, J. (2012). *Global policing*. SAGE
Bradford, B., Loader, I., Jauregui, B., et al. (2016). *The SAGE handbook of global policing*. SAGE.
Bruinsma, G. (2015). *Histories of transnational crime*. Springer.
Burawoy, M. (2001). Manufacturing the global. *Ethnography*, 2(2), 147–159.

Chan, J. (2011). Racial profiling and police subculture. *Canadian Journal of Criminology and Criminal Justice, 53*(1), 75–78.

Chan, J. B. (1997). *Changing police culture: Policing in a multicultural society.* Cambridge University Press.

Charman, S., & Bennett, S. (2022). Voluntary resignations from the police service: The impact of organisational and occupational stressors on organisational commitment. *Policing and Society, 32*(2), 159–178.

Christensen, M. J. (2021). Battles to define the Danish police. In Mbuba J. (ed) *Global Perspectives in Policing and Law Enforcement.* Rowman & Littlefield

Cockcroft, T. (2020). *Police culture: Research and practice.* Policy Press.

Collins, R. (2008). *Violence: A micro-sociological theory.* Princeton University Press.

Dansk_Politi. (2018). *Redaktionens fokus—DANSK POLIT—flot og fjernt.* Retrieved May 18, from https://dansk-politi.dk/nyheder/redaktionens-fokus-dansk-politi-flot-fjernt

De Bolle, C. (2020). The role of Europol in international interdisciplinary European cooperation. *European Police Science and Research Bulletin, 19*, 17.

Deflem, M. (2002). *Policing world society: Historical foundations of international police cooperation.* Oxford University Press.

Deflem, M. (2006). Europol and the policing of international terrorism: Counter-terrorism in a global perspective. *Justice Quarterly, 23*(3), 336–359.

Den Boer, M., & Bruggeman, W. (2007). Shifting gear: Europol in the contemporary policing era. *Politique Européenne, 23*, 77–91.

Emerson, R. M., Fretz, R. I., & Shaw, L. L. (2011). *Writing ethnographic fieldnotes.* University of Chicago Press.

Ericson, R. V. (1981). *Making crime: A study of detective work.* Butterworths.

Farrell, G., & Clark, K. (2004). What does the world spend on criminal justice? HEUNI Paper No. 20.

Fassin, D. (2017). Boredom: Accounting for the ordinary in the work of policing (France). In D. Fassin (Ed.), *Writing the world of policing: The difference ethnography makes* (pp. 269–292). University of Chicago Press.

Feldman, G. (2019). *The gray zone: Sovereignty, human smuggling, and undercover police investigation in Europe.* Stanford University Press.

Fielding, N. (1994). Cop canteen culture. In T. Newburn & E. Stanko (Eds.), *Just boys doing business* (pp. 46–63). Routledge.

Franko, K. (2019). *Globalization and crime.* SAGE Publications Limited.

Franko, K. (2021). The two-sided spectacle at the border: Frontex, NGOs and the theatres of sovereignty. *Theoretical Criminology.* https://doi.org/10.1177/13624806211007858.

Gill, M., & Hart, J. (1997). Exploring investigative policing: A study of private detectives in Britain. *The British journal of criminology, 37*(4), 549–567.
Guild, E., & Bigo, D. (2017). Policing at a distance: Schengen visa policies. *Controlling frontiers* (pp. 233–263). Routledge.
Hartmann, M. R. K., Hestehave, N. K., Høgh, L., et al. (2018). Knowing from within. *Nordisk Politiforskning, 5*(01), 7–27.
Hestehave, N. K. (2017). Predicting crime?: On challenges to the police in becoming knowledgeable organizations 1. *Moral issues in intelligence-led policing* (pp. 62–80). Routledge.
Hobbs, D. (1988). *Doing the business: Entrepreneurship, the working class, and detectives in the east end of London*. Clarendon Press.
Holdaway, S., & O'Neill, M. (2006). Institutional racism after Macpherson: An analysis of police views. *Policing and Society, 16*(4), 349–369.
Holmberg, L. (1999). *Inden for lovens rammer*. Gyldendal.
Holmberg, L. (2003). *Policing stereotypes: A qualitative study of police work in Denmark*. Galda & Wilch.
Holmberg, L. (2014). Nordisk politiforskning–udfordringer og muligheder. *Nordisk Politiforskning, 1*(01), 24–40.
Holmberg, L. (2015). Challenges to Nordic police research. In: R. Granér & E. Helgren (Eds.), *The past, the present and the future of police research: Proceedings from the fifth Nordic police research seminar,* 43.
Hunt, J. (1984). The development of rapport through the negotiation of gender in field work among police. *Human Organization, 43*(4), 283–296.
Innes, M. (2003). *Investigating murder: Detective work and the police response to criminal homicide*. Oxford University Press.
Justitsministeriet. (2016). *Danskerne har stor tillid til politi og domstole*. Retrieved February 1st 2023, from http://www.justitsministeriet.dk/nyt-og-presse/pressemeddelelser/2016/danskerne-har-stor-tillid-til-politi-og-domstole
Kingshott, B., & Prinsloo, J. (2004). The universality of the 'police canteen culture'. *Acta Criminologica, 17*(1), 1–16.
Kraska, P. B. (2007). Militarization and policing—Its relevance to 21st century police. *Policing, 1*(4), 501–513.
Kruize, P. (2016). Omrejsende kriminelle i Danmark. Det Juridiske Fakultet, Københavns Universitet. Retrieved February 1st from: https://www.justitsministeriet.dk/sites/default/files/media/Arbejdsomraader/Forskning/Forskningspuljen/Omrejsende%20kriminelle%20i%20Danmark%2009-2016.pdf

Kruize, P., & Sorensen, D. W. M. (2017). Det danske indbrudsniveau. *Det Kriminalpræventive Råd*. Retrieved February 1st 2023 from: https://dkr.dk/materialer/indbrud/det-danske-indbrudsniveau

Lemieux, F. (2013). *International police cooperation: Emerging issues, theory and practice*. Routledge.

Loftus, B. (2009). *Police culture in a changing world*. Oxford University Press.

Loftus, B. (2019a). Normalizing covert surveillance: The subterranean world of policing. *The British Journal of Sociology, 70*(5), 2070–2091.

Loftus, B., & Goold, B. (2012). Covert surveillance and the invisibilities of policing. *Criminology & Criminal Justice, 12*(3), 275–288.

Loftus, B., Goold, B., & Mac Giollabhui, S. (2015). From a visible spectacle to an invisible presence: The working culture of covert policing. *British Journal of Criminology, 56*(4), 629–645.

Manning, P. (2006). Detective work/culture. *Encyclopedia of Police Science, 2*, 390–397.

Martin, J. T. (2018). Police culture: What it is, what it does, and what we should do with it. In *The anthropology of police* (pp. 34–53). Taylor and Francis.

Marx, G. T. (1988). *Undercover: Police surveillance in America*. University of California Press.

McCulloch, J. (2001). *Blue army: Paramilitary policing in Australia*. Melbourne University Publish.

Mutsaers, P. (2019). *Police unlimited: Policing, migrants, and the values of bureaucracy*. Oxford University Press.

Nadelmann, E. A. (2010). *Cops across borders: The internationalization of US criminal law enforcement*. Penn State Press.

Olwig, K. F., Grünenberg, K., Møhl, P., et al. (2019). *The biometric border world: Technology, bodies and identities on the move*. Routledge.

Pakes, F. (2012). *Globalisation and the challenge to criminology*. Routledge.

Punch, M. (1979). Observation and the police: The research experience. In *Policing the inner city* (pp. 1–18). Springer.

Punch, M. (1989). Researching police deviance: A personal encounter with the limitations and liabilities of field-work. *The British Journal of Sociology, 40*(2), 177–204.

Reiner, R., & Newburn, R. (2007). Police research. In R. King & E. Wincup (Eds.), *Doing research on crime and justice*. Oxford University Press.

Robinson, W. I. (2020). *The global police state*. Pluto Press

Ruggiero, V. (2013) Organised and transnational crime in Europe. *The Routledge handbook of European criminology*, 154.

Safjański, T., & James, A. (2020). Europol's crime analysis system—Practical determinants of its success. *Policing: A Journal of Policy and Practice, 14*(2), 469–478.

San, S. (2022). Transnational policing between national political regimes and human rights norms: The case of the Interpol red notice system. *Theoretical Criminology.* https://doi.org/10.1177/13624806221105280

Sausdal, D. (2014). Cultural culprits: Police apprehensions of pickpockets in Copenhagen. In B. Petterson & P. Bevelander (Eds.), *Crisis and migration: Implications of the eurozone crisis for perceptions, politics, and policies of migration.* Nordic Academic Press.

Sausdal, D. (2020a). Everyday policing: Toward a greater analytical appreciation of the ordinary in police research. *Policing and Society,* 1–14.

Sausdal, D. (2020b). Police bullshit. *Journal of Extreme Anthropology, 4*(1), 94–115.

Sausdal, D. (2023). A collaborator? Ethnographic issues of police and peer suspicion. In Fleming, J & Charman. S (eds) *Routledge International Handbook of Police Ethnography.* Abingdon, Oxon: Routledge

Sheptycki, J. (2000). *Issues in transnational policing.* Routledge.

Sheptycki, J. (2002). *In search of transnational policing: Towards a sociology of global policing.* Ashgate.

Sheptycki, J. (2004). The accountability of transnational policing institutions: The strange case of Interpol. *Canadian Journal of Law and Society, 19,* 107.

Sheptycki, J. (2005). Transnational policing. *The Canadian Review of Policing Research,* 1.

Sheptycki, J. (2017). *Transnational crime and policing: Selected essays.* Routledge.

Sheptycki, J. (2018). Transnational organization, transnational law and the ambiguity of Interpol in a world ruled with law. In M. J. Christensen & N. Boister (Eds.), *New perspectives on the structure of transnational criminal justice* (pp. 65–86). Leiden.

Siegel, D. (2014). *Mobile banditry: East and central European itinerant criminal groups in the Netherlands.* Eleven International Publishing.

Sollund, R. (2007). Canteen banter or racism: Is there a relationship between Oslo Police's use of derogatory terms and their attitudes and conduct towards ethnic minorities? *Journal of Scandinavian Studies in Criminology and Crime Prevention, 8*(1), 77–96.

Stalcup, M. (2013). Interpol and the emergence of global policing. In W. Garriott (Ed.), *Policing and contemporary governance* (pp. 231–261). New York, NY.

UNODC. (2010). *The globalization of crime: A transnational organized crime threat assessment*. United Nations Office on Drugs and Crime.

van Hulst, M. (2013). Storytelling at the Police Station the canteen culture revisited. *British Journal of Criminology, 53*(4), 624–642.

Van Maanen, J. (1973). Working the street; a developmental view of police behavior. *Working paper (Sloan School of Management)*.

Vigh, H., & Sausdal, D. (2021). *Global crime ethnographies: Three suggestions for a criminology that truly travels* (p. 171). Oxford University Press.

Von Lampe, K. (2012). Transnational organized crime challenges for future research. *Crime, Law and Social Change, 58*(2), 179–194.

Waddington, P. A. (1999). Police (canteen) sub-culture. An appreciation. *British Journal of Criminology, 39*(2), 287–309.

Westmarland, L. (2015). Outsiders inside: Ethnography and police culture. In *Introduction to policing research* (pp. 163–173). Routledge.

2

Xenophobia

In thinking about how global policing and criminal trends affect a local police force, one of the first things that come to mind is the problem of xenophobia (or prejudice, discrimination, racism, etc.). As much research in both Denmark (Holmberg, 2003) and beyond (cf. Chan, 1997; Loftus, 2009; Fassin, 2013) has shown, police forces tend to be nationalist conservative organizations with, if not a direct dislike of foreign elements, then at least a skepticism toward them (for a newer Danish study on this subject, see Kammersgaard et al., 2022). It therefore makes good sense to think that a major problem of a growingly globalized local police is that it may trigger and further add to issues of police xenophobia. In having spent a considerable time with a group of Danish detectives, who increasingly have to police foreign nationals, I can conclude that this is exactly what seems to happen. Both the detectives at Task Force Burglary (TFB) as well as Task Force Pickpocketing (TFP) frequently voiced their deprecation of the many Poles, Romanians, Chileans, Moroccans as well as other foreign nationalities they encountered in their investigations. "I really don't like these people. They're real bastards who should go

---

This chapter is a reworked version of a previously published article: Sausdal, D. (2018). Pleasures of policing: An additional analysis of xenophobia. *Theoretical Criminology, 22*(2), 226–242.

back to the countries and caves they come from, if you ask me", one detective for example put it, not at all hiding his aversion.

Pondering his and the many similar views on foreign nationals I encountered during my fieldwork, this chapter may be read as a confirmation of what earlier studies have shown or suspected; namely that local police forces are places where intolerant attitudes tend to thrive, and, furthermore, that there is a risk of such attitudes propagating as the police increasingly deal with various international-cum-foreign matters (Bowling & Sheptycki, 2012, 2016; Weber & Bowling, 2013; Bowling & Westenra, 2018; Feldman, 2019; Olwig et al., 2019). While also being a confirmation thereof, this chapter, however, is first and foremost an attempt to add to our scholarly ideas about the causes and consequences of police xenophobia rather than simply substantiating them. In it, I draw attention to a much less debated source of police negativity toward foreign nationals—a source of xenophobia seldom debated in the literature, but nevertheless something I experienced as central to the detectives' disliking. Although I encountered several different examples thereof, the following incidence was what initially caught my interest:

> **Vignette 2**
>
> One late April afternoon at Station South, TFB Police Detective Jensen[1] comes into the office waving a yellow post-it note in front of me and his colleagues. "So guys, I was just talking to Gabriel [a Romanian liaison officer] who's been listening through some of the hours of tape we have on an old case. Apparently, the primary suspect was on the phone with some other Romanian guy who asked if he could help get 'a discrete means of transportation'. You know, he was asking for some wheels to use for break-ins. Gabriel gave me the number so maybe we should set up a wiretap?"
>
> I'm sitting in the corner of their small-ish office, watching Detective Jensen, who is somewhat pleased about the possibility of running "a good case" as the detectives tend to call it. However, his eagerness dwindles rather quickly when he is met by what appear to be a couple of colleagues who don't immediately share his interest. Detective Pedersen doesn't even look up from behind his computer, as he continues with his work in an almost demonstrative fashion.

(continued)

---

[1] All of the detectives' surnames used in the book are pseudonyms.

> **Vignette 2** (continued)
>
> A short moment later, however, Detective Andersen reacts, sitting at her desk across from Detective Pedersen. Without initially saying anything, she looks skeptically at the post-it that Detective Jensen is still waving in his hands in anticipation of a reply. "What do you think?" he asks her. Detective Andersen, gives it a quick thought, and then replies simply and rather sharply: "Hell no! Forget it. I don't care about those damn foreigners. I don't want anything to do with them. They are no fun. Like, seriously, don't we have another case that we can do instead? I'm sick and tired of these damn Romanians, Moroccans or whatever. They make me so angry!"
>
> Detective Jensen agrees, "Hmm … yeah, I know what you mean. But no, I don't have anything better at the moment … so, what do you think?" "I say no", Detective Andersen answers, "unless we really really have to; I prefer to stick with the cases we already have". "And you?" Detective Jensen asks Detective Pedersen, who then, for the first time, looks up only to say that he agrees with Detective Andersen. "Alright. Another time then", Detective Jensen concludes, tossing the post-it into the nearby bin whilst actually not looking overly disappointed with the group having decided not to pursue an investigation into a suspected Romanian burglary ring operating in Denmark. He sits down and turns to me in order to explain what just happened. "Yeah, to be honest, although the cases against these Romanians can be very good and although they are important, so that we can stop them from coming up here, I'm also kinda fed up".

As I sat there, just next to the three TFB detectives, following their conversation up close, I was quite baffled. Much research is pointing to the existence of the opposite, namely the police's willingness to (over) police foreigners and minorities if given the choice (cf. Weber & Bowling, 2013; Solhjell et al., 2019; Aliverti, 2021). Yet, here was a contradictory example. Detective Jensen was handing Detective Andersen and Pedersen a group of Romanian burglars on a silver platter. Even so, his colleagues didn't feel inclined to seize the opportunity. And not just that. The reason to them not wanting to take on the case did not appear to be that it, for example, was a particularly difficult case to solve or that they were already overworked. No. The reason provided was apparently that the Romanian suspects were "no fun"; that the detectives were "kinda fed up".

Refusing to take on a case because it is "no fun" sounds unprofessional. And in some ways, it might have been. This is not the point however. Rather, what I aim to discuss in this chapter is how a contributing reason to the detectives' dislike of foreign nationals (and thus a contributing reason to their concerns about the globalization of local policing) might have something to do with a decreasing vocational fulfilment. In other words, the problem is not that foreign criminal suspects themselves are less "fun", but, rather, that the work involved in investigating them is experienced as less rewarding and more frustrating—a frustration making the detectives detest the people believed to be the cause of it. In the following pages, I will provide different empirical examples of this process. However, in order to be able to understand how such an explanation of police xenophobia differs from and adds to already existing explanations, I will first be outlining how policing research has normally theorized the existence of police xenophobia.

Traditional Explanations of Police Xenophobia

Vignette 3

"Can someone please go and pick up Ioana and drive her back here for questioning? Her lawyer is coming later today so we need to make sure she's here", the TFB management reminds the detectives at the end of this Wednesday's morning briefing. Nobody reacts. Waiting in vain for someone to volunteer, the management turns to Detective Axelsen, ordering Detective Axelsen and his partner Detective Carlsen to do it. "Sure", Detective Axelsen says, obviously not thrilled to have been chosen for this, to them and to most others, boring transporting task.

Later that day, I'm in the back of the car while Detectives Axelsen and Carlsen drive toward the prison where the Romanian citizen, Ioana, is being held in custody. "These damn gypsies! I'm sure she's gonna give us nothing but trouble", Detective Carlsen says as we approach the prison. Meanwhile, the radio broadcasts a news story on how shoplifting has become an increasing problem in Denmark. Listening to the radio and sighing rather heavily, Detective Carlsen turns around and looks at me: "You see, David … I guess you and I don't share the same political views but if you knew what we knew … Like, seriously, I promise you that a major reason for this crime problem is that we have an asylum center up here around the corner where the foreigners who live there are basically allowed to come and go as they please. No control whatsoever! I promise you that if we spent just a couple

(continued)

Vignette 3 (continued)

of minutes waiting outside the asylum center, and if we searched or followed people coming and going, then we would be able to arrest several of them. Maybe even all of them. Seriously! Without doubt! To them, the Danish law and the entire criminal justice system is one big joke. That's why they are here. They don't give a shit. They have a completely different way of seeing things. To them all of this is just one big criminal opportunity". Without saying so, it is obvious that Detective Axelsen agrees as he is nodding during the entire conversation.

Some few minutes later, I am sitting next to Ioana, a woman in her forties perhaps fifties, who has spent every second since we picked her up complaining loudly about her arrest and imprisonment—also including a lot of crying and shrieking. "Why?!" she screams in broken English. 'I haven't done anything!'. At first, the detectives don't answer her. They are giving her the silent treatment. A minute later, however, Ioana suddenly announces that she wants another lawyer than the one she has at the moment and that, if she doesn't get a new one, and preferably the same one as her husband who is also a suspect in the same case, she will refuse to be interrogated today. Legally, she is within her rights to do so, the detectives tell me in Danish, but they are counting on her to change her mind before reaching the station. "It's just a stupid performance", they add, making sure that Ioana doesn't understand, but that she does understand that we are speaking about her. Detective Axelsen looks at me in the rear-view mirror with his eyebrows raised:

"You get what we mean, David? Right? It's always like this. These damn gypsies make things so dramatic and difficult. It's so infuriating this damn gypsy thing. She's guilty and she knows it. We know. The evidence is there. But she is still crying and behaving like some insane child. Seriously! What a fucking joke! You never see this with the Danes, let me tell you".

Situations and sentiments like these were common during my time with the task forces; situations and conversations filled with irritation and with what can hardly be described as anything other than negatively stereotyped attitudes toward, in this case, a Romanian citizen. Derogatory words were frequently used. So was comparison to the animal kingdom alongside atavistic associations. The question remains, however; how we may interpret such xenophobic if not racist attitudes among police officers? In the literature, two prevailing explanations seem to exist, that is a "cultural explanation" as well as a more "political explanation".

Of the two, the arguably most common way of explaining police xenophobia is by using a (sub)culture framework, a framework captured by the rich and long-standing research on "police culture(s)" (cf. Loftus, 2009; Cockcroft, 2020). In this particular strand of thought, police negativity toward foreigners is habitually explained as being caused by the existence of racial or otherwise cultural prejudice. Bowling et al. (2004), for example, have provided a telling summary thereof which remains relevant (see also Keith, 1993). In locating the roots of police xenophobia and racism more broadly, Bowling and his colleagues track the cultural foundations of police prejudice from its smallest component of the police organization (the individual) to the larger context of which the police organization is a part (society). And in doing so, they outline the following three well-known explanations as to why "racial discrimination, xenophobia, intolerance and the abuse of power are problems in police forces in many parts of the world" (Bowling et al., 2004, p. 4): At the individual level, the "bad or rotten apple theory" explains police xenophobia as a phenomenon caused by "the result of the actions of a small number of rogue police officers who actively discriminate against ethnic minorities" (Bowling et al., 2004, p. 10). At the organizational level, "occupational culture theory" views negative attitudes toward foreign nationals and ethnic minorities as the product of a specific police culture "in which concentrated forms of racism and xenophobia are prevalent" (ibid:12). Thirdly, shifting the focus to the larger culture of which the police are a part, the "reflection of society theory" argues that "racial prejudice and discrimination in the criminal justice system simply reflect widely held beliefs and behaviors among the general population" (ibid:11). This third theory, or explanation, obviously builds on and includes wider arguments about institutional or structural racism in society (cf. Waddington, 1999a; Holdaway & O'Neill, 2006; Banton, 2018; Feagin, 2013; Rowe, 2012; Bosworth et al., 2008)

Looking at the police's everyday practices more specifically, the cultural explanation of xenophobia is also at the center of the long-standing debate about "police discretion" (cf. Davis, 1975; Brown, 1981; Holmberg, 2000; Mastrofski, 2004; Lipsky, 2010). As many a study has contemplated, the fact that everyday police work frequently allows officers the possibility of themselves choosing a course of action, unavoidably also includes the risk of turning cultural prejudices into practices of discrimination. In a specific Danish context, for example, Holmberg has demonstrated how the line between discretion and discrimination is indeed rather fluid as frontline officers tend to act on their ideas about "typological guilt" (1999, p. 187); a term Holmberg uses to denote how the police tend to see certain foreigners and minorities as inherently criminal without there necessarily being any sufficient evidence to back such a claim (Holmberg, 2000). The police officers simply "know" they are guilty, he writes, thereby disregarding whether there is any immediate proof thereof (see also Choongh, 1998). That police discretion is inevitably tied to issues of police discrimination is also why Mastrofiski among others has made the question of "controlling street-level police discretion" (2004) central to their work as a means of curtailing xenophobic prejudice and partiality.

While the above explanation has its basis in (un)conscious cultural sentiments, located in society at large, the organization or in the individual officer, a second prevalent explanation of police xenophobia is somewhat less normative and more instrumental. In this theoretical framework, negative attitudes toward foreigners are viewed as not only reflecting cultural partialities but are also understood as being a case of cynical politics. A most exemplary study in this regard is Hall et al.'s *Policing the Crisis* (2013: [1978]). In their study, Hall and his Birmingham School colleagues famously examined the 1970s "moral panic" about "mugging" in British media and society and the subsequent increasing policing of ethnic minorities. Instead of merely understanding this as an example of a British xenophobic (police) culture, Hall et al. argued that the escalating fear of mugging had to be read through a larger political and economic lens. They specifically proposed that the increasing disapproval and subsequently policing of ethnic minorities was caused by a "crisis of legitimacy" (ibid.). 1970s England was a time of political and economic turmoil and in this time of crisis the state needed a "scapegoat" by means of which the focus could be redirected and a societal consensus and consciousness restored. The manifest fear and policing of proverbial foreigners, the argument went, was therefore to be understood as an example of a politics of belonging—politics whereby a given society, by casting certain minorities as dangerous and even unworthy, was able to view itself and its citizens as virtuous and worthy. Similar kinds of "political analyses" of policing—with various nuances of course—have also been used frequently in more contemporary criminological studies, particularly in the recent work on "crimmigration" (Stumpf, 2006; Franko, 2019) and "the criminology of mobility" (Pickering et al., 2015) (see also Aas, 2007, 2013, 2014; Bosworth et al., 2016; De Genova, 2010; Gundhus & Franko, 2016; Melossi, 2015; Weber, 2013; Aliverti, 2021). In these studies, xenophobia functions less as a cultural and more as a socio-political differentiator, serving to enforce the margins between the haves and have-nots, the insiders and the outsiders.

Echoing this "scapegoat framework", other well-known criminologists have focused on how the foreign is habitually used as a "suitable enemy" in political fearmongering (Christie & Bruun, 1985; Tham, 1995; Wacquant, 1999). For example, ethnic minorities and migrants are frequently linked to issues of crime and insecurity and, more recently, to terrorism. And in promoting and even exaggerating this link, "moral entrepreneurs" (Becker, 1995), such as the media, politicians, policy makers or, in the case of this book, policing actors are understood to be capitalizing on this self-induced xenophobia (Andersson, 2014; Andreas & Nadelmann, 2006; Bowling & Sheptycki, 2012; Flyghed, 2002). In this less cultural and more political reading of things, foreigners thus become a center of negative attention and attitudes not only because of ingrained beliefs that they are truly lesser persons but also because xenophobia is politically advantageous—a useful political tool which police organizations are not blind to.

Toward More Work-related Explanations

That the existence of police xenophobia and racism is explainable with reference to widespread cultural attitudes as well as policing politics is beyond doubt. Many studies have confirmed this—and I myself observed several examples thereof during the time I spent with the Danish police. Relating the existing theories to my ethnographic experiences, they do however also seem to fall short of fully explaining the different kinds of xenophobia I encountered. Recalling the introductory example of the

TFB detectives expressing their dislike of foreign nationals with reference to a lack of fun and frustration, what indeed seemed to be at the heart of the task force' detectives' prejudice was often the work involved more than the people themselves. To be sure, this was not the first nor the last time I witnessed the detectives complain along these lines, complaining about how ungratifying and even infuriating it was to investigate foreign nationals. Instead of them randomly airing racist viewpoints, their xenophobic attitudes almost always came up in the concrete course of them working cases involving foreign nationals—or when proposed the possibility to open a case on, say, suspected Romanian, Polish or Chilean burglars. More than therefore "just" being a case of ingrained cultural prejudice or even political strategy, the detectives' xenophobia seemed to be more directly related to their daily casework and its potentially enraging qualities. The question that remained to be answered, however, was why this was happening? How, in other words, was I to explain the existence of police xenophobia as it related to the tasks and troubles of daily police work?

Looking at the literature, there are unfortunately not many comprehensive studies on the different ways in which police officers value their daily work, including how such valuations may be the cause of either satisfaction or negativity. Those that do exist are often framed as studies of "police culture", but they remain mostly concerned with how frontline officers particularly value and enjoy catching criminals alongside other more action-oriented aspects of police work (Manning, 1978; Loftus, 2010; Fassin, 2013, p. 59ff; Newburn & Stanko, 1994; Cain, 2015). Furthermore, such action-based, crime-fighting is not only understood as a particularly appreciated part of the police vocation, it is often promoted by police officers worldwide as being emblematic of "real" police work (Manning, 1978). Even though the reality of police work involves much more than catching criminals (such as a lot of paperwork and, as Banton famously put it, "peacekeeping" (1964)), crime-fighting seem to remain not only a symbol but an actual valuation of what police work is really about. This was also frequently confirmed by the Danish detectives, who would zealously celebrate being able to "get out there and catch some criminals instead of just sitting on our arses, staring at our computer screens". As such, a correlation between emotional appreciation and vocational worth was forged—a correlation which, as McWilliams has argued, is not only typical of the police but of most professional vocations in which the everyday gratifications of one's job are what make the work both enjoyable and, importantly, meaningful (1999). This is indeed a standard conclusion in both the psychology and sociology of work with regard to job satisfaction, and the phenomenon is perhaps particularly pronounced in today's post-industrial work settings (Casey, 1995; De Botton, 2010; Kahn, 1990)

Though the Danish detectives did very much value crime-fighting as one of the primary gratifiers and meaning-makers of their work, this was by no means the sole source of professional satisfaction. By paying even closer attention to their daily work, it became clear to me that less outwardly exhilarating parts of their job were also perceived as professionally gratifying—gratifying when things went well but maddening when they were made difficult. A similar observation has recently been made by Fassin on the basis of his ethnographic study of policing in Parisian banlieues and his observations of the considerable amount of time his police interlocutors spent not catching criminals (2013, 2015, 2017b). Pondering the vocational significance of the more non-eventful police work, Fassin argues that such mundane aspects "may not have benefitted from all the attention [they] deserve … as a banal fact of life" even though, he asserts, they might actually be "key to the understanding of policing" (2015). On a more general note, one is even tempted to conclude that too much focus in the study of "police work" has been on the alluring "police part" rather than on the more humdrum "work part" of the equation—perhaps both from a police and scholarly perspective (Sausdal, 2020a). As Van Maanen (1978b) indeed argued many years ago, this may be explained because of how scholars are tempted to follow suit when police officers so often and openly speak of crime-fighting and other more spectacular aspects of their work as both the most thrilling and "real" part of their vocation. Nevertheless, this chapter (and this book in general) includes an attempt to demonstrate the great importance of also paying careful attention to the more mundane work (dis)pleasures of policing (Fassin, 2017a, 2017b; Sausdal, 2020b). And as I now aim to illustrate, it was exactly by observing the Danish detectives' apparent as well as more rudimentary work valuations that I got closer to an understanding of their dislike of foreign nationals. Three examples are presented below, including the normal pleasure the police (and prosecutors) take in seeing their work coming to fruition, the usual off-the-cuff fun of interrogating suspects and, lastly, the gratification that typically comes from listening to otherwise monotonous wiretap recordings.

The (Dis)satisfaction of Convictions

> It's a win! This is why we work hard and put the time in. I know it might appear distasteful to an outsider, seeing us openly celebrating throwing people in prison for several years. Yet you have to understand that it is one of the few tangible ways in which we can measure if we've done a good job or not. That's also why I feel rather satisfied when I get to see how the harsh realities of life suddenly dawn on the criminal when he realises that he is going away for a long time. Like, let's be honest, why shouldn't I be happy about putting away a serial burglar. Right?

These were words of joy relayed to me just after a judge had sentenced two Moroccan burglars to three years of prison. The vocational pleasure that law enforces experience as a result of putting away criminals (sometimes even letting the end justify illegitimate means) has frequently been demonstrated in police research (see Skolnick, 1982, p. 43). And as I also experienced, the two task forces' detectives found it similarly gratifying. Putting away criminals were seen as particularly emblematic of successful and satisfactory work. They were fighting crime and a convicted criminal equaled a battle won. And as a result, the detectives would openly celebrate what they also called "good convictions" when they were announced during briefings, via email, or in the police station's kitchen. Such good news would put a smile on their faces and make for a good day at work.

On the other hand, the detectives would become angry and at times even disheartened if a judge had ruled against them, for instance only sentencing criminals to a shorter time in prison than the prosecutor had asked for or, even worse, acquitting them. Such bad news would taint the entire day at both task forces, becoming the center of discussions and causing passionate outbreaks, detectives announcing how "it's all worthless. No matter what we do, the law is so lenient that it doesn't really matter. It's a joke. They [the foreign criminals] are laughing at us. Seriously, they are laughing right in our faces", which was how TFP Detective Madsen responded when, in this case, he felt that a group of Polish pickpockets had gotten off all too easily.

In this way, a lot of vocational worth was focused on a case being successful, which essentially meant that the case produced what the detectives viewed as a satisfyingly harsh conviction. Yet, in discussing the (dis)pleasures of convictions I am not so much focusing on the quantitative aspects of sentences, although such aspects evidently remain central to police officers' assessments of their work. "Three years are better than one year, and six years better than three", as their logic dictates. Instead, my observations of the detectives' work (dis)satisfactions eventually led me to consider some of the more qualitative aspects of convictions—qualitative aspects also appreciated by the detectives as symbolic markers of meaningful versus meaningless police work. What I want to draw attention to are the aspects found toward the end of the introductory quote. Here, a detective speaks of the particular gratification he felt when the newly convicted person "finally realised what was happening"; "when the harsh realities of life suddenly dawn[ed]" on him. As I frequently experienced, although the Danish detectives did quite often secure a seemingly good and harsh sentence in quantitative terms (or as good as the law allowed for), this didn't always mean that the sentenced person exhibited that he or she also felt it to be a harsh sentence. Frequently, the detectives experienced the opposite, namely that a foreign criminal, now convicted, seemed largely indifferent to the fact that the police had caught him and that he was going to prison. The detectives would sit in the court room, looking at the suspects' faces and gestures, yet failing to see them feel properly dismayed as the honorable judge eventually passed her ruling. This disconnect between the felt quantity and quality of convictions, this seeming lack of despair among criminals even when convicted, was the focus of much debate and frustration among the task forces' detectives, a frustration much more common when cases involved foreign nationals. "They often just sit there, looking like they were just given a day pass to

Tivoli rather than three years in the slammer", Detective Gustavsen complained to his colleagues after yet another example thereof.

Detective Gustavsen's words are certainly illustrative of a kind of work frustration that foreign nationals were believed to be the cause of them turning the normal celebration of a conviction into something of a felt forfeiture. And there are many examples to choose from. Two particular telling examples come to mind, however; the first being one I experienced first-hand, involving a Romanian citizen held in custody awaiting trial, and the second being an example of a Polish suspect talking about the, to him, minute threat of getting caught and imprisoned in Denmark.

Vignette 4

Detectives Ibsen, Detective Thorsen and I are in Vestre Jail, waiting by the front desk. Vestre Jail is Copenhagen's largest jailhouse, not far from the city center. We're there to pick up the Romanian citizen, Christi who is a suspect in a big TFB case. Christi has just been arrested a few days ago and is supposed to have his fingerprints and photo taken today at the nearby police station, Station City. The detectives talk to the prison officer working at the prison's front desk, letting her know why they are there.

A few minutes later, Christi comes out, escorted through a massive iron door by another prison officer. Christi is all smiles and greets us. "You look tremendously happy", Detective Ibsen remarks, "Why is that? There's no reason to be happy about what've you done and your situation". Christi nevertheless continues to smile, and then says in bad but fairly comprehensible English "Yeah, it's hard not to be happy, you guys. Instead of living under a motorway bridge, and having to search for food all day, I now get a bed to sleep in, and", he laughs, "here I also get three different porn channels on the telly! So, what's not to like?!" The detectives put up a laugh, seeing the amusement if not the absurdity in how a Danish prison is providing a Romanian suspect with such offerings as free pornography. Yet as they later tell me, "It's also madly provocative to see him smile like that and talk about porn. It's like he couldn't care less. And seriously, that's how it is. You heard him. Here they get food, shelter, a PlayStation, free dental service and other healthcare things beyond their wildest dreams and so on. So even if they get convicted, it's not really a real punishment to them, right? Like, look at him", Detective Thorsen points to Christi who is now getting his fingerprints taken by Detective Ibsen, "he's yakking away like some happy kid although we are in a cold and ugly police station basement. I mean, that seems a bit off, right?"

Whether Christi really was so happy and unconcerned is another question. When I chatted with him later that day, the two of us sitting in the backseat of the police car on our way back to the jail, his cheerful manner had changed into something sadder. He was now telling how he wouldn't be able to talk to and see his family if he was convicted and had to spend a considerable amount of time in a Danish prison far away from home. Nevertheless, his initial cheery ways had been enough to upset the TFB detectives. "It's too often like that. We spend all this time putting a case together, only to face a Romanian, Polish or whatever suspect who doesn't give a damn, who smiles instead of showing any signs of sadness. It's makes you question whether this is worthwhile, to be honest". Detective Ibsen admitted to me, as him and I discussed the incident one of the following days. "Trust me, it's not just me, not just us", he elaborated. "This is one the most annoying parts of policing these foreigners—something we all experience". To be sure, the next example tells a similar story about the Danish detectives' frustrations in relation to a felt lack of fear (if not respect) of the police and punishment in Denmark.

> **Vignette 5**
>
> During a lunch break, a group of TFB detectives are discussing why so many foreign burglars travel to Denmark. "There's a lot to steal here", Detective Pedersen suggests, "and it's pretty easy to travel to Denmark from Eastern Europe". The others agree. "And we Danes don't protect our houses properly", Detective Andersen argues. Again, people agree. "And then we have the big question about how soft the punishment is here in Denmark compared to what they're used to", Detective Jensen says. "For instance, on this older case in which we were investigating a ring of Polish burglars, we", Detective Jensen carries on, "had set up a wiretap on one of the primary suspects. The investigation had gone on forever before eventually, when we thought we had the required amount of evidence, we arrested him and his crew. Now, as we were listening in on the wire, we were also able to overhear that the suspect seemed aware that he was on the verge of getting caught. Since he was thinking like this, he said to his wife on a phone call we intercepted: 'Hey love, don't worry. It's not that bad. Not that bad at all. There's no actual punishment up here. Prisons are like kindergartens. There's nothing to worry about.'"
>
> As the detectives kept on talking about how not only Polish but most other foreign suspects saw Danish prisons as kindergartens and how "ridiculous but also true from a Polish perspective" this was, Detective Jensen eventually turns toward me.

(continued)

> **Vignette 5** (continued)
>
> "David, you wouldn't believe how normal it is to hear foreign suspects not only telling their wives about the leniency of Danish criminal law and punishment but also using this as an argument when trying to recruit fellow countrymen/criminals". "The fact is that they openly talk about how good prison conditions are in Denmark. Seriously, since we know this, this needs to change. I tell you, it's so frustrating to see that they don't think of it as punishment at all—of what we do as punishment. They don't care. It's laughable to them. I mean, this is obviously a problem in terms of deterrence, if suspects don't in any way feel frightened about the prospect of going to prison in Denmark. Yet it is also very frustrating for us as it becomes a provocative and patronizing remark on the value of our efforts when we see them, say a Polish, Romanian or whatever citizen, joking or smiling about the prospect of going to prison in Denmark. It's not motivating at all, let me tell you".

Again, whether or not the Danish detectives are right in assessing that foreign nationals don't fear or perhaps even enjoy going to prison in Denmark, is not the point of interest here. Remembering how Christi was obviously upset about the prospect of not seeing his family, I believe the reality to be more nuanced than the detectives described it. Disregarding what is right or wrong, the point however remains that this was how the detectives experienced things—an experience that had a significantly negative effect on their appreciation of their work as well as the foreign nationals. To the detectives, what was once seen as the ultimate and professionally gratifying culmination of their work was losing its punitive powers (see also Sausdal, 2023). The detectives were indeed often successful in catching and convicting them, but, as Detective Christensen brashly admitted "it just doesn't feel like winning if they don't give shit".

The (Dis)satisfactions of Interrogations

As already discussed, catching and convicting criminals are in many ways emblematic of most police officers' ideas about "real" and, consequently, rewarding police work. Seeing the judge rule in favor of the state is where the police's crime-fighting efforts come to full fruition. Yet, before there can be any chance of a conviction, there is a lot more and often less ostentatious work to be done. One of these more run-of-the-mill tasks, a task which took up a lot of the Danish detectives' time, was the on-going questioning and interrogations of suspects.

Interrogations, understood in terms of both casual conversations and formal questioning, were also one of the few work situations in which the detectives and their suspects were face to face for a sustained amount of time, and therefore also one of the few social scenes in which the police and policed could get to know one another a little more profoundly (an actual encounter which the increasing use of surveillance and information technologies are making more and more rare, something I return to in Chap. 3). Though one might think that the police find interrogations tiresome, I found it to be one the work practices that many of the Danish detectives tended to appreciate. As I was allowed to sit in on several of their interrogations of criminal suspects, it became clear to me that the detectives took particular pleasure in what they would also call "a good or nice interrogation". However, it also became obvious that the detectives tended to find the interrogations much less pleasurable when they involved foreign nationals. More than allowing for the usual contentment, interrogations and other forms of conversations with foreign suspects were often the cause of much negativity.

As I was starting to notice this pattern, and as TFP Detective Larsen had just finished interrogating a suspect, I decided to ask him explain to me what he believed to be particularly rewarding about this kind of work:

Vignette 6

I actually think it's quite fun. It's like a game. Like, how I go about it is that I often like to establish a connection so that it feels like we're also just two people talking about life. As you just saw me do before as I was talking to this guy, I'll go outside on the balcony, have a smoke and chat about normal things, talking about family, football, getting them to understand that I'm basically a normal guy. It's about being able to relate, right? That to me is a good interrogation.

"But," he continued, "when an interrogation turns into a simple 'yes and no thing' it becomes tiresome, it rarely produces anything of worth. Sure, if the suspect just says 'I did it', that's also good, but when it's hard to get anything out of the suspect and they won't talk, it's just an annoying waste of time".

(continued)

> **Vignette 6** (continued)
>
> A few weeks later, Detective Larsen's description of a good interrogation resembles what TFB Detective Axelsen tells me as him and I later are driving to the Western fringes of Copenhagen to scope out a house in which a group of suspected Romanian thieves are thought to be living. "One thing is of course whether it is of any use or not. That's a given", "But", he continues, "that's not all. I also find it quite meaningful to be able to engage in good conversations with people".
>
> Sitting in the car, killing time, he elaborates, now talking about his work as a dedicated source handler:
>
> "In order to really connect with sources, you really have to take an interest in what they tell you. Like if he's having problems with his wife, kids, friends and so on, I need to know that. Similarly, I need to offer him a part of me. Like, if I'm an hour late, I need to tell him it was because of my kid who was sick and not tell him some bullshit about the traffic or something. I need to be honest so that he confides in me. It should feel like we're having a genuine relationship ... Now, it's much the same for normal interrogations, when questioning suspects. You have to be able to create a situation in which it feels like you're just having a nice and sincere chat. That's when it becomes fruitful".

According to these detective Larsen and Axelsen—and many of their detectives colleagues I should add—a good and "fruitful" interrogation involves establishing a "genuine relationship". Their preference for genuine relationships very much mirrors existing research conducted into how interrogations are supposed to be carried out. Here "establishing rapport" and the ability to create a "positive atmosphere" have been identified as key ingredients (Hartwig et al., 2005). Although the research on this subject is predominantly preoccupied with how a good interrogation may lead the suspect to want to confide in the interrogator, in just the way described by Detective Axelsen, the same ingredients seem to comprise the Danish detectives' definition of what constitutes not only a useful but also an otherwise meaningful and even enjoyable interrogation—a perhaps understandable correspondence between the product and process.

Bearing the described features of a good interrogation in mind, we can now turn to its opposite, namely the earlier-mentioned displeasures of interrogating foreign criminal suspects and, keeping in mind the chapter's focus, the possible xenophobia these may produce. In doing this, and in order to demonstrate the difference between a good and not-so-good interrogation, I present another example of Detective Larsen, this time interrogating a Polish suspect. As the example shows, rather than being meaningful and thus cause of work satisfaction, this interrogation ended up in a lot of frustration:

Vignette 7

Together with the suspect, a Polish citizen in his late thirties, Detective Larsen and I take the elevator up from the downstairs holding cells to the TFP office on the fifth floor. Not long before picking up the Polish man from his holding cell, Detective Larsen had let me know that he would try to see if he could get him to not only plead guilty, since the case against him wasn't the strongest, but, as Detective Larsen elaborated, "also get him to tell a bit about his accomplices and the criminal environment in Poland". "David", he continued, "you'll see, I'll try to chat him up a bit. So, please keep in the background so that he doesn't feel too overwhelmed". Standing in the elevator, Detective Larsen first tries to make small-talk in English.

Unfortunately, the attempt to create ease in the situation fails as the suspect barely understands the detective. Instead, some incoherent German words are exchanged, a language both parties speak poorly. After some moments of awkward silence and staring at the elevator wall, we finally get to the office and Detective Larsen places the Polish suspect on a chair next to his desk and calls in the interpreter. Just before the interpreter comes in, Detective Larsen turns to me again and says in a rather unsatisfied tone, "Yeah, that didn't go so well. It's hard to chat when you don't speak the same language, no?" With this slight disappointment in the back of his mind, the interrogation starts.

Detective Larsen: Can you tell me a little bit about yourself?
Suspect: Why?
Detective Larsen: I just like to know who I'm talking to.
Suspect: I'm just a tourist. Just here to explore.
Detective Larsen: Sure you are … Like, where are you from in Poland? Do you have a family? A job?
Suspect: [Doesn't really care about answering but after a while he says] I'm from Kielce. I have a wife and a boy. And I work in construction.
Detective Larsen: OK. It's not the first time we've met someone from Kielce. How is it down there?
Suspect: What do you want me to say? It's Poland. We're poor.
Detective Larsen: But you have a job. You just told me. So, you don't need to steal?

(continued)

Vignette 7 (continued)

   Suspect: Exactly. I'm a tourist. I'm here to explore and see friends.
   Detective Larsen: Don't give me that silly tourist bullshit.
   Suspect: I don't know what you're talking about.
   Detective Larsen: So even if I show you this picture of you standing right next to one of the victims, you'll still say you're a tourist.
   Suspect: It's not me [looking out the window].
   Detective Larsen: Look at me when I talk to you! It's not you? Are you kidding me? Everyone can see it's you … You're going to have to talk. It'll make things a lot easier. Now, I'm going to go through all the different charges and you're going to tell me whether you admit to them or not.
   Suspect: I don't understand … How can I admit to something when I don't know why I'm here? I'm just a tourist. I don't understand anything.
   Detective Larsen: You are here because you're a thief. And don't give me that provocative "I know nothing, I'm a victim" attitude. You're really starting to irritate me.
   Having escorted the suspect back to his cell, Detective Larsen turns to me again and says: "God damn Polacks! God damn idiots! They only know how to steal and lie. Like, it was impossible to have a proper conversation with him. How hard can it be? He can even choose to say that he doesn't want to talk but instead he's badly behaved and all over the place. It's like he was downright dumb. And he probably is with all the vodka they drink. We see this all the time. All the time!"

The above conversation exemplifies, in condensed form, the ways in which talking to and questioning foreign suspects often ended up being perceived as a bad rather than a good interrogation, resulting in police irritation and prejudiced utterances. Of course, becoming angry could and would happen with Danish (speaking) suspects as well, but the general perception, which was both confirmed by my observations and often openly admitted by the detectives themselves, was that it happened more often with foreigners. "They are just harder to have a normal, earnest conversation with", the detectives would conclude.

As above example also indicates, the detectives' difficulties in establishing rapport and creating a positive atmosphere in interrogations with foreigners seemed to be largely due to three recurrent work-related problems: (1) gaps or barriers in language, (2) gaps in knowledge and (3) social gaps—gaps which the detectives themselves spoke of or otherwise expressed their frustrations in relation to. That there is a language barrier is self-evident. The Danish detectives do not, for instance, speak Polish and the foreign suspects did not speak Danish and only rarely decent English. In this way, given that the possibility of establishing rapport is reliant on conversational techniques such as small-talk (Abbe & Brandon, 2014), the simple fact that the parties involved cannot communicate very easily produces its own problems. And as research has also shown (Muir, 1979; Bayley & Bittner, 1984), the ability to converse both in order to obtain information and to calm down difficult situations—to keep the peace—is one of the police officer's central tricks of the trade. This application of this trick however frequently failed with foreign suspects, as is for example evident in the way that Detective Larsen was unable to engage the Polish suspect in any kind of chit-chat.

Additionally, language barriers become amplified by significant gaps in police knowledge about foreign suspects' specific backgrounds and lives. When questioning a domestic citizen, the detectives would often be able to acquire a lot of additional information about the suspect both prior to and after the interrogation. They would for example check different national registers (crime, taxes, health, current address, motor vehicle, etc.), thereby developing a better idea of the individuals' criminal histories, where they live, where they are from, who they know, their family relations, and so on. Moreover, this register-based data often becomes supplemented by what one detective described as "the shared knowledge that comes from having been brought up in the same country by more or less the same institutions"—from the idea that they belong to a sort of shared "imagined community" (Anderson, 2006). As the detectives experienced it, these different kinds of prior knowledge were believed to give them both a conceptual and conversational resource which they could put to use during interrogations and otherwise encounters with suspects, providing things to talk about as well as providing the means to interpret what the suspect said.

When it comes to foreign nationals, however, the detectives didn't feel that they had the same prior knowledge about the suspects (real or imagined)—something they considered to be a considerable hindrance in their efforts to make conversation and keep it going. The example presented above demonstrates this problem. Detective Larsen is seeking to gather some knowledge about who the Polish suspect is, but fails as the suspect is not particularly able nor interested in saying very much about himself. A supposed lack of knowledge about the suspects therefore made interrogations "difficult" or "bumpy", as the detectives would put it. When interrogating foreign suspects they simply found it increasingly difficult to create a situation in which the conversation flowed—a flow which they viewed as an essential part of not only a useful but also enjoyable interrogation. To borrow from Goffman's (1957) definition of the core rule of a "good conversation", the detectives' difficulties in relation to being able to actually talk with (language gap) as well as having things to talk about (knowledge gap) would stifle the otherwise needed "spontaneity" of the conversation. It became, as a TFP Detective Cluasen rather eloquently put it, "less like a conversation and more like a questionnaire".

Finally, the detectives' interrogations and other communications with foreign suspects may also be said to include a potential "social gap"—a social gap which in turn affected and was affected by the language and knowledge gaps. The troubling existence of a potential social gap concerns what the detectives would also describe as "the foreigners not knowing how to behave", talking about foreign suspects' believed tendency to misbehave in meetings and conversations with the police. This is also evident in the above example, where Detective Larsen grew annoyed by the way in which, as he perceived it, the Polish suspect did not follow the normal behavioral rules of an interrogation. This perceived social "misbehavior" of foreign suspects was indeed a recurring phenomenon during my field study, in which I continuously observed the detectives becoming irritated with foreigners, commenting on how they wouldn't behave when, for example, being interrogated, when detained or when they were in court. As TFB Detective Ibsen commented, having spent an entire day in court where a group of Romanian citizens were on trial:

> Jesus! Did you see how she was getting her "gypsy" on? She was throwing her hands up in the air, rolling her eyes, and screaming all sorts of gibberish. She was so hysterical. They all are. All of the damn gypsies. This happens every time we catch them for the many crimes they commit. Honestly, that behavior really pisses me off. It's infuriating.

Whether Detective Ibsen and his detective colleagues were right in assessing that the foreign suspects were misbehaving more than Danish suspects is not relevant to the argument made in this chapter. What is relevant is simply that the foreign suspects were not thought to be behaving according to the police's behavioral standards. Following on from this, it is well-established in situational/interactionist police research that interactional failure gives rise to police resentment. One of the best-known examples of this is Van Maanen's paper, "The Asshole" (1978a) being a symbolic interactionist analysis of the genesis of various police typologies. In his analysis, Van Maanen explores the underlying reasons for police negativity toward groups of individuals, such as foreigners and ethnic minorities, whom the police often speak of as "assholes". The asshole, he argues, is viewed as a particular pestilence because of his exact "failure to meet police expectations arising from the interaction situation itself" (1978a, p. 224), the police's negative sentiments therefore being based, Van Maanen argues, more upon "situational contingencies [t]han upon certain individuals" (1978a, p. fn. 4). Or as Goffman (1961, p. 18) would have put it, negativity surfaces because the conversations between the foreigner and the detectives lack a "we rationale" whereby both parties come to acknowledge how the conversation should be conducted. To be sure, the believed absence of this "we rationale" became evident in how the task forces' detectives would, in contrast, often praise Danish suspects for "behaving well" or "knowing the game". Here, a social gap was not thought to exist. Sadly though, in the eyes of the Danish detectives, many of the foreign nationals they interrogated and elsewise encountered in their work failed to know and respect the game, making it difficult for the police to play and enjoy the game, and, ultimately, making the foreigner a more frowned-upon opponent.

Lastly, it was not only the foreigners themselves who were at fault. A central reason to the Danish detectives' bigger dislike of interrogating foreign suspects was (as the above example didn't really touch upon) the fact that an interpreter had to be present. This was yet another aspect that the detectives found to be stifling the possibility of having a good and

> **Vignette 8**
>
> Detective Christensen: So, I'll ask you again, do you know these two people? It seems like you're working together. Look, you're right there next to them on this photo we have of you guys.
> Interpreter: [Speaking Romanian to the suspect]
> Suspect: [Answering in Romanian]
> Interpreter: [Continuing to talk to the suspect in Romanian]
> Suspect: [Speaking Romanian]
> Interpreter: He says no.
> Detective Christensen: What do you mean no? What were you two talking about? He just said no? Really? Listen, I need to know what he said exactly. Don't interpret, just translate! Understand?!
> Following Detective Christensen questioning of the Romanian suspect, I asked him how he thought it had gone.
> "Hmmm...", he said, "I guess we got what we needed actually, although it's annoying as hell not speaking the same language. You're never quite sure that you understand each other. There's always that annoying uncertainty. And that interpreter... like, she's sweet and all, but I'm sure she misinterpreted several things. And it makes me skeptical when I don't understand what they're talking about. I have no control over that. It's fucking annoying. But it's often like that when using interpreters. It makes it difficult to have a proper conversation. Like, I want him to talk with me man-to-man instead of talking with her".

gratifying interrogation. The following is a short example taken from an interrogation with a Romanian suspected of pickpocketing:

Having to use an interpreter made it even more difficult for the detectives. In the detectives' understanding of things, the inevitable use of an interpreter added yet another layer of possible misunderstanding. And, given that the detectives defined a professionally gratifying and meaningful interrogation in terms of the ability to have this "genuine relationship", to relate "man-to-man", the detectives who interrogated foreigners often felt that they became lost in translation. Potentially good conversations turned bad—and so did the attitude of the detectives. As one TFB detective wittily put it, "Having to have an interpreter present is like going on a date with a chaperon. Nobody likes that".

The (Dis)satisfaction of Wiretaps

The use of wiretaps is another aspect of police/detective work that may offer excitement. This was also true of the Danish detectives, whose investigations frequently involved them sitting in their offices for hours on end with their headphones on, waiting for things to happen, waiting for suspects to out themselves. However, since criminal suspects spend most of their days doing something else than committing crimes, a large percentage of the information that the detectives obtained from the wiretaps simply involved calls and messages about rather mundane matters. The suspects would call and have conversations with family members or friends about everyday things such as the weather, the news, what to buy from the supermarket, the latest football match, their sex/love lives, and so on. In this way, the detectives' wiretap work involved them listening in on many apparently irrelevant conversations about non-criminal matters, and, yet, their tireless efforts became worth it when something of investigational interest eventually occurred (although sometimes it never did).

However, what made wiretaps interesting for the detectives was not only when a criminal suspects eventually revealed something of relevance to the case the police were building against them. Indeed, much of the otherwise tedium of listening in on suspects' mundane conversations and chinwags was made less trivial by the almost voyeuristic pleasures of this type of work; by the way in which detectives would enjoy obtaining insights into the lives (and secrets) of their suspects - or, stated differently, by the detectives' feelings of satisfaction in closing the knowledge gap described above. Listening in on the many non-criminal and mundane conversation that the suspects were having served as a way for the detectives to develop an interest in their suspects that extended beyond their delinquency. Here is an example:

> **Vignette 9**
>
> It is late afternoon at TFB. Detective Pedersen and I are the only ones left at the office as the operations they are running are not giving them much in terms of evidence. "They are not using their phones that much. Maybe they have acquired new phones. Or maybe they are just resting a bit", Pedersen explains, looking at me from across the desk. "And when they do talk, they mostly talk about girls—or with them", he adds. Fifteen minutes later he waves me over. "Come over here, David. Listen to this young guy talking to his dad". He swiftly puts his headphones on my head and presses start.
>
> Dad: Hey. What's this I've been hearing? You in trouble again?
>
> Suspect: What? Who said that? No, not at all, dad. I'm just hanging out with my friends. Everything's fine, Dad. Don't worry.
>
> Dad: You sure? It doesn't matter who said it [...] You know you can tell me anything. I just don't want you to waste your life. You need to tell me if you're in trouble.
>
> Suspect: Dad, don't worry. I haven't always made the best choices, but right now everything's good.
>
> After listening to the suspect's conversation with his dad, Detective Pedersen remarks:
>
> "This is typical. Like, even though he's an idiot, it's hard not to get some sympathy for the kid when you hear him talking to his dad. Even though he's lying, it's obvious that he doesn't want to disappoint his dad. We all know what that's like. These boys are trying to be tough guys whilst trying to appear as good boys in relation to their families. We see this all the time [...] Actually, even though it might not be directly relevant for me to listen through recordings of this guy talking to his dad or whoever, I like doing it. It might reveal something that we can use, yet it's also nice as it gives me a better understanding of who he is".

Throughout my fieldwork I noticed how the detectives enjoyed acquainting themselves with their suspects. As already mentioned earlier, they did this by checking available police and other national databases or registers, or by browsing social media, by continuously discussing their suspects with their colleagues (as well as me) and, if given permission by a judge, by using wiretaps or other forms of surveillance. They even spent considerable time producing and decorating print-outs of the criminal groups they were investigating (see also Sausdal, forthcoming), and, as these print-outs would also show, they often spoke of the suspects using the suspects' first names in a way that signalled a certain familiarity. One could say that for the detectives, this gave their work an added meaning, not only seeing and listening to the criminals as criminals but also relating to them as "normal people" (see also Björk, 2008). Indeed, this appeared to be an integral way for the detectives to experience themselves as not only one-eyed officers of the law but, mirroring Loftus et al.'s findings, "becoming observers of the larger human condition [e]ngrossed in, and occasionally sympathetic to, the lives of those they are investigating" (2015, p. 636).

However, when it came to the many foreign nationals they were investigating, the aforementioned language and knowledge gaps meant that the detectives did not have the same opportunities to familiarize themselves with these suspects. The detectives did not have the same contextual data available to them, and they did not have the same opportunities in getting to know the suspects through the wire. I asked Detective Pedersen how this affected his work:

> **Vignette 10**
>
> "Hmm … I must admit that I often develop a much more cynical view. When I listen in on Danes I get to hear them talk about a lot of different things. Like, they talk to their mom, their dad, their friends, and so on. Just like normal people, they talk about everyday stuff. But when it's a foreigner we need an interpreter who'll most often only translate the case-related criminal matter. In this way, I never get the bigger picture but only the criminal one […] This might be why I like catching Danes. I get the bigger picture. Like, when I go and arrest Johnny it's like I already know him. I'll be like 'Hey Johnny, how's it going with your mom?!' If his name's Petrescu or something, I'll probably be less understanding".
>
> Related to this, one of the other TFB detectives admitted that:
>
> "When I go out and arrest a Danish burglar, it might be someone I know from a prior case. Like, I know what he's about […] And even if I don't know him I know of him […] I mean, we've all grown up with someone named Kasper who had a difficult childhood […] But when it's these foreigners it's different. We know almost nothing about them".

Among other things, this begs the question of why knowing a suspect is more satisfying and not knowing them less so? The most frequently and perhaps obvious use of the police having an extensive knowledge of suspected criminals is that it may be of either preventive or investigational use (Dean et al., 2006; Skogan & Antunes, 1979). Knowing a suspect, who he is, where he lives, what he does, who he knows and how he thinks, may help the police prevent his crime or, alternatively, catch him. However, observing the Danish detectives' daily work and arguments, this was not the only satisfaction that came with an added insight into their suspects' lives. Instead, the detectives often spoke of what may also be understood as "sense-making". In other words, the detectives seemed to find it both professionally and personally giving for them to be able to, at least somewhat, understand the broader intent and purposes of the criminals they investigated. And as I experienced it, and as Detective Pedersen words hinted at, if they were not given this opportunity, they were likely to become more contemptuous and cynical.

That cynicism and dislike may indeed be the outcome can be related to Van Maanen's (1978a, p. 228) old illustration of how the police's difficulties in not properly understanding suspects are well-known triggers of negative sentiments, since, as he elaborates, the suspects' actions become understood as "so senseless [t]hat recognizable and acceptable human motives are difficult for the police to discover". In other words, while listening in on a suspected Danish person also became a form of what might be termed "anthropological work" for the detectives, listening in on the non-Danish speaking foreign suspects often just made for merely instrumental, investigative police work. And, as the above examples demonstrate, this mere instrumentality entailed the risk that the detectives would, quite literally, think less of the suspect (see also Björk, 2005). Instead of allowing them some sort of insight into the lives of their suspects, the wiretaps they ran on foreign suspects made the detectives more thoughtless than thoughtful.

It is one thing how the detectives found themselves growing more cynical when running wiretaps on foreign suspects. Another problem were how wiretaps and a wider knowledge of the people they investigated would usually allow for another central satisfaction of everyday police work. Known as "canteen culture" (Fielding, 1994; Waddington, 1999b; Kingshott & Prinsloo, 2004; Sollund, 2007; van Hulst, 2013; Sausdal, 2020c), police officers are (in)famous for telling stories and bantering. Knowledge about suspects here acts as a key ingredient as the police use their extensive insights into their suspects lives and doings to tell good stories and thereby entertain one another. Also, one might add, this is not just "entertainment" understood in its most common sense. Instead, it should also be understood in its old etymological sense as in "*entretenir*", originating from Old French, meaning that which "holds things together". Wider knowledge (false or true) about criminal suspects simply constitutes a fun as well as an everyday basis for collegial conversations—a sort of commonplace police vocabulary used to lighten up the boring downtime that constitutes the majority of police/detective work. But when the police, like the Danish detectives, do not have a substantial knowledge about "their" criminals, they will lack a needed literary substance for their on-the-job storytelling. As a result, the risk is that the police's stories about the people they encounter become both uninteresting *and* uninterested, boring *and* crude.

Finally, knowing one's suspects is arguably not only important in terms of sense-making or as a means of storytelling, for the detectives, it was also a key ingredient in terms of internal, organizational prestige. As research has shown, among police officers, and detectives in particular, there is a great deal of cachet associated with "intelligence hoarding", that is, having a wider knowledge of the criminals and suspects. Truly knowing one's suspects is seen as being career-promoting and, not least, something that makes for much collegial respect (Sheptycki, 2004). Between the Danish detectives, it was obvious that this aspect also played a significant role in why working with foreigners were a less liked activity. As Detective Gustavsen explained it:

> There's definitely still a police hierarchy in terms of what makes up the most prestigious work in our organization. Drugs and gangs are still the types of crimes that'll give you a name. There many mythical stories being told in the Danish police about this and that person who knew everything about and everyone in, for instance, the Hells Angels. Like, you can walk down the hall and talk to some of the guys down there whose job it is to handle sources and informants. They know everything. But, if you want to talk about the problem of cross-border criminals, about some foreign issues, then I know for certain that they'll have very little to say. They know no one. Cross-border crime policing is still not "sexy" police work.

Why "No Fun"? Why "Fed Up"? Why Xenophobic?

Why were Detective Andersen and her colleagues so reluctant to take on a new case including a potential Romanian burglary ring? Why did they—as well as many other of their Danish detective colleagues—say that they were "fed up", that they didn't "care about those damn foreigners", that they were "no fun"? These were the questions initially asked in this chapter; questions where we should now be in a better position to provide an answer. Though the introductory example led the detectives to shy away from taking on a new case, this was not what usually happened. In fact, most of the task forces' cases involved foreign nationals, and increasingly so. And most of the time, the detectives neither could nor would refuse the opportunity to investigate. They were professionals, and as professionals they felt obliged to solve the cases put in front of them. Also, it is important to note that the detectives very much shared in the not only Danish but wider international political and criminal justice discourse that highlights cross-border crime as a particular and grave societal problem. In this way, most of the detectives were passionate about bringing foreign nationals to justice—a passion which was often fortified through their xenophobic ideas about the lesser worth and natural-born delinquency of the many Romanians, Chileans, Poles and Moroccans they were investigating.

As such, the point here has not been to argue that foreign nationals get off the hook more easily in Denmark because of how the police find them less exciting. They don't. Neither has the point been to argue against or neglect the aforementioned traditional ways of theorizing police xenophobia as a predominant cultural and/or political phenomena. The Danish police, like many other police forces worldwide, is also the home of negative attitudes toward foreigners and ethnic minorities. And it wouldn't be far off the mark to say that Danish criminal justice politics as well as the Danish police strategically use non-Danish dangers for their own advantage. Instead, the simple yet important point of the chapter has been to point to the different and daily on-the-job issues that occur when Danish detectives investigate and police foreign suspects. What I have tried to illustrate is how and why the detectives experienced how different aspects of their workday were made difficult and even frustrating when involving foreign nationals. This was why they were "fed up". This was why it was "no fun". In this way, more than such sentiments only being an expressed deprecations of the foreign nationals themselves, these were sentiments related to the process of usually gratifying work practices turning sour. In a strictly practical investigational sense, the Danish detectives did often have the means and knowledge to investigate and apprehend the foreign suspects. Yet, given the more meagre knowledge they had of—and were able to obtain on—foreign suspects in a wider anthropological sense, the detectives often found it difficult to truly comprehend their actions, to engage in interesting encounters with them, tell good stories about them or, for that matter, use foreign criminals as a token of organizational prestige. In short, working cases involving foreign nationals didn't always provide the detectives with the same workaday satisfactions as investigations involving Danish nationals did.

Now, one could of course choose to be uninterested in whether a group of Danish detectives find policing foreigners satisfactory or not. However, this would be a faulty kind of thinking. Because, as I have here tried to exemplify, the detectives' experienced decrease in job happiness often came with the risk of them projecting their frustrations, blaming the persons involved rather than the practices themselves. Moreover, the negativity the Danish detectives felt toward the foreign nationals were not just a matter of them projecting—of them (un)consciously blaming Romanian or Polish suspects for having made their work lives less interesting. As I also have tried to clarify, the detectives' xenophobia was directly related to them finding themselves unable to fully connect and relate to their new and more global suspect pool—the detectives not being able to connect and relate in the same way as they believed they normally could when policing Danish suspects. One may therefore say that the detectives did not only find the work less gratifying but also more superficial. They could not understand what the foreign suspects were saying on the wire. They could not understand and chat with them. And the detectives had a harder time procuring information about the suspects' whereabouts as well as getting to know what they were about. Rather than seeing them as human beings that were also criminals, they tended to see them as only criminal. The difficulties the detectives experienced thus quite literary led them to think less of the foreign suspects. This explanation of police xenophobia might then add to the traditional explanations, especially in a world of increasingly globalized local policing. Indeed, as much of the wider literature on the origins of xenophobia argues (see Banton, 1994, 1996), prejudice is often reinforced by the xenophobe only having a crude and thus caricatured knowledge about a group of people. Spending time with the Danish detective, this seemed to be at the heart of the issue. The local police workers I studied were already skeptical of foreign elements, and the work itself only intensified this feeling. To me, this serves as reminder to not only study the cultural and political foundations of (police) xenophobia, but to also look at the workaday, situational aspects thereof. It offers a way to also study xenophobia as an interactional process more than it just being a finished cultural product or political scheme.

Bibliography

Aas, K. F. (2007). Analysing a world in motion: Global flows meet 'the criminology of the other'. *Theoretical Criminology, 11*(2), 283–303.

Aas, K. F., & Bosworth, M. (Eds.). (2013). *The borders of punishment: Migration, citizenship, and social exclusion.* Oxford University Press.

Aas, K. F. (2014). Bordered penality: Precarious membership and abnormal justice. *Punishment & Society, 16*(5), 520–541.

Abbe, A., & Brandon, S. E. (2014). Building and maintaining rapport in investigative interviews. *Police Practice and Research, 15*(3), 207–220.

Aliverti, A. (2021). *Policing the borders within.* Oxford University Press.

Anderson, B. (2006). *Imagined communities: Reflections on the origin and spread of nationalism.* Verso Books.

Andersson, R. (2014). *Illegality, Inc.: Clandestine migration and the business of bordering Europe.* University of California Press.

Andreas, P., & Nadelmann, E. (2006). *Policing the globe: Criminalization and crime control in international relations.* Oxford University Press.

Banton, M. (1964). *The policeman in the community.* Basic Books.

Banton, M. (1994). *Discrimination.* Open University Press.

Banton, M. (1996). The cultural determinants of xenophobia. *Anthropology Today, 12*(2), 8–12.

Banton, M. (2018). The concept of racism. In Banton (ed) *Race and racialism* (pp. 17–34). Routledge.

Bayley, D. H., & Bittner, E. (1984). Learning the skills of policing. *Law and Contemporary Problems, 47*(4), 35–59.

Becker, H. S. (1995). Moral entrepreneurs: The creation and enforcement of deviant categories. In N. Herman (Ed.), *Deviance: A symbolic interactionist approach* (pp. 169–178). Lanham, MD.

Bosworth, M., Bowling, B., & Lee, M. (2008). Globalization, ethnicity and racism: An introduction. *Theoretical Criminology, 12*(3), 263–273.

Bosworth, M., Hasselberg, I., & Turnbull, S. (2016). Punishment, citizenship and identity: An introduction. *Criminology and Criminal Justice, 16*(3), 257–266.

Bowling, B., Phillips, C., Campbell, A., et al. (2004). Policing and human rights: Eliminating discrimination, xenophobia, intolerance and the abuse of power from police work. *Identities, Conflict and Cohesion (2000–2005), United Nations Research Institute for Social Development, 3–5 September 2001, Durban, South Africa*. 3–26.

Bowling, B., & Sheptycki, J. (2012). *Global policing*. Sage.

Bowling, B., & Sheptycki, J. (2016). Transnational policing and the end times of human rights. In *The Routledge international handbook of criminology and human rights* (pp. 431–442). Routledge.

Bowling, B., & Westenra, S. (2018). 'A really hostile environment': Adiaphorization, global policing and the crimmigration control system. *Theoretical Criminology*. https://doi.org/10.1177/1362480618774034

Brown MK (1981). *Working the street: Police discretion and the dilemmas of reform*. The Russell Sage Foundation

Cain, M. E. (2015). *Society and the Policeman's role*. Routledge.

Casey, C. (1995). *Work, self, and society: After industrialism*. Psychology Press.

Chan, J. B. (1997). *Changing police culture: Policing in a multicultural society*. Cambridge University Press.

Choongh, S. (1998). Policing the dross: A social disciplinary model of policing. *The British Journal of Criminology, 38*(4), 623–634.

Christie, N., & Bruun, K. (1985). *Den goda fienden: Narkotikapolitik i Norden*. Rabén & Sjögren.

Cockcroft, T. (2020). *Police culture: Research and practice*. Policy Press.

Davis, K. C. (1975). *Police discretion*. West Group.

De Botton A (2010). *The pleasures and sorrows of work*. Knopf Doubleday Publishing Group,

Dean, G., Fahsing, I. A., & Gottschalk, P. (2006). Profiling police investigative thinking: A study of police officers in Norway. *International Journal of the Sociology of Law, 34*(4), 221–228.

De Genova NP (2010). *The Deportation Regime: Sovereignty, Space, and the Freedom of Movement*. Durham, NC: Duke University Press.

Fassin, D. (2013). *Enforcing order: An ethnography of urban policing*. Polity Press.

Fassin, D. (2015). *Instituttseminaret SAI: Didier Fassin 'Boredom: The temporality of policing and the politics of time'*. Retrieved January 29, 2017, from http://www.sv.uio.no/sai/forskning/aktuelt/arrangementer/instituttseminaret/2015/desember-02-fassing.html

Fassin, D. (2017a). Boredom: Accounting for the ordinary in the work of policing (France). In D. Fassin (Ed.), *Writing the world of policing: The difference ethnography makes* (pp. 269–292). University of Chicago Press.

Fassin, D. (2017b). *Writing the world of policing: The difference ethnography makes*. University of Chicago Press.

Feagin, J. (2013). *Systemic racism: A theory of oppression*. Routledge.

Feldman, G. (2019). *The gray zone: Sovereignty, human smuggling, and undercover police investigation in Europe*. Stanford University Press.

Fielding, N. (1994). Cop canteen culture. In T. Newburn & E. Stanko (Eds.), *Just boys doing business* (pp. 46–63). Routledge.

Flyghed, J. (2002). Normalising the exceptional: The case of political violence. *Policing and Society, 13*(1), 23–41.

Franko, K. (2019). *The Crimmigrant other: Migration and penal power*. Routledge.

Goffman E (1957). Alienation from interaction. *Human relations, 10*: 47–60.

Goffman E (1961). *Encounters: Two Studies in the Sociology of Interaction*. Indianapolis: Bobbs-Merril.

Gundhus, H. O., & Franko, K. (2016). Global policing and mobility: Identity, territory, Sovereignty. In B. Bradford, B. Jauregui, I. Loader, et al. (Eds.), *The SAGE handbook of global policing*. SAGE Publications.

Hall, S., Critcher, C., Jefferson, T., et al. (2013). *Policing the crisis: Mugging, the state and law and order*. Palgrave Macmillan.

Hartwig, M., Anders Granhag, P., & Vrij, A. (2005). Police interrogation from a social psychology perspective. *Policing and Society, 15*(4), 379–399.

Holdaway, S., & O'Neill, M. (2006). Institutional racism after Macpherson: An analysis of police views. *Policing and Society, 16*(4), 349–369.

Holmberg, L. (1999). *Inden for lovens rammer*. Gyldendal.

Holmberg, L. (2000). Discretionary leniency and typological guilt: Results from a Danish study of police discretion. *Journal of Scandinavian Studies in Criminology and Crime Prevention, 1*(2), 179–194.

Holmberg, L. (2003). *Policing stereotypes: A qualitative study of police work in Denmark*. Galda & Wilch.

Kahn, W. A. (1990). Psychological conditions of personal engagement and disengagement at work. *Academy of Management Journal, 33*(4), 692–724.

Kammersgaard, T., Søgaard, T. F., Kolind, T., et al. (2022). 'Most officers are more or less colorblind': Police officers' reflections on the role of race and ethnicity in policing. *Race and Justice*. https://doi.org/10.1177/21533687221127445

Keith, M. (1993). *Race, riots and policing: Lore and disorder in a multi-racist society*. Ucl Press.

Kingshott, B., & Prinsloo, J. (2004). The universality of the 'police canteen culture'. *Acta Criminologica, 17*(1), 1–16.

Lipsky, M. (2010). *Street-level bureaucracy: Dilemmas of the individual in public service*. Russell Sage Foundation.

Loftus, B. (2009). *Police culture in a changing world*. Oxford University Press.

Loftus, B. (2010). Police occupational culture: Classic themes, altered times. *Policing and Society, 20*(1), 1–20.

Loftus, B., Goold, B., & Mac Giollabhui, S. (2015). From a visible spectacle to an invisible presence: The working culture of covert policing. *British Journal of Criminology, 56*(4), 629–645.

Manning, P. K. (1978). The police: Mandate, strategies, and appearances. In P. Manning (Ed.), *Policing: A view from the street* (pp. 7–31). Goodyear Publishing Company.

Mastrofski, S. D. (2004). Controlling street-level police discretion. *The Annals of the American Academy of Political and Social Science, 593*(1), 100–118.

McWilliam, E. (1999). *Pedagogical pleasures*. P. Lang.

Melossi, D. (2015). *Crime, punishment and migration*. SAGE Publications Ltd.

Muir, W. K. (1979). *Police: Streetcorner politicians*. University of Chicago Press.

Newburn, T., & Stanko, E. A. (1994). *Just boys doing business?* Routledge.

Olwig, K. F., Grünenberg, K., Møhl, P., et al. (2019). *The biometric border world: Technology, bodies and identities on the move*. Routledge.

Pickering, S., Bosworth, M., & Aas, K. F. (2015). The criminology of mobility. In S. Pickering & J. Ham (Eds.), *The Routledge handbook on crime and international migration*. Routledge.

Rowe, M. (2012). *Policing, race and racism*. Routledge.

Sausdal, D. (2020a). Everyday policing: Toward a greater analytical appreciation of the ordinary in police research. *Policing and Society*, 1–14.

Sausdal, D. (2020b). *On the workaday origin of police callousness*. Society of the Anthropology of Work.

Sausdal, D. (2020c). Police bullshit. *Journal of Extreme Anthropology, 4*(1), 94–115.

Sausdal, D. (2023). Dirty Harry gone global? On globalizing policing and punitive impotence. In J. Beek, T. Bierschenk, A. Kolloch, & B. Meyer (Eds.), *Policing race, ethnicity and culture: Ethnographic perspectives across Europe*. Manchester University Press.

Sheptycki, J. (2004). Organizational pathologies in police intelligence systems: Some contributions to the lexicon of intelligence-led policing. *European journal of criminology, 1*(3), 307–332.

Skogan, W. G., & Antunes, G. E. (1979). Information, apprehension, and deterrence: Exploring the limits of police productivity. *Journal of Criminal Justice, 7*(3), 217–241.

Skolnick, J. H. (1982). Deception by police. *Criminal Justice Ethics, 1*(2), 40–54.

Solhjell, R., Saarikkomäki, E., Haller, M. B., et al. (2019). 'We are seen as a threat': Police stops of young ethnic minorities in the Nordic countries. *Critical Criminology, 27*(2), 347–361.

Sollund, R. (2007). Canteen banter or racism: Is there a relationship between Oslo Police's use of derogatory terms and their attitudes and conduct towards ethnic minorities? *Journal of Scandinavian Studies in Criminology and Crime Prevention, 8*(1), 77–96.

Stumpf, J. P. (2006). The crimmigration crisis: Immigrants, crime, and sovereign power. *American University Law Review, 56*, 367.

Tham, H. (1995). Drug control as a national project: The case of Sweden. *Journal of Drug Issues, 25*(1), 113–128.

van Hulst, M. (2013). Storytelling at the Police Station the canteen culture revisited. *British Journal of Criminology, 53*(4), 624–642.

Van Maanen, J. (1978a). The asshole. In P. K. Manning & J. Van Maanen (Eds.), *Policing: A view from the street* (pp. 221–238). Goodyear Publishing.

Van Maanen, J. (1978b). On watching the watchers. In P. K. Manning & J. Van Maanen (Eds.), *Policing: A view from the street* (pp. 309–309). Goodyear Publishing.

Wacquant, L. (1999). Suitable enemies. *Punishment and Society, 1*(2), 215–222.

Waddington, P. A. (1999a). Discretion, 'Respectability' and Institutional Police Racism. *Sociological Research Online*.

Waddington, P. A. (1999b). Police (canteen) sub-culture. An appreciation. *British Journal of Criminology, 39*(2), 287–309.

Weber, L. (2013). *Policing non-citizens*. Routledge.

Weber, L., & Bowling, B. (2013). *Stop and search: Police power in global context*. Routledge.

3

Orwellianism

> **Vignette 11**
>
> "Trust me, David!" TFP (Task Force Pickpocketing) Detective Christensen promises, as he has promised and himself so many times before, "I know we need to work more closely together with the National Police, Europol and so on, and, hell, even the local post office if we're to improve our chances of tracking down these cross-border criminals".
>
> "And, yes", he carries on saying, now tapping his index finger on the top of his computer screen, "I know that we need to be better at using computers and sharing the info we gather. It's definitely the way to go in the battle against the problems of globalization. We know that. We need new technologies; something that allows us to better track and identify who and where the suspects are. But [pausing for a bit], I must also admit that when it comes to us actually developing and doing all this new and needed surveillance work, it quickly becomes a different story."

In Chap. 2, I discussed issues of police xenophobia as they relate to a globalizing of local policing and to the everyday work of a group of Danish detectives. This chapter goes in another direction, turning from

---

This chapter is a reworked version of a previously published article: Sausdal, D. (2020). Everyday deficiencies of police surveillance: A quotidian approach to surveillance studies. *Policing and Society, 30*(4), 462–478.

© The Author(s), under exclusive license to Springer Nature Switzerland AG 2023
D. Sausdal, *Globalizing Local Policing*, Transnational Crime, Crime Control and Security, https://doi.org/10.1007/978-3-031-18919-7_3

the more perceptual to the practical. Rather than focusing on how Danish detectives feel displeased with increasingly having to investigate international criminals, Chap. 3 focuses on different practical developments that are supposed to make local policing more successful in a time of growing globalization. As TFP Detective Christensen underlines in the above quote, there is indeed in the Danish Police a shared understanding of the importance of developing their capacity and ability to police more global and complex forms of criminality—a professional policing development that fundamentally includes a focus on increasing collaborations with external and especially international partners as well as a growing implementation and use of various information and surveillance technologies (see also Bowling & Sheptycki, 2012; Ratcliffe, 2016; Fyfe et al., 2017; Egbert & Leese, 2021).

While Danish police management and its Danish frontline officers are often very outspoken about the importance of expanding and developing their surveillance capacity, my study of the two task forces also revealed another and somewhat conflicting story. Here, we may again return to the issues raised in the opening quote by Detective Christensen. Being part of TFP, tasked with investigating organized pickpocketing and credit card fraud committed by foreign nationals in Denmark, Christensen and his colleagues were constantly reminded by the management of the importance of collaborating with international partners and to keep their computer databases updated. The detectives were reminded thereof because of how cross-border collaboration and sharing of criminal intelligence were seen as, as the management would stress,

> the *only* way of making sure that we can keep an eye on and catch these cross-border criminals. If we don't extend our possibilities of following them across borders, to the next country or back to Romania or Africa or wherever they belong, it's all too easy for them to escape us nowadays.

Similar words resounded throughout Task Force Burglary (TFB), with international burglars being among their main suspects. TFB had its own undercover stake-out team, they had on-going collaborations with other countries' law enforcement, they had offices and cars fitted with state-of-the-art surveillance equipment, and they frequently communicated with international policing bodies such as Europol, Eurojust and Interpol. Indeed, as the TFB management lectured me on one of the first days I spent with them; "here at TFB, to be successful, we need ways of shadowing these cross-border criminals that are as mobile as they are".

With the above in mind, it was therefore not a big surprise to hear Detective Christensen and many of his colleagues talk about the great importance of them working "more closely together with the National Police, Europol [and] be better at using computers and sharing the info we gather", as he put it. What *was* unexpected, however, was how they in their daily work often didn't follow suit. As the introductory quote is meant to illustrate, the task forces' highly skilled and specialized detectives would willingly mirror recurrent calls for a growth of police surveillance *yet*, when push came to shove, they would habitually avoid answering these calls. As Detective Christensen admitted it himself, the otherwise affirmative story about the police developing and dedicating themselves to new and increasing types of surveillance work in a time of globalized and complex crime became a less Orwellian story when looking at their actual workday. Why, this chapter essentially asks, was there such a discrepancy between the official surveillance discourse and the detectives' daily doings? What made the Danish detectives echo the emphasis on making policing more omnipresent and even surreptitious, only then to circumvent doing so in practice?

In the following pages, different examples of why that is are offered. On the one hand, these examples serve as a reminder that the everyday reality of present-day police and surveillance work may not necessarily be as efficient and thought-through as some scholarship on the matter may lead us to believe. In noting this, the chapter also adds to the similar findings of the growing number of ethnographic and otherwise qualitative studies of "the quotidian [or] even banal character of surveillant practices" (Friesen et al., 2012, p. 73)—studies which seek to highlight the everyday reality of (police) surveillance as well as how it does not always match the graveness and grandeur of policy statements (see also Friesen et al, 2009). Speaking directly to the book's overall focus on local police concerns in a globalizing world, the chapter demonstrates how a group of Danish detectives did not only not follow the stated policies, but sometimes even actively bemoaned and opposed them. Contrary to the idea that policing and surveillance actors all appreciate new and ever-more obstruse Orwellian opportunities, the Danish detectives I spent time with frequently saw them as a hindrance to what they liked about their work.

Surveillance Theories

> Social control has become more specialized and technical and, in many ways, more penetrating and intrusive ... There is the danger of an almost imperceptible surveillance creep. (Marx, 1988, p. 2)

To gauge the differences between the doctrinal versus the daily doings of the Danish detectives, it is worth revisiting the current state of (police) surveillance theory. Doing so, we may go back to Marx's influential book on undercover police surveillance, and surveillance more generally in which he warned about not only a growing "surveillance creep" but an emerging "cult of surveillance" (ibid.). Though 30 years have passed since his work was published, Marx's warning has been continuously echoed in much police and surveillance research as well as in wider criminological studies. Studies differ in both scope and substance, yet they stand united in arguing that present-day surveillance and control has dramatically and problematically increased. Applying a variety of custodian concepts to diagnose the development, for example "panopticon" (Gordon, 1987; Mathiesen, 1997; Fox, 2001; Haggerty, 2006), "ban-opticon" (Bigo, 2008), "prepression" (Schinkel, 2011), "assemblage" (Haggerty & Ericson, 2000), "network" (Jones & Newburn, 2006), "web" (Brodeur, 2010) or even "surveillance society/culture" (Lyon, 1994, 2018; Mathiesen, 2013), they tell a story of governmental surveillance having become both more pervasive and intrusive, more inescapable as well as inequitable.

In essence, this is a twofold story. First, scholars point to how policing actors are less sectorial than they used to be. Rather than merely minding their own territories, we are seeing a significant growth in both public and private policing collaborations across international borders as well as institutional boundaries. Public police forces increasingly cooperate bi- or multilaterally or via international institutions, and they are partnering up with non-policing actors, for instance when seeking out illegal immigrants via collaborations with Customs or Immigration as well as private and civic actors (cf. Aliverti, 2013, 2014, 2021; Weber, 2013, Franko, 2019). In this way, by extending their collaborative reach, the police's surveillance and control mechanisms are becoming more wide-reaching. Secondly, another and even bigger reason why present-day surveillance has become more ubiquitous is the expansion and integration of various surveillance and information technologies. Among other things, this includes new technological means of tracking people via, for example, audio or video surveillance, recorded biometrics or via the digital footprints we leave behind when using our electronic devices. Ultimately, such (both overtly and covertly) obtained intelligence and information become digitalized data subsequently shared with relevant policing partners, thereby bettering the police's chances of monitoring and finding otherwise itinerant and hard-to-locate suspects in a globalized world. To reuse Haggerty and Ericson's critical conclusion from their celebrated article on "The Surveillant Assemblage", contemporary surveillance may thus be understood as being "driven by the desire to bring systems together, to combine practices and technologies and integrate them into a larger whole" (2000, p. 610)—a disquieting Orwellian development that 11 years later led Haggerty, Wilson and Smith to declare that

> Western societies appear to be in the midst of a world historical transformation in terms of the amount and intensity of surveillance. This is an overdetermined development, one that is obviously related to the rise of new information technologies and visualizing devices … As we look to the future it is easy to anticipate that the role of surveillance in crime control is only apt to increas[e]. (Haggerty et al., 2011, pp. 235–236)

To be sure, according to many scholarly predictions and concerns, the future is one where not only criminal suspects but all of us can expect to be increasingly if not constantly monitored—be it in person or as a "data double" (Haggerty & Ericson, 2000). Of course, the question is whether the future is really the future or if the future isn't already here?

A More Quotidian Approach

Studies of present-day Orwellianism have been important to our current understanding of the wide-reaching and often discriminatory developments of policing and surveillance. Although studies may differ and disagree, they all succeed in bringing attention to the, as Marx initially put it, "surveillance creep" which many a politician have ungrudgingly endorsed and which policing actors are progressively employing, also including Danish politicians and police. This chapter is therefore not written as a critique of these studies. Instead, the aim is to look for an additional perspective; to follow the still few yet thought-provoking studies of what Monahan has described as "quotidian" studies of "surveillance as cultural practice" (2011). As he explains this alternative approach, then

> [r]ather than analyzing surveillance technologies, for instance, as exogenous tools that are mobilized by actors to deal with perceived problems or needs, studying surveillance as cultural practice [is] an approach [m]ore likely to try to comprehend people's experiences of and engagement with surveillance on their own terms, stressing the production of emic over etic forms of knowledge [and thereby] offer[ing] vital insights to surveillance. (Monahan, 2011, p. 496)

Here is an alternative methodology to the study of (police) surveillance. As Monahan suggests, new and vital insights may be offered if we force ourselves to forget the established canon of political and police discourse on surveillance in an attempt to examine how surveillance is actually practised and perceived by those tasked with developing/doing it—proposing a bottom-up rather than top-down approach (see also Lyon, 2018). Looking at the practice rather than principles of surveillance, the question thus becomes a matter of how surveillance actors, in the workaday lives, "combine practices and technologies and integrate them into a larger whole", to reuse Haggerty and Ericson's words, rather than unquestioningly accepting the existence of the larger whole.

Though studies are still limited, more and more bottom-up, ethnographic studies have come to the fore in recent years, including studies of both police actors (Sheptycki, 2004; Kruger & Haggerty, 2006; Manning,

2008; Franko & Gundhus, 2015; Loftus et al., 2015; Fyfe et al., 2017; Feldman, 2019; Olwig et al., 2019) and, for instance, CCTV operators (McCahill & Norris, 1999; Wilson & Sutton, 2003; Smith, 2009). On a more encompassing level, Schuilenburg has recently outlined and argued for a study of the daily "patchwork" of the securitization of society (2017). By using the concept of patchwork, Schuilenburg exactly highlights how Orwellian types of surveillance exist not as a detached and stable a priori entity; instead present-day surveillance and securitization is enacted or, indeed, patched together through daily and often routinized social interactions—a view mirrored in Lyon's newest work on the everyday culture(s) of surveillance (2018). Serving as both an empirical supplement as well as an analytical correction to prevalent conceptualizations, these bottom-up studies highlight how it is imperative not to automatically confuse discourse with daily life, nor policy with practice. In short, they illustrate the simple importance of examining how different kinds of surveillance and control practitioners *actually* carry out and experience their work—a scientific endeavor increasingly important as, in Friesen et al.'s words, a "response to the increasingly quotidian, even banal character of surveillant practices in postindustrial societies" (2012, p. 73).

Quotidian Problems We Already Know Of

Existing studies of surveillance as an everyday, cultural practice make up this chapter's theoretical as well as methodological point of departure. Moreover, they provide not only a guiding framework but also a few particularly interesting analytical inspirations. For example, in their qualitative study of Frontex, Franko and Gundhus (2015) explored the daily effects of international police cooperation as they interviewed a number of Norwegian police officers engaged at Frontex. While Frontex, on the one hand, is an apparent instantiation of how present-day policing is expanding beyond the nation-state (both in practice and digitally via the European Border Surveillance System), Franko and Gundhus point our attention to the everyday complications of such cross-border cooperation. When the Norwegian officers were interviewed, they did, just like their Danish colleagues, amenably speak of the need for increasing international collaboration. However, as Franko and Gundhus' study shows, they also spent a lot of time pointing to a number of mundane factors that complicated the effectiveness of the cooperation. The Norwegian officers spoke of how they found it difficult to communicate with other Frontex officers as they didn't necessarily speak a mutual language (ibid., p. 1). The Norwegian officers also spoke of problematic cultural differences, both in terms of how officers from different countries went about behaving professionally as well as privately, and of how these differences in opinion frequently led to serious disagreements (see also Larsson, 2006; Lemieux, 2013; Christensen, 2017; Basic & Yakhlef, 2022).

Additionally, Franko and Gundhus' (2015) study points to another particularly important issue that much international police cooperation entails, namely the issue of "police (dis)trust". As research has consistently shown, the police's work culture is very often characterized by a strong in-group trust and similarly strong out-group distrust (ibid.). Police officers tend to only truly confide in their closer colleagues and simultaneously be highly skeptical of any outsider, leading them to approach most people with a certain amount of suspicion, especially if the people in question are not already well-known to them. As Franko and Gundhus illustrate, this ingrained mechanism of (dis)trust has an unfortunate effect on international police cooperation as unknown international colleagues, although also being police, are often regarded with skepticism. This is obviously not something that allows for a productive work environment. And it is therefore also the reason why Lemieux in his larger study on exactly the problems of international police cooperation has argued that the "cultural heterogeneity inherent in international cooperation introduces the potential to aggravate the ever-present lack of trust in police subcultures" (2013, p. 4). Consequently, while a well-functioning cooperation between international policing partners is seen as integral to a spread of police surveillance and the globalization of policing more broadly (cf. Bowling & Sheptycki, 2012), it is continuously made difficult by various linguistic and cultural problems—with one of these paradoxically being located at the heart of police culture itself, that is that police officers tend to treat people whom they don't already have close knowledge of, including international partners, with suspicion (see also Ross, 2004).

Where Franko and Gundhus as well as Lemieux primarily focus their study on trans-/international police cooperation, other studies are looking at how traditional, local police work is affected by the growing implementation of surveillance, information and other investigational technologies (Sheptycki, 2004; Kruger & Haggerty, 2006; Manning, 2008; Loftus et al., 2015). On the one hand, they reveal the same push toward the implementation of technologies in order to combat developments in crime and other global risks. Yet, mirroring the interest of this chapter, they also shine a light on some considerable issues when it comes to the everyday use of policing technologies. As Gundhus (2013) for example illustrates in her study of the Norwegian police, Norwegian police officers often find that the work involved in information technologies differs problematically from their usual way of thinking and working. Speaking of the increased use of surveillance and information technologies in policing as either "evidence-based policing" (cf. Fleming, 2018), "intelligence-led policing" (cf. Ratcliffe, 2016) or "knowledge-based policing", as Gundhus prefers, such new police work promotes "a concept of knowledge", she asserts,

> that indirectly threatens the police officers' traditional experience-based knowledge and professional discretion ... Knowledge-based policing emphasizes a logic based on evaluation of codified, standardized information-systems, rather than an experience-based, action-oriented, and collegial logic. (Gundhus, 2013, p. 178)

Gundhus is not alone in her observation. As other studies have also shown (cf. Egbert & Leese, 2021), frontline officers tend to find an increasing reliance on computers, data and analysis to be somewhat in conflict with their believed ability and wish to rely on their own wits. One could even say that frontline officers' skepticism toward an increasing use of data and technology more than personal experience is related to the earlier-mentioned skepticism among police officers in relation to working with more or less unknown colleagues. Police officers, it seems, tend to trust and prefer that and those which emanate from their own personal involvement—disregarding whether it is matter of computer-generated insights or international partnerships.

Lastly, studies have also demonstrated that it is not just conventional normative or cultural preferences that cause problems in relation to the police's daily use of technology. As Sheptycki has illustrated, there are many other inherent "pathologies in police intelligence systems" (2004). Among other things, these "pathologies" are due to the stark hierarchical nature of police organizations as well as the tendency for knowledge to be generated, and thus also biased, in relation to the interest at hand. Although the ultimate success of information technologies as an efficient tool of surveillance and police work is dependent on the horizontal extension of information, police organizations tend to funnel information vertically up and down their hierarchical structures, generating what Sheptycki calls "information silos" (ibid., p. 320). Knowledge becomes compartmentalized rather than spread, and the practices and products of surveillance risk becoming haphazard and insubstantial (see also Manning, 2008). Adding to this problem, studies have shown how police officers tend to have a quite selective approach to knowledge generation (see Sheptycki, 2004). If you investigate murders, for example, you will find certain information to be of interest. If you investigate property crime, other observations might be that which catches your eye. And, as my study showed me, if you are one of the relatively few Danish detectives investigating cross-border criminality, then you are at risk of being one of the few within the organization finding this and the work it includes to be of specific importance, inevitably tainting the quantity *and* quality of the gathered intelligence and data.

The Orwellianism of Danish Detectives (Or Lack Thereof)

In 2010, the Chief of Copenhagen Police declared that Danish citizens were to "expect more surveillance in the future". This is a surveillance positive statement that has subsequently been echoed by many a Danish politician and police representative. For example, former Danish Prime Minister, Lars Løkke Rasmussen, has announced that even though "we don't want to live in a surveillance society", there should be a discussion of how "we may extend the space and means of surveillance" in order to "keep a keen eye on some of the forces in our society that constitute a risk". It was therefore with great pride and satisfaction that Police Commissioner Svend Larsen in February 2017 was able to warn criminals and reassure worried citizens by declaring that the Danish police had acquired a new "super weapon". This super weapon, which was also—and has been since—termed both a "revolution" and "a quantum leap toward a modernized Police", was a state-of-the-art and very expensive pre-crime computer system named "Polintel" developed by Palantir Technologies.

As mentioned at the beginning of this chapter, it was not only the politicians and police management who were wishing for a new computerized super weapon, for a quantum leap. The view that the future of policing would necessarily have to be that of more technologized and internationally oriented work was repeatedly echoed among the task forces' detectives. As we were sitting together at a remote location on the outskirts of Copenhagen from where the Danish railways' CCTV cameras can be monitored, Detective Madsen yet again shared his and his colleagues view on the matter:

> In this new global world, we need more global means of policing. When crime and criminals move more, then we also need to be able to do that. That's why we need to have systems that can trace such movements. If we don't develop new methods, we'll be left behind.

Having heard both the Danish police management and the Danish detectives so routinely expressing their fear of being "left behind" and, thus, their desire for a, to paraphrase the police commissioner, "future of surveillance", I indeed became very surprised when the detectives' daily activities did in fact often not work toward this future but at times even seemed to go against it. To be sure, the reasons for this gap between a seeming panoptic ideal and practical everyday considerations were many and ranged from the more openly explicit to the unconscious and rather banal. In the next section, I will make an effort to provide some telling examples of some of the main reasons why the Danish detectives, at the end of the day, didn't so easily appreciate the described policing and surveillance developments. Much inspired by the aforementioned research into the everyday practices of surveillance, I have divided the examples into three explanatory categories of, respectively, "cultural problems", "technological problems" and "private problems"—problems that all stemmed from the detectives' workday considerations rather than wider ideological demands or desires.

Cultural Problems

The "cultural problems" of the Danish detectives' surveillance work are related to the issues mentioned earlier. Specifically, they concern how police cooperation and technology runs the risk of sparking the inherent distrust in police workculture toward people and phenomena that individual officers lack personal experience of, be it a foreign colleague or "foreign" data on a computer screen.

The fact that personal experience is preferred over the perceived detachment of information technologies and international cooperation was made abundantly clear to me when I was given the opportunity to visit the Danish representation at Europol in The Hague, also known as "The Danish Desk".

> **Vignette 12**
>
> Even before I have had the opportunity to sit down and enjoy the lukewarm coffee I have just been offered, Officer Poulsen starts talking. As I am sure he has already heard of my research interests, he straightaway tells me that one of the biggest challenges to a functional international police cooperation is what they down in Europol call "the cousin police":
>
> "Let me just tell you how it is; the problem when it comes to securing a well-functioning international police partnership is that much policing itself is based on suspicion if not downright distrust. You simply only trust that which you have experienced first-hand yourself or the people you've met. We call this 'the cousin police' down here in The Hague. The thing is, that many of our colleagues back home might call us, but they don't really trust the stranger on the phone, even though he is also police, and even if he is also Danish. It's all the same to them. They don't know me. They don't fully trust me".

The problems described by the Danish Europol officer as that of "the cousin police", and the major hindrance these placed in the way of police cooperation, resonated well with the observations I made during my time at TFB and TFP. Spending day and night with them, I got to see how the task forces' detectives often reacted with a certain degree of hesitancy—hesitancy I would otherwise not notice in their more conventional day-to-day work. In line with previous research, their hesitancy or even outright distrust particularly showed itself when, respectively, the detectives were being pushed to work with externally developed information/intelligence or when having to cooperate with more-or-less unfamiliar colleagues.

> **Vignette 13**
>
> "You just don't readily believe some numbers you see on the screen. Nor do you simply buy everything that's written on a piece of paper that you haven't yourself had a chance to double-check. You always treat such information with caution. Always!"
>
> Reading yet another report from the one of the National Police's intelligence unit, these are the conclusions drawn by TFB Detective Andersen. She is venting her frustration to me, as she had spent most of the day going through the report. Earlier that day, the management had asked her to read it. Actually, the management had been asking Andersen and her colleagues about the report for several weeks now ever since it had found its way into their inboxes.
>
> "Today is the day", Andersen had announced after the morning briefing. Unfortunately, having now browsed more than actually read the report, her conclusion is that she is "not getting anything out of it besides a headache". As the report outlines current developments of different serious organized crimes of specific interest to her and her colleagues' work, one could have expected a more positive outcome.
>
> "Listen", she says, "it's not that we don't understand the value of these things. We kinda do. But we very often experience a big disconnect between our practical reality and these general illustrations and theories". The other colleagues in the office agree. "She's right", Detective Pallsesen says in support. "I feel the same. It's a pity, but that's how it is. We sit here with these reports and analyses, often with the sense that they bring about more questions than answers".

Andersen and Pallesen weren't alone in thinking like that. In general, the task forces detectives weren't easily impressed by the otherwise increasing amount of criminal intelligence and analyses they were receiving—in writing or on their computers. The following example provides further evidence that this was the case:

> **Vignette 14**
>
> For a long time, the detectives at TFB had been complaining about the lack of "useful intelligence" as they put it. This morning however, Detective Jensen had received an interesting email from Europol. The email, as he now shows me, contains information about a suspected Romanian burglar on his way to Denmark. There is a name, photo and a brief description of the burglar's MO. "This could be what we've been waiting for", Detective Jensen says, explaining to Detective Pedersen what he just received.
>
> Later, after lunch, I ask Detective Jensen about the intel and what they will be doing.
>
> "You seemed pretty thrilled about the Europol intel you got earlier … ?" I query. "Hmm … yeah … there's some decent intel here … [he hesitates] …. but then again … [hesitating again] … here's the thing; where should we start? Right? I often feel like this when we receive this kind of intel from Europol", Detective Jensen explains whilst staring at the picture of the suspect. "When you haven't yourself got any real experience of these people, like who they are and how they work, but only this scarce, generalized info, it becomes hard to work with. It's like a bone without any flesh on it".

Detective Jensen's hesitation ended up leading him and his colleagues to conclude that their resources were better used elsewhere. And, similarly, the earlier-mentioned intelligence report from the National Police ended up giving Detective Andersen more of a headache than inspiring her. Indeed. What the examples are meant to illustrate is that even though the detectives were seemingly yearning for useful intelligence and help from national and international colleagues, they often had a hard time getting themselves to react when receiving it. Their phone would ring, an email would tick in or a report would be delivered, making the detectives hopeful, yet, nevertheless, often deciding against putting it to use. In theory, it felt like a good idea. But in practice, the detectives had a hard time relating the received intelligence to their own everyday experiences.

"We also call this the snowball-method—or the snowball-problem", I was later told by Detective Pedersen:

> There is definitely a tendency in police work to simply work from case to case, using one case as the starting point for the next. So, if potentially good but unknown intelligence comes along, detectives will be a bit apprehensive about taking it up. Maybe that's stupid but it's the truth. The cases you've just worked seem more familiar and safer, and also easier to be honest, which will ultimately make you choose them over these other more abstract ones.

Furthermore, the task forces' detectives not only had what they would also speak of as "a healthy skepticism" toward intelligence and insights that they themselves had not been involved in producing. Their skepticism also very much included potential colleagues whom they hadn't had the chance to work with before.

Confirming what prior research have also found, I have many examples thereof, the earlier-mentioned "cousin police" notion being one of them. One way of further appreciating this issue is however to recount what the task forces' detectives answered when I asked them about how many national and international colleagues working with cross-border crime they knew? During my fieldwork, I would also interview these colleagues, and the two things that I had consistently been told were that further cooperation between the local and the (inter)national level was "absolutely necessary", but also that the parties involved in fact had very limited contacts with each other. Thus, in asking the detectives about whom they knew, I didn't expect them to be able to provide many names. My expectations were met. One task force detective was able to give me the names of two relevant colleagues, another detective one name, but most of them were unable to recall a single name when it came to their (inter)national colleagues who were also involved in policing cross-border crimes. Knowing that collaboration is key to cross-border crime policing, this didn't seem promising. However, the task forces' detectives uniformly explained this (away) by saying that

> yeah, we should be better at working together. Tracking cross-border criminals becomes difficult if we don't. Yet, we honestly never hear from them. And when we ask them for help, it often turns out to be unproductive.

Thereby again, the detectives were echoing the idea that external help sounds like a good idea but that it "honestly" is often of little actual use. Though there might be some truth to this, what was curious about this statement was that colleagues at both the Danish National Police and Europol said the exact same thing when I asked them why they didn't work more closely with one another. To them, collaboration was equally troubled by a lacking engagement and expediency, not on their behalf, of course, but because of the frontline detectives. Hence, while a lack of coordination and productiveness might explain some of the task forces' detectives' hesitancy toward more and wider collaboration, it doesn't seem to explain it in full. Instead, it once again seems to be the police's ingrained suspicious demeanor which is at fault.

Later in my fieldwork, I observed one specifically evocative example of this when I was with TFB. TFB was running a large-scale investigation into a suspected Romanian criminal group, suspected of not only bringing burglars into the country but of human trafficking. Due to the cross-border nature of the investigation, TFB had established contact with Europol and Eurojust to seek help from Romanian authorities. As many of the criminal suspects TFB dealt with were from Romania, the TFB management and its detectives would indeed frequently talk about "the importance of securing assistance from the Romanians". Meanwhile, I also observed a constant skepticism about the possibility of such a collaboration.

> **Vignette 15**
>
> "It would be great for the case but we're also afraid that our efforts will be futile. We shouldn't get our hopes up. Let's be honest, it's not the most well-run country down there. Corruption and stuff, right?", the TFB management announces before a planned video conference call with the Romanian national prosecutor. "And then there's the question of why they should want to help us. I mean, is it really in the Romanian authorities' best interest to help us catch Romanians?", he reminds everyone just a second before their Romanian colleague appears on the slightly pixelated screen.
>
> "The meeting went alright, don't you think?" one of the leading detectives concludes. The conference call is over and everyone seems happy. "I was honestly convinced that they wouldn't want to help at all—that they would be taking the piss—but it did actually seem like they might want to help out after all. Let's see. Fingers crossed".

Indeed, statements like "they probably don't want to help" were common. To the detectives as well as its management, talking to and asking for help from international partners was often a daring endeavor filled with apprehension. This again may be viewed as the perfect example of the general distrust they had of policing partners whom they didn't personally know, coupled with ingrained prejudice about many international police forces capabilities as well as credibility. As TFP Detective Madsen also explained to me, describing why he did not reach out more often to Europol or the National Police despite the fact that he recognized the importance of building up these relationships:

> I don't really know these guys. Maybe if I'd worked with them before I'd contact them more. But when you don't know them it feels a bit weird. You don't know what to expect. It feels a bit like you're losing control of the situation … So, instead, we often just reach out to people we already know. And if we don't know anyone, it kind of ends there to be honest …

The seemingly endemic issue of (dis)trust with local police organizations limits the way in which they work—and arguably even more so when working with more global criminal matters that inevitably push the police to work with materials and persons more foreign to them.

This brings us to the next, and related, "cultural problem", being that of the notorious police "nose" or "gut". As we all know from having watched endless hours of police series on Netflix, the "nose" or the "gut" are emic police concepts that speak of their predilection for knowledge that has been personally embodied rather than technologically disseminated—something which is not just an occupational preference but also heavily linked to the police's assessment of their own professional worth. Here is an example:

Vignette 16

I'm sitting in the foyer of one of Copenhagen's larger hotels with TFP Detective Larsen. We are undercover, in plain clothes, drinking coffee, looking for "breakfast thieves". "Breakfast thieves" are the detectives' fitting label for thieves who steal hotel guests' bags whilst the guests are enjoying the breakfast buffet. The detectives have told me that it is difficult to know exactly where these breakfast thieves will be, thieves who are, I'm told, most often from Chile.

"How do you know where to look for them?" I ask Detective Larsen. Detective Larsen doesn't take much time thinking about my question as he instantly points to his nose. "This. That's how. You know because of the experience you get from having done this for a long time." "But", I ask in a slightly critical tone, "Wouldn't you be able to know better if you did some sort of analysis of the data you have?" "Nah ... " he replies, "These criminals don't follow a specific route. Like, the only thing we know is that they travel from Chile to Denmark somewhere during summertime. Also, we know that if they were here yesterday, then they're probably not coming here today".

"But", he says, having paused for a good second, "then again, because it's so stupid and insane to return to the same hotel the following day maybe it's actually the smart thing to do, right? So, you know, this is what I'm saying. The only thing we can do is to follow this [pointing to his nose again]".

Pointing to their noses, or in other ways referring to having a well-developed, embodied sense of where criminals might be, was a normal way for both the TFB and TFP detectives to explain how they worked. It was also a habitual way for them to explain what they believed to be the limitations of the technologies and wider means of intelligence and analyses that were otherwise made available to them when going on their surveillance stake-outs. As earlier described, they would frequently receive reports and analyses from Europol, the National Police or from their own district, in which crime patterns were studied and dissected, also often including practical recommendations. The detectives would even themselves speak of how they at times even longed for "some good analyses that can optimize our surveillances and investigations". However, mirroring Detective Andersen's earlier words, when they received the analyses, the normal thing for them to do was to briefly skim them, and then ignore them. Here is an example:

> **Vignette 17**
>
> "Shouldn't we get the Department of Analytics to look at these Polish pickpockets?" the TFP management ask its detectives, with me listening from my usual spot in the corner. "Sure! If they can put something together about who these damn Poles work with, their MO, etc., that'd be amazing", Detective Larsen answers quickly.
>
> About two weeks later, Detective Larsen receives the requested analysis. He prints out a copy to read and share with the other detectives. He comes back from the printer quickly flipping through the pages. He looks at it some more and then he puts it to the side. None of the other detectives ask for it. Surprised by their lack of enthusiasm, remembering how keen they had all been on getting such a report, I ask him what he thought of it.
>
> "Hmm ... first of all, we got it a bit late. Two weeks is a long time. Secondly, it just outlines how some of our suspects might be connected, but it's really not that different from what we already know. So, yeah, I can't see how this helps us." The other detectives concur. And the report is quickly placed on the dusty window shelf together with other documents that they have apparently deemed unfit for actual police work.

One might well ask if the Danish detectives were right in their reading of this report, and much other intelligence they received, as being practically useless? It does seem fair to note that a report that is not received until two weeks after cross-border criminal activities have been detected—criminal activities which often involve suspects swiftly leaving the country—is rather unusable and that the reports thereby often fell short in terms of what the detectives needed. However, the detectives' reluctance to use intelligence analyses and other surveillance reports went beyond such explanations. In my experience at least, it had a lot more to do with their fondness of their "noses", than the alleged nonsense of the report.

That the notorious "police nose" was a hindrance to a more globally oriented police work was well-known to one of the primary producers of such reports, a seasoned detective working at the National Police's "Centre of Investigations" named Gustavsen. Gustavsen and the small intelligence team he belonged to were tasked with collecting and analyzing intelligence on cross-border crime at the national and international level. They were, I was told, the Danish police's "absolute experts" when it came to this. Being the Danish experts, the team was making many efforts in disseminating their knowledge to their frontline colleagues. As Gustavsen told me, they had for example written a small and, according to him, "very accessible" pamphlet on what Danish officers should do when investigating and encountering suspected cross-border criminals. Among other things, the pamphlet included what information to acquire in order to ensure that the Danish police had accurate and useful data on the matter. Detective Gustavsen and his colleagues had even included a little description of how to read a Romanian ID card to ensure that frontline officers didn't write down the suspect's last name as his/her first name or vice versa:

> "Making that mistake is common", Gustavsen says. "Let me tell you. "And if the guys out there make a mistake, we won't be able to recognize the person in our systems the next time we meet him .... Seriously, this pamphlet could be understood by your grandma. I've been on a tour around the country, telling detectives and officers how important it is that our data are generated correctly. But ... yeah ... I know I've done it in vain. They're stuck in their usual ways. They pretend to listen, but they don't."

Here we may again return to the issue of "the nose". As Punch has also noted in his description of what the police recognize as "a nice piece of work", the police have a tendency to invoke bodily concepts such as "a 'feeling' or a 'nose' for the unusual or suspicious" (1979, p. 46). In a Danish context, the former Head of National Murder Investigations, H. J. Bonnichsen, confirms this in his book on police investigation and interrogation methods, where he describes how one of the central qualities of a murder detective is that they have "a nose for" murder (2012). Recalling Gustavsen's above words, this is indeed "their usual ways"—a preference for a personalized way of policing over albeit clever pamphlets which is core to police and especially "detective culture" (cf. Ericson, 1981; Innes, 2003; Manning, 2006; Bacon, 2017; Feldman, 2019). As Gundhus has therefore argued, the problem is not whether or not new technologies and practices are in fact useful but, more so, that they clash with deep-seated police ideas about what constitutes "real police work" (2013). Police officers, she explains, are both used to and prefer to work using "traditional experience-based knowledge and professional discretion", whereas "a logic based on evaluation of codified, standardized information-systems" is not only different from their normal vocational practice but threatens to undermine the individual police officer's feeling of professional worth (Gundhus, 2013, p. 178). To be sure, this is closely related to Smith's argument that information technologies might "empower the watcher" whilst simultaneously "disempowering the worker" (2009).

Following from this, though surveillance technology may grant practitioners a bigger perspective, there is a risk that this will also streamline and thus simplify the daily, practical engagements which many practitioners find to be specifically meaningful. This, I believe, is why it is important to remember that what Danish detectives point out, when pointing to their noses or guts, is not just that they are reactionaries, instinctively reluctant to take onboard new ways of working. They are also pointing to what they believe to constitute not only good but gratifying police work. Stated differently, when detectives feel that they have less discretion as a result of the more mechanical and external nature of information technologies, and that their personal/professional experience is being made somewhat obsolete, they become skeptical. Speaking of their noses or guts, or refusing to read a pamphlet, should therefore not only be gauged as a simple conservative preference on the part of some police officers who revel in and romanticize the past. Nor should it only be understood as a simple or even stupid suspicion toward computerized data or the work of foreign colleague. In order to truly understand why the local police remains skeptical, their seeming obsession with bodily metaphors may also be appreciated as a manifestation of general apprehensiveness toward the way in which new developments in policing and surveillance negatively affect what they understand as being at the heart of their professional worth.

Technological Problems

Another recurring hindrance to the task forces' detectives' use of information and surveillance technologies had less to do with cultural issues and more with the technology itself. One rather basic yet very significant issue the detectives had was that the technologies were so many—and that only more were being bought and implemented. The sheer quantity and continuous flux of, for example, new intelligence and investigative computer programs made for a slight schizophrenia among them. The detectives' celebrated their arrival while feeling both disoriented and embarrassed for not being up to speed. Knowing that this concerned them, I one day asked Detective Jensen to draw me up a list of the different computer programs he knew of and mostly used. This is the list he provided:

> **Vignette 18**
>
> - KR—The national crime registry, POLSAS—The police's case management system
> - PED—The police's investigation database
> - FR—The national population registry
> - CRM—The national motor vehicle database
> - POLMAPLITE—A search engine which combines POLSAS with geographical maps and graphs
> - The informant registry
> - TARGET360—a surveillance system
> - The firearms registry
> - "I believe these are the most relevant ones But there are many others. Trust me. And new ones are being developed all the time", TFB Detective Jensen explains to me, sounding more forewarningly than excited. "But, to perfectly be honest" he quickly carries on saying, looking at the list he just created, "most days most of us only use a couple of them, to be honest".

After having listed all the programs—and also telling me about a couple more he suddenly came to think of—Detective Jensen also took the time to log on to and go through all the different programs with me. In doing so, I was given an immediate understanding of the simple challenges posed by the existence of such a large number of computer programs. To a novice like me it felt overwhelming. Using these different programs and systems was of course part of the detectives' job, meaning that one would expect them to have a better of understanding of the programs, which they certainly had. Yet, even though they were not novices, it was however obvious how the very multitude of programs and interfaces felt fairly overwhelming. Learning to know and navigate each and every one of them took time the detectives' neither could nor would afford. Instead, they tended to "rely on the most central and old systems that we do know", as many of the task forces' detectives in one way or another admitted—one of these systems being the KR-registry (i.e. the national crime registry), which was developed for the 1980s' MS-DOS operating system!

The already sheer quantity and constant introduction of new systems were perhaps also why the detectives were not easily persuaded when the management encouraged them to use a new intelligence computer program named POLKON. One day, when the detectives turned up for work and turned on their computers, a small pop-up window designed in the form of a slot machine would playfully encourage the detectives to use this new-fangled intelligence and investigation system. "Do you want to catch an internationally wanted criminal?", the pop-window said, enticing the detectives to pull the lever and use this new computer program. Yet, even though I was studying the work of detectives whose job it precisely was to catch international criminals, I never experienced them pulling the lever and using this system (as is also revealed by the absence of the system from Detective Jensen's list). For some weeks, the pop-up window was there. And then it was gone. Truth be told, it was almost like the detectives never really noticed it. "Yeah, I did see it, but I didn't really pay it any attention. Just clicked the x and moved on", Detective Axelsen said, as I had brought up the question over lunch.

The problems produced by an overload of computer systems in relation to getting the police to actually use them is one of the central "pathologies" of policing surveillance systems as earlier noted by Sheptycki. "[The] multiple recording of data on multiple systems and at multiple levels is a contributing factor" to why the systems do not necessarily function in practice, he argues (Sheptycki, 2004, p. 316). Elaborating further, Sheptycki goes on to note that the

> tendency to systemic overload in the intelligence system is [further] exacerbated by its voracious appetite for data. Intelligence-led policing predicated on widespread system surveillance has a tendency to demand "more data" rather than "better data". (ibid.)

Within the Danish task forces, quality also seem to give way to quantity—a rapid technological development which in my experience left the detectives dumbfounded more than enabled. They detectives seemed to be experiencing the counterproductive feeling that comes as the result of having too many options—options they had a hard time choosing from but, even more so, properly understanding.

One thing was the quantity of options. Another thing was the detectives self-admitted technological illiteracy. Contrary to what one may think when thinking of a group of highly skilled and seasoned detectives investigating cross-border crimes in the twenty-first century, the Danish detectives did not think of themselves as specifically technologically gifted. The detectives spoke openly of how they didn't feel like they had the necessary skills to operate the different systems and technologies available to them, and especially so when it came to those that were seen as most important in their endeavor to surveil and catch cross-border criminals. For example, the detectives knew that using the computer program PED (the police's investigation database), and thereby building up and sharing criminal intelligence and evidence, was essential in keeping track of suspected cross-border criminals' whereabouts. At TFB, for example, the management therefore more than once ended the morning briefing by stressing how extremely important it was that the detectives actually used PED when registering their investigations. "It's the only way for us to get a consistent overview", they would say. Although encouraged/ordered by their bosses, few of the detectives used PED, or at least used it properly. This was either because they didn't prioritize it or simply because they didn't know how to.

> **Vignette 19**
>
> Leaving one of TFB's morning briefings, with the echo of the management's words still ringing in his ears, Detective Axelsen steps out of the meeting room. Waiting until he has gone far enough for the management not to hear him, he whispers to his usual partner, Detective Thorsen: "Damn, I've been doing it differently from how the bosses want it. Shit! Honestly, I'm kind of lost when it comes to this thing".
>
> Detective Thorsen tells him not to worry. He is on the same page. "Same here", he says, just as I pass them on the stairs leading down to the kitchen. "I also still have no idea how it works. I just do it the best I can. And having talked to the others, I think most of us are kinda lost".

The lack of a general aptitude amongst the detectives was particularly evident in the way that officers at both TFB and TFP identified a single person as being "our in-house PED expert", thereby admitting their own inability (see also Manning, 2008). At TFB, when I queried about the detectives' actual use of PED, I was told to contact Detective Sørensen, who was jokingly but respectfully referred to by her colleagues as "the Danish police's Queen of PED". In talking with her and observing her work, she showed me how he she had built up different folders and categories in the computer program which she used to go through reported crimes, and if a known suspect could be identified, she would make sure to make a data entry. "In this way", she explained,

> we make sure that we don't only get cross-border criminals for the crimes they just recently committed. By using the program properly to track and catalogue cases we can make a case against a cross-border criminal that includes, say, 150 charges instead of just one or two. In doing this, we make sure that we get them with a harsher sentence. Doing what I do is the future.

Her colleagues were inclined to agree. This was something they especially admitted when they with great frustration otherwise sifted through many of the old-school, physical folders that they kept on the shelves behind their desks, searching for crimes that they were certain a given suspect had committed but that they couldn't easily find.

Given that that all detectives agreed that a greater and more systematized use of computer and data systems was the future, it appeared rather absurd that the detectives were not more invested in using these technologies. One simple explanation for the detectives' lack of tech savviness had to do with the minimal amount of training they received. The rolling introduction of different electronic hard- and software obviously demanded that the detectives acquired at least a basic understanding of them. Of this, both task forces' management were well aware. The detectives were therefore sent on various training courses on which they were introduced to new technologies. "How-to manuals" were also produced and distributed. Still, even though the detectives attended courses and read, or perhaps rather skimmed through, manuals, they still felt ill-equipped to fully engage with these often quite complex computer systems. As Detective Clausen explained to me the day before he was to attend one of these courses:

> Tomorrow, I'm attending a course on this new, I think, Israeli surveillance program the police have just bought. Or was it American. Can't remember. Anyhow, it sounds like something we can use to track the foreign criminal networks beyond the streets and outside of Denmark's borders. It sounds very promising. [pausing]. However, I also know that a two-day course is close to being useless if we don't end up using it in our everyday work. And I bet you, that's how it's gonna be.

Many of his colleagues also frequently mentioned the scant usefulness of the different courses and lectures they attended: "We get this simple introduction and then the expectation is that we'll go ahead and use it—but the reality is that we don't", Detective Christensen reasoned. And adding to the limited use of their training, I also repeatedly observed instances where the detectives were supposed to attend a course only to have their attendance postponed indefinitely because of how they were needed elsewhere: "That's just how it is", the TFB management told me, "That's the reality of police work. We have to start with the base of things, crimes that suddenly occur etc., before we move toward the more complex parts"—thereby also hinting at how traditional, local policing issues would often trump, for example, the more complicated, global ones (see also Chaps. 4 and 5).

Another and already mentioned reason for what the detectives would also sometimes humorously call their "technological idiocy" probably had less to do with them being overwhelmed or untrained. Instead, it seemed to be more related to the vocational partialities described earlier as the detectives would also use their proclaimed lack of interest in technologies to signal what they, by contrast, believed to constitute "real police work" (see also Manning, 1996). This, for example, was echoed in a comment made by Detective Larsen.

> **Vignette 20**
>
> Just like all his colleagues, Detective Larsen is also frequently reminded by the management of the importance of using the newly acquired computer systems. This day, the management has him corned outside the TFP office. "Larsen", his manager says in a stern voice, "you promised us that you would do this—that you would systematize things on the computer. Of the guys in TFP, you are the one who supposedly know how to do this, right? Is it ever gonna happen?"
> "Sorry boss. I'm a very old man". Detective Larsen says, grinning. "It's not really something I know how to do. I'm much more about doing actual police work, getting out there and shipping criminals to prison, you know".

Detective Larsen was only in his late thirties and in other ways he was more than capable of using modern-day technology. He did also end up promising his bosses that he would do it. But, to the best of my knowledge, he never did. Nor did the management seem to really blame him for it.

Private/Personal Problems

A third and last reason for the Danish detectives' reluctance to fully engage themselves in international collaborations and with modern-day technologies concerns something rarely discussed in the academic literature, namely the police's personal and private lives. Though at times studied, such issues are mostly looked at from the vantage point of how the strains of job might (negatively) affect police officers' personal life, including the risk of stress, mental health issues, substance abuse as well as marital issues (Burke, 1993; Garbarino et al., 2013; Queirós et al., 2020). What is of interest here however is the opposite process, that is how non-work-related matters affect police work, an area of study which has received even less interest.

Much like anyone's working day, the detectives work consisted in them sometimes having to leave early to, for instance, take care of a sick child or even to go grocery shopping, as they were responsible for that evening's dinner. It was also not a rarity to observe the detectives coming in late because they had attended a school meeting, been to the dentist, or perhaps they had overslept. Indeed, my observations of the two task forces, just like any other police ethnography I am sure, were filled with such personal and even private matters. These were matters that, at first, seemed rather humdrum and scientifically irrelevant to me. But as I started to pay more attention to them, I also started to notice the many ways in which they would influence the detectives' work and, in the case of this chapter, influenced their daily engagement with the development of coherent policing and surveillance systems and practices. The following examples illustrate this point:

> **Vignette 21**
>
> The TFP detectives have just brought in a group of suspected Polish pickpockets and placed them in custody. While two of the suspects have prior convictions in Denmark, which means they can probably be prosecuted for a violation of their entry-ban (i.e. that they have entered Denmark even though they aren't legally allowed to), the detectives don't have sufficient grounds to charge and detain the remaining two. Knowing this, the management comes into the office to tell the detectives to "cut them loose". The detectives know that this is their only option, but it nevertheless heavily frustrates them. "I hate when this happen", Detective Christensen says. Detective Clausen and Larsen loudly agree.
>
> Later that day, the management comes back into the office. "You know, these two Polish assholes you just released, remember to register and upload the info you got on them. Then our international colleagues will keep an eye out for them". Detective Christensen concurs and tells the management that he "will do it straight away, boss!"
>
> Five minutes later, however, he gets up from his chair, puts on his jacket and walks out the door. "Did you update the system?" his boss asks, as he walks by. "Nah, didn't have the time, gaffer. Gotta pick up the kids. No worries though, I'll do it tomorrow".
>
> A week later, the paper with the information on the Polish men is still lying on his desk. Another week passes and the paper is now either gone or, at least, hidden beneath some other papers that have been stacked on top of it.

Fairly ordinary examples of this kind occurred more times than I could count during my time with the task forces. At TFB, for instance, Detective Jensen was a divorced single parent (which several of them were) and during the weeks when he had the kids, he couldn't stay late at the office irrespective of how urgent a given situation might be. They could have several wiretaps and video surveillance running. But he would still have to leave. His colleagues respected his situation. They themselves had young children and were also often forced to leave work to pick them up, cook dinner, attend meetings at school, or for some form of activity at the local sports club, and so on. On another occasion, one of the detectives even left work early as he was going on a date(!), something his colleagues also respected.

Admittedly, mentioning the detectives' personal and private matters might be viewed as a comparatively insignificant matter, or even as silly. When talking about the proliferation of cross-border crimes or the Orwellianism of the supposed increasing amount of police surveillance, who cares about some Danish detectives' personal lives, or lack thereof? To be sure, we policing scholars most often don't care, or we at least don't think about these things in our analyses. But, even though the few examples I have presented here appear rather banal when compared with the larger drives of an expanding means of police surveillance, they are inevitably something that the detectives have to care about. In the context of their everyday lives, picking up the kids is not simply more important, it is necessary. Minding and furthering systems of surveillance is not. So, although the detectives readily admitted that their preferences might appear ill-advised, they nevertheless commonly chose—out of obligation or desire—to prioritize their personal and private lives, even though they knew this was not optimal in relation to the chances of tracking and apprehending suspects—especially in a global era where criminals may potentially escape out of sight. "We just got our second child", as TFB Detective Christensen explained it, describing why he couldn't work overtime during the weekend, even though some fresh, new surveillance intelligence had indicated that a group of Chilean pickpockets were becoming increasingly active on Friday and Saturday nights. "I have to be at home with the family. That's just how it is". Though it is banal to mention it, the fact that private and personal matters had such a bearing on the detectives' work serves as a useful reminder that even the most doctrinal discourse, in this case that of otherwise needed surveillance in a globalizing world of crime and policing, inevitably competes with the banality of people's quotidian existence.

Not So Orwellian, Not So Satisfactory

What may be learned from this chapter's description of Danish detectives' lack of proper participation in various global surveillance developments? Before answering this question, it is important to remember that it is true that there are many policies that are promoting an increase in police surveillance, and that many steps have already been taken to realize these policies. It is also true that authorities and the police themselves, in this case a number of Danish detectives, openly speak of the necessity of such developments and that they even dream about the ways in which more Orwellian practices and technologies will help them catch, for example, otherwise hard-to-apprehend cross-border criminals. New both collaborative and technological means of policing and monitoring people are arguably at the very center of the globalization of local policing. Yet, even though this is true, and while it is therefore perfectly understandable that the criminological convention is to point to and often warn against a proliferating means of surveillance of this kind, it is not necessarily true that the everyday practices of police surveillance will follow this narrative. Looking at the daily practices and perceptions of a group of local, Danish surveillance practitioners, the reality I experienced was at least somewhat different. Here, workaday issues frequently outweighed the otherwise outspoken importance of developing contemporary surveillance practices. One may even say that the detectives' daily work revealed how (Danish) police surveillance is perhaps not so ubiquitous and systematic after all…

Lastly, while it is true that the (Danish) police's means of surveillance have grown—having extended their reach through new partnerships and new technologies—this chapter was also written to demonstrate how this logic similarly applies to the individual police officers involved in this Orwellian apparatus. Albeit for different reasons, Danish police detectives also feel the presence and pressures of the expanding, global surveillance apparatus, as they too look for ways in which to escape—finding ways to avoid having their sense of professional discretion and worth (as well as personal lives) constrained by the threads of this spreading web. Here we may therefore again recall Smith's astute reminder that surveillance technologies might "empower the watcher" yet "disempower the worker"

(2009). In many ways, this is exactly what the detectives were experiencing. Contrary to what some studies argue (cf. Loftus et al., 2015; Loftus, 2019) and contrary to our gut might tell us, the months I spent with a group of Danish detectives showed me that more police surveillance did not equal more professional satisfaction. Instead of feeling all-seeing and all-powerful, a growing Orwellianism had them complaining.

Bibliography

Aliverti, A. (2013). *Crimes of mobility: Criminal law and the regulation of immigration*. Routledge.
Aliverti, A. (2014). Enlisting the public in the policing of immigration. *British Journal of Criminology, 55*(2), 215–230.
Aliverti, A. (2021). *Policing the borders within*. Oxford University Press.
Bacon, M. (2017). *Taking care of business: Police detectives, drug law enforcement and proactive investigation*. Oxford University Press.
Basic, G., & Yakhlef, S. (2022). Anomie and collaboration in intelligence and operational police and border guard work in the Baltic Sea area: In-group mentality and construction of the other. *Policing and Society*, 1–21.
Bigo, D. (2008). Globalized (in)security: The field and the ban-Opticon. In D. Bigo & A. Tsoukala (Eds.), *Terror, insecurity and liberty: Illiberal practices of liberal regimes after* (pp. 10–48). Routledge.
Bonnichsen, H. J. (2012). *Tvivl på alt og tro på meget: Jagten på sandhed-Politiets afhøringsmetoder*. Rosinante & Co.
Bowling, B., & Sheptycki, J. (2012). *Global policing*. Sage.
Brodeur, J.-P. (2010). *The policing web*. Oxford University Press.
Burke, R. J. (1993). Work-family stress, conflict, coping, and burnout in police officers. *Stress and Health, 9*(3), 171–180.
Christensen, M. J. (2017). Crafting and promoting international crimes: A controversy among professionals of Core-crimes and anti-corruption. *Leiden Journal of International Law, 30*(2), 501–521.
Egbert, S., & Leese, M. (2021). *Criminal futures: Predictive policing and everyday police work*. Taylor & Francis.
Ericson, R. V. (1981). *Making crime: A study of detective work*. Butterworths.
Feldman, G. (2019). *The gray zone: Sovereignty, human smuggling, and undercover police investigation in Europe*. Stanford University Press.

Fleming, J. (2018). How do the police respond to evidence-based policing? In R. A. W. Rhodes (Ed.), *Narrative policy analysis* (pp. 221–239). Springer.

Fox, R. (2001). Someone to watch over us: Back to the panopticon? *Criminology and Criminal Justice, 1*(3), 251–276.

Franko, K. (2019). *The crimmigrant other: Migration and penal power*. Routledge.

Franko, K. and Gundhus, H.I., 2015. A divided fraternity: transnational police cultures, proximity, and loyalty. *European journal of policing studies*, 3(2), 162–184.

Friesen, N., Feenberg, A., & Smith, G. (2009). Phenomenology and surveillance studies: Returning to the things themselves. *The Information Society, 25*(2), 84–90.

Friesen, N., Feenberg, A., Smith, G., et al. (2012). Experiencing surveillance. In A. Feenberg and N. Friesen (eds) *(Re)inventing the Internet* (pp. 73–84). Brill

Fyfe, N., Gundhus, H. O., & Rønn, K. V. (2017). *Moral issues in intelligence-led policing*. Routledge.

Garbarino, S., Cuomo, G., Chiorri, C., et al. (2013). Association of work-related stress with mental health problems in a special police force unit. *BMJ Open, 3*(7)

Gordon, D. R. (1987). The electronic panopticon: A case study of the development of the National Criminal Records System. *Politics and Society, 15*(4), 483–511.

Gundhus, H.O., 2013. Experience or knowledge? Perspectives on new knowledge regimes and control of police professionalism. *Policing: a journal of policy and practice*, 7, 178–194. https://doi.org/10.1093/police/pas039

Haggerty, K. D. (2006). Tear down the walls: On demolishing the panopticon. In *Theorizing surveillance: The panopticon and beyond* (pp. 23–45).

Haggerty, K. D., & Ericson, R. V. (2000). The surveillant assemblage. *The British Journal of Sociology, 51*(4), 605–622.

Haggerty, K. D., Wilson, D., & Smith, G. J. (2011). Theorizing surveillance in crime control. *Theoretical Criminology, 15*(3), 231–237.

Innes, M. (2003). *Investigating murder: Detective work and the police response to criminal homicide*. Oxford University Press.

Jones, T., & Newburn, T. (2006). *Plural policing: A comparative perspective*. Psychology Press.

Kruger, E., & Haggerty, K. D. (2006). Review essay: Intelligence exchange in policing and security. *Policing and Society, 16*(1), 86–91.

Larsson, P. (2006). International police co-operation: A Norwegian perspective. *Journal of Financial Crime, 13*(4), 456–466.

Lemieux, F. (2013). *International police cooperation: Emerging issues, theory and practice*. Routledge.

Loftus, B. (2019a). Normalizing covert surveillance: The subterranean world of policing. *The British Journal of Sociology, 70*(5), 2070–2091.

Loftus, B., Goold, B., & Mac Giollabhui, S. (2015). From a visible spectacle to an invisible presence: The working culture of covert policing. *British Journal of Criminology, 56*(4), 629–645.

Lyon, D. (1994). *The electronic eye: The rise of surveillance society*. University of Minnesota Press.

Lyon, D. (2018). *The culture of surveillance: Watching as a way of life*. John Wiley & Sons.

Manning, P. (2006). Detective work/culture. *Encyclopedia of Police Science, 2*, 390–397.

Manning, P. K. (2008). *The technology of policing: Crime mapping, information technology, and the rationality of crime control*. New York University Press.

Marx, G. T. (1988). *Undercover: Police surveillance in America*. Univ of California Press.

Mathiesen, T. (1997). The viewer society Michel Foucault's panopticon' revisited. *Theoretical Criminology, 1*(2), 215–234.

Mathiesen, T. (2013). *Towards a surveillant society: The rise of surveillance Systems in Europe*. Waterside Press.

McCahill, M., & Norris, C. (1999). Watching the workers: Crime, CCTV and the workplace. In *Invisible crimes* (pp. 208–231). Springer.

Monahan, T. (2011). Surveillance as cultural practice. *The Sociological Quarterly, 52*(4), 495–508.

Olwig, K. F., Grünenberg, K., Møhl, P., et al. (2019). *The biometric border world: Technology, bodies and identities on the move*. Routledge.

Punch, M. (1979). Observation and the police: The research experience. In *Policing the inner city* (pp. 1–18). Springer.

Queirós, C., Passos, F., Bártolo, A., et al. (2020). Burnout and stress measurement in police officers: Literature review and a study with the operational police stress questionnaire. *Frontiers in Psychology, 11*, 587.

Ratcliffe, J. (2016a). *Intelligence-led policing*. Routledge.

Ross, J. E. (2004). Impediments to transnational cooperation in undercover policing: A comparative study of the United States and Italy. *The American Journal of Comparative Law, 52*(3), 569–623.

Schinkel, W., 2011. Prepression: the actuarial archive and new technologies of security. Theoretical criminology, 15, 365–380. https://doi.org/10.1177/1362480610395366

Schuilenburg, M. (2017). *The securitization of society: Crime, risk, and social order*. New York University Press.

Sheptycki, J. (2004). Organizational pathologies in police intelligence systems: Some contributions to the lexicon of intelligence-led policing. *European journal of criminology*, 1(3), 307–332.

Smith, G. J. D. (2009). Empowered watchers or disempowered workers. In K. F. Aas, H. O. Gundhus, & H. M. Lomell (Eds.), *Technologies of InSecurity: The surveillance of everyday life*. Routledge-Cavendish.

Weber, L. (2013). *Policing non-citizens*. Routledge.

Wilson, D., & Sutton, A. (2003). *Open-street CCTV in Australia*. Australian Institute of Criminology Canberra.

4

Terrorism

"Terror is ruining the Danish police" - Danish police detective —*Danish Police Detective*

In late February 2015, Denmark was hit by a terror attack dubbed the "2015 Copenhagen Shootings". The culprit, a young Danish citizen with Palestinian parents named Omar El-Hussein, tried but failed to shoot one of the "Muhammad cartoonists", the now otherwise deceased Swede, Lars Vilks. Later that day, while still on the loose, El-Hussein attempted to break into the Copenhagen Synagogue. He did not manage to do this either, but he did succeed in killing two civilians and wound five police officers during his horrific rampage, only to be shot and killed by the police later that day.

Following the Copenhagen Shootings and in the wake of previous terror attacks and threats in other cities around the world, the threat level was heightened in Denmark and the Danish police were ordered to increase their counterterrorism efforts—a threat level and

---

This chapter is a reworked version of a previously published article: Sausdal, D. (2021). Terrorizing police: Revisiting "the policing of terrorism" from the perspective of Danish police detectives. *European journal of criminology*, 18(5), 755–773.

© The Author(s), under exclusive license to Springer Nature Switzerland AG 2023
D. Sausdal, *Globalizing Local Policing*, Transnational Crime, Crime Control and Security, https://doi.org/10.1007/978-3-031-18919-7_4

counterterrorism focus which have now become the new standard in Danish policing and society. All this happened just two weeks before I started my fieldwork and became something that greatly affected what I was to observe during my time spent with the two task forces.

So far, I have described some concrete examples of how the task forces' detective experienced their work being "globalized"—and how they often felt concerned about it. As Chaps. 2 and 3 respectively illustrated, the globalization of the Danish police came with issues of xenophobia as well the need of increasing collaborations and a growing technologizing of police/detective work. This chapter continues in this vein focusing on how another global issue affected the detectives' daily work. Yet, where one may have foreseen the other chapters' focuses, this ethnography being a study of two detective task forces and their investigation of cross-border (property) crimes, this chapter homes in on a largely unanticipated matter. Rather than focusing on the detectives' investigations of cross-border crimes per se, this chapter focuses on how the entire Danish police—and therefore also Task Force Pickpocketing (TFP) and Task Force Burglary (TFB)—have increasingly been required to spent a considerable number of daily resources on the policing of terrorism. This, of course, is not a unique Danish development. As Deflem (2004, 2010) among others has described, terrorism policing is no longer the single task of committed counterterrorist units or intelligence services, but something that entails and affects much if not most everyday police work.

Policing of Terrorism

Reading the available literature, one could be tempted to conclude that a growing terrorism policing must also be a development appreciated by a group of Danish detectives and many of their policing colleagues. It is, for example, the thinking that underlines much of the literature published on the matter as it discusses the increasing "militarization" of the public police forces (Kraska, 1996, 2007; McCulloch, 2001, 2004). Matching the police's well-documented preference for action and crime-fighting, the deduction is that police organizations and officers welcome this newer call to arms. In their influential treatise on *Global Policing,*

Bowling and Sheptycki, for example, argue that police officers often have little hesitation in endorsing the terrorism narrative because it aligns itself with "the dualistic world view [of] labelling others as 'you' or 'them'" prevalent in police cultures worldwide (2012, p. 127). "The label 'terrorist' provides", they elaborate, "a powerful image of a suitable enemy legitimating any and all paramilitary policing efforts" (2012, p. 127).

In following the ebbs and flows of the task forces' work, I did also experience how the detectives would buy into the omnipresent fear and threat of terrorism and, hence, the importance of policing it. The detectives would regularly contemplate whether a Moroccan or Turkish citizen suspected of property crime "is in fact connected to ISIS..?" "Do you think he's using the money he steals to fund terrorist activities?", they would ask each other, though little or no evidence existed to prove this besides their guesses and gut-feelings. The detectives also eagerly accepted the both popular and political belief that a new terrorist attack was imminent, that "it will happen sooner rather than later", and that many and drastic steps therefore had to be taken to prevent this from happening. In this sense, the task forces' detectives confirmed much conventional as well as scholarly thinking on the matter.

However, though instinctively supportive, when it came to the detectives experiencing how these drastic and daily steps to counter terrorism would affect their work lives, their support for an increase in anti-terrorism policing seemed to wane. This is not to say that the wider political and institutional context in which the detectives worked was not increasingly geared toward combatting terror, and that this "war on terror" didn't trickle down into everyday police practices. It was. It did. And it still does. Knowing this, the simple point I wish to further here (mirroring the learnings of Chaps. 2 and 3) is that a difference exists between the reasonings of the Danish Police as a societal institution vis-a-vis the day-to-day thinking and doings of its individual police officers—or, as Van Maanen and Kolb (1982) argued in relation to the importance of (police) ethnography, that a difference exists between dominant policing representations and that of everyday police work (Bacon et al., 2020; Sausdal, 2020). Where the former, in and beyond a Danish context, is officially and evidently engaged in a mounting war on terrorism, the latter—for reasons this chapter describes—lags behind. Indeed, for task forces' detectives, the policing of terrorism appeared more troubling than reinforcing. Whereas more dedicated counterterrorism and intelligence units perceivably (though I wouldn't know as I did not study them) experienced the policing of terrorism as worthwhile and professionally giving, most of the other Danish frontline officers I encountered during my fieldwork seemed to see it as a vocational burden.

In the pages that follow, I will further develop why the Danish detectives did not necessarily feel the martial draws of counterterrorist warfare, but, instead, felt that this new global policing tendency was, even though also needed, a nuisance. I will do so by providing three empirical examples thereof—examples that both separately as well as together may explain why (the policing of) terrorism is something of a bother to (Danish) police work. Specifically, the examples include illustrations of how the detectives themselves felt "terrorized" by, first, regularly repeating "incidents" that halted their daily work; secondly, anti-terrorism oriented "practices" which they were increasingly asked to do; and, third, how the detectives in more general terms felt that their "working conditions and private life" suffered. Phrased in a more overall theoretical manner, the provided examples follow and confirm Cottee and Hayward's (2011) approach to what they conceptualize as a more existential and emotive study of terrorism and, by extension, counterterrorism efforts. Cottee and Hayward argue that an existential and emotive study of (counter)terrorism entails an orientation toward: (1) the desire for excitement, (2) the desire for ultimate meaning and (3) the desire for glory that terrorism might offer and satisfy. These are the three "existential desires" (ibid.)—existential desires which Cotteeand Hayward believe to be key motivators of (counter)terroristic behavior. Although I am well aware of how Cottee and Hayward's emotive approach to terrorism studies is developed to provide an understanding of why people become/do not become terrorists, they do in fact develop their theory *not* from studies of terrorism but from wider conflict and military studies of violent and armed behavior more generally. This explains why their proposed threefold could, feasibly, also help explain the vocational (de)motivations of a group of Danish detectives as they face a growing amount of terrorism threats and fears.

The Usual Arguments

First, a few words on how the issue of (policing of) terrorism has typically been analyzed. As Mythen and Walklate argue in their summarizing paper on "Criminology and Terrorism" (2006b), the conventional criminological approach is to "critique the ways in which the terrorist threat is being *discursively* and *materially* shaped by law and order institutions" (2006b, p. 379, emphasis added). Indeed, One of the primary ways of analyzing the fear/threat of terror, as for example manifested by politicians, the media or law enforcement, is to scrutinize its symbolic representations. Without neglecting the danger, scholars often criticize how threats are exaggerated and fears exploited. A prototypical example in this regard is Altheide's "Terrorism and the Politics of Fear" (2006). In the article, Altheide discusses how 9/11 has given way to continuous representations in the media and by politicians that link terrorism to existing fears of victimization in ways that "often decontextualize rather complex events to offer simplistic explanations" (2006, p. 417). This one-dimensional coupling, Altheide concludes, has made it easier for "moral entrepreneurs … to market to audiences anchored in fear" (2006, p. 434). Pointing to the terrorist threat thus becomes a means by which willing actors may "harnes[s] a culture of fear" (Mythen & Walklate, 2006a). Or, as Pickering has simply put it, the fear of terror is repeatedly "consciously mobilized for political point scoring" (2004, p. 223).

In more direct relation to the question of policing, scholars have similarly reasoned that, even though it is undeniable that a terror threat exists, the threat is being symbolically exploited by many a policing actor (cf. Mueller & Stewart, 2016; Pickering, 2004). As Flyghed for example argues, discussing the policing of terrorism in particular:

> [T]he manufacture of dangerous situations [such the threat of terrorism] constitutes one means of promoting efforts to normalise the use of extreme weapons and spectacular policing methods … This too constitutes an example of the normalisation of coercive measures. (Flyghed, 2002, p. 35)

Viewed from the perspective of Flyghed's analytical framework, the police knowingly promote and even overstress the terror threat as a means of "normalizing the exceptional" (ibid.), thereby allowing them to retain often provisional resources and rights allocated to them. Considering the Danish context, in which the police, alongside politicians, continuously represent the threat of (Islamist) terror as being omnipresent, Flyghed's Swedish-based assertion rings true. For example, Danish studies have pointed to the widespread existence of islamophobia and its incessant use in parliamentary politics as well as in a growing policing of borders, foreign nationals and ethnic minorities (see Højer et al., 2018; Rytter & Pedersen, 2014). Seen in a broader criminological perspective, and in relation to global policing studies more specifically, critiques of political as well as police representations have been repeated more broadly by Bowling and Sheptycki, who remind us of the importance of

> acknowledg[ing] that appearances can be deceptive and [that] it is not always the case that the social actors [i.e. the police] claiming to be "good guys" and pointing fingers at the "bad guys over there" have anyone's best interests in mind other than their own. Indeed, we would even go so far as to say that it is more important to unmask the taken for granted assumptions, because the rhetoric of "war on terror" … ha[s] well documented harmful effects. (2012, p. 135)

Shifting perspectives, though the criminological discourse on terrorism has often engaged itself with symbolic matters, the declared war on terror has palpably led to a large number of concrete governmental and policing initiatives—and many more than the space of this chapter allows. Nevertheless, there seems to be one development, if not caused then carried forth by the war on terrorism, which most scholars seem to agree on. This is the notion that the fear of terror has become the very foundation of present-day "expansions in real-world panopticon surveillance [and the] endors[ement of] calls for |m]ore prisons, more data checks and greater police powers" (Coleman & McCahill, 2010, p. 28). Or, as Lyon has repeatedly pointed out, "the war on terror" has been the primary catalyst in "the growth of globally networked surveillance" (2007, p. 30). Terrorism alongside other alleged "dark sides of globalization" (Heine & Thakur, 2011) thereby drives the on-going widening of legislation, surveillance technology expansion, the increase of police tactical resources as well as the proliferation of international law enforcement and wider criminal justice cooperation around the world (see also Altheide, 2006; Brodeur, 2007; Ericson & Haggerty, 2006; Lyon, 2003).

In scrutinizing this Orwellian and otherwise penal-oriented expansion, many criminological analyses focus on its problematic (side-)effects. A recurring critique here is that voiced by the likes of recently deceased Thomas Mathiesen (2013). In his work on contemporary surveillance and international policing efforts, Mathiesen has expertly criticized the way in which the expansion of various transnational European surveillance systems—which together amount to a "surveillance monster", he argues (2013, p. 177)—is not truly effective in relation to its proclaimed targets, that is to increase surveillance in order to prevent cross-border crime and terrorism. Instead, Mathiesen directs our attention to how (too) much of this public monitoring is actually used to track political opposition, to solve more petty and traditional criminal justice cases, or used in relation to more or less ordinary public order issues. Rather than actually becoming a terrorism policing as such, or a policing of other larger global criminal threats, the surveillance systems put in place often become a policing of much more mundane matters (see also Brodeur, 2007; Kroener & Neyland, 2012, p. 143ff). What this tells us is that the people who are often most affected by the increasing policing of terrorism are actually not necessarily potential terrorists or transnational criminals but "ordinary" citizens of the world—people who are now incessantly monitored and controlled, both overtly and covertly. Among other things, this (mis)appropriation of surveillance has led to stark criticism of the legitimacy of many counterterrorism initiatives, particularly in relation to how the expansion of surveillance involves violations of general human and civil rights (Flyghed, 2002; Mathiesen, 2013). As an example, it has been widely documented that the expansion of police surveillance and control frequently includes issues of discrimination. As Morgan and Poynting (2016) argue, fear and terror, and the practices produced in their name, are directly tied to a rising Islamophobia in the West—a prejudiced and stereotyped connection that has "[negatively] affected the Muslim community" (Hörnqvist & Flyghed, 2012, p. 319).

This is not the only reported problem of an increasing terrorism policing. Although it is obvious that there has been an increase in surveillance and other means of overseeing the public in the name of terror, there is simultaneously a conspicuous lack of public knowledge about the inner workings of this panoptic increase (see Bowling & Sheptycki, 2015; Coleman & McCahill, 2010, p. 28). As Ericson and Haggerty describe the paradox,

> [t]he ongoing war on terror accentuates how the state is … concerned with carving out a sphere of privacy, even as it tries to render the actions of others more transparent … Hence, legal claims to privacy are being invoked as a means to render actions of powerful interests more opaque …. (2006, p. 10)

This panptioc double-standard is also vividly present in the Danish context, where parliament in the wake of 9/11, again in 2006, and then following the 2015 Copenhagen Shootings, passed anti-terror bills that have included the allocation of several 100 million Danish Kroner, of which the lion's share has been given to the Danish Intelligence Service Agency, whose work largely remains beyond public and even political scrutiny (Kublitz, 2021). In Denmark, as in other countries, when it comes to the policing of terrorism efforts, this deliberate obfuscation is most often excused by the necessity of following suit. That is, the argument goes, the state and its relevant security and law enforcement agencies must, just like their dangerous criminal opponents, work in the shadows in order to be properly effective. Although there is some practical truth in this, it nevertheless gives rise to significant problems of accountability. As Bowling and Sheptycki have concluded in relation to a worldwide increase in many global and often surreptitious policing measures, this development "is antithetical to transparent and democratically accountable policing" (2012, p. 71)—a type of policing which many local, public police forces otherwise rest and pride themselves on.

Police Militarization

What the above illustrates is that areas of "high policing" or "political policing" (Brodeur, 2007) have been significantly endowed with extra resources and rights in the name of terror. Yet, as Mathiesen's study (2013) also showed us, there is evidence that conventional law enforcement, or "low policing" (Brodeur, 2007) is also marshalled by contemporary terrorism politics, and perhaps even more so (see Murray, 2005; Pickering, 2004; Stuntz, 2002). A core argument here is that "most constitutional limits on policing are transsubstantive—they apply equally to suspected drug dealers and suspected terrorists" (Stuntz, 2002, p. 2140). It thus follows "that when courts approve police tactics designed to fight terrorists, they will also be sanctioning use of the same tactics against other sorts of criminals" (2002, p. 2140). To be sure, the possible spill-over or trickle-down effect of criminal justice and security politics is nothing new. The transsubstantive nature of law, and thus its spread to areas for which it was not initially intended, has been documented by many other researchers—including not only studies of anti-terror legislation but studies of anti-narcotics legalization (Nadelmann, 2010; Farber, 2021) as well as migration law (Stumpf, 2006). In Denmark specifically, problematic spill-over effects from terrorism politics and legalizations have also been noted and criticized by several legal and human rights scholars (Hansen, 2011).

In following this transsubstantive analysis of the spread of counterterrorism policing measures, scholars are therefore arguing that the many policies and practices introduced in the name of terror should be critically assessed as constituting a growing "conflation of crime and national security concerns" (Pickering, 2004, p. 212); as a conflation of high and low policing. The most well-known and emblematic example of this is found in the fact that the various forms of governmental work intended to prevent terrorism are repeatedly framed as warfare rather than as a manifestation of criminal justice—it is not just a crime but a societal attack. Such a war-like framing, it is argued, has "significant consequences for the expansion of national security issues into traditionally internal policing domains, and the utilisation of external military apparatus for non-war functions involving international policing tasks" (Pickering,

2004, p. 212). In its most dramatic form, this perspective includes the increasingly popular police "militarization" or "para-militarization" thesis (Kraska, 2007; McCulloch & Pickering, 2009), that is the argument that otherwise traditional public police are increasingly becoming not just the proverbial "boys in blue" but a regular "blue army" (McCulloch, 2001). Policing and criminological scholars here point to how not only the continuous labelling of various criminal justice issues as "wars" (war on drugs/crime/terror, etc.), but the legislation as well as police tactics and equipping that it has given rise to, have made both the police and policing methods more extensive and aggressive—a blue *army* indeed.

Terrorizing Danish Police Detectives

> [T]he domestic war on terrorism is ... affecting local police departments' ability to deal with more typical sorts of crime. A lot of police manpower has been diverted to various forms of homeland security, such as guarding at-risk public spaces and responding to reports of possible attacks. (Stuntz, 2002, p. 2139)

> [There is something] peculiar about police work against terrorism relative to other efforts in the wider constellation of counterterrorism. All too often, sweeping statements can be heard about counterterrorism that are based on interpretations of very specific aspects of certain responses to terrorism, without clarifying which institutions and agents play a part in these practices and how they might differ from other efforts. (Deflem, 2010, p. 5)

While sympathetic, Stuntz and Deflem here raise an important critique of previously mentioned studies. They argue that criminologists and scholars of policing more specifically have tended to conflate their analyses of exceptional counterterrorism activities with the much wider realities of everyday police work—sometimes unfairly taking discourse, policies, legislation and other extraordinary measures as exemplary of how the policing of terrorism is actually practised and, not least, perceived in the ordinary life of a police department (see also Sheptycki, 2017). In Deflem's reading, the police, especially regular criminal justice officers such as police detectives and patrolmen, actually tend to resist external pressures and the politicization of this issue, and thereby also the rhetoric of war, as they "continue [to carry out] counterterrorism activities that rest on an efficiency-driven treatment and depoliticized understanding of terrorism" (2004, p. 75). Or as Deflem has more bluntly stated it, to the regular police "the 'War on Terror' is no war at all" (2004, p. 87), making him go on to argue that "the policing of terrorism presents an as-yet relatively unexplored and often not properly understood topic of research" (2010, p. 1).

When it comes to ethnographic and otherwise qualitative studies of the daily and different ways in which the policing of terrorism is actually carried out, Deflem's words still ring true. Such studies are few and far between—and those that do exist tend to remain more or less singularly focused on the exceptional combative and discriminatory nature of the work rather than also looking at its broader everyday makeup (see Drotbohm & Hasselberg, 2015; Maguire et al., 2014; Pickering et al., 2008; Mueller & Stewart, 2016). Indeed, similar to Deflem, my ethnographic study of the Danish police also revealed how the war on terror was most commonly not a war at all. Following Cottee and Hayward's (2011) contention that the psycho-social draw of both terrorism as well as counterterrorism actions is founded on a particular emotive and motivational engagement, the Danish detectives I observed tended to find the policing of terrorism acutely unproductive—immobilizing rather than mobilizing, bad rather than good for police morale. To further substantiate how and why this is, I will now go on to provide some expounding empirical descriptions of three specific ways in which terror (negatively) affected, or indeed "terrorized", the detectives' day-to-day police work.

Terrorizing Incidents

The belief in Denmark, as well as across many Western countries, is that terrorists will ultimately strike if given the chance. This lingering fear had many consequences for the Danish police, who, among other things, had been ordered to be extra vigilant toward even the slightest hint of a possible attack. Below is an example of how such alertness would recurrently affect the detectives' work:

Vignette 22

No one's around when I step into the TFP office just before 6 am. I hang my jacket on the coat rack behind the door while wondering where the detectives are. Yesterday, before going home, I had agreed to come in early "to go hunt for breakfast thieves" as the TFP detectives put it. The detectives, in other words, were planning to go and scope out different downtown hotels, looking for a particular brand of international thieves who steal rich hotel guests' belongings as the guests are otherwise occupied with eating their breakfasts. However, looking around the office and elsewhere on the fifth floor, everything seems deserted. I'm the only one there. Suddenly, I see what looks like the shadow of Detective Larsen with Detective Mikkelsen just behind him. "David, we're downstairs", he shouts to me from down the hall.

I join them and we walk to one of the station superintendents' offices downstairs. Detectives Clausen, Christensen and Madsen are already there alongside a couple of police officers from other units. The superintendent immediately starts explaining why he has summoned us (and hence why the TFP detectives are not preparing to go out and catch the aforementioned "breakfast thieves").

"We need you all to stay here at the station so that you can be prepared to help out if needed … As you have no doubt already heard, this morning a Danish Railway Company employee was found tied up inside a train carriage that was being cleaned and prepared for service. He was placed on a chair and his hands and body were tied together with duct tape and, as the employee himself explained it to the first-responders, he had been attacked by two unidentifiable assailants while he was trying to clean the train. The guy also said that he heard the assailants talking about how they wanted to blow something up. [pausing]. So, gentlemen, as a result of this possible terror threat, Copenhagen Central Station has been shut down and all traffic has been halted for now. It's a pretty major decision as this disturbs the morning rush hour, but it's our only option. We have to take the threat seriously. Right now, we have people searching and sweeping the whole area looking for anything suspicious, people or explosives. Until we know more, I need you to stay put and for you to be prepared to help with the investigation if needed and, God forbid, help out if the whole thing blows up".

After listening and taking stock of the superintendent's report, the TFP detectives and I leave his office and walk back upstairs. Detective Mikkelsen doesn't seem convinced. "No doubt it's a hoax", he says. "It's the work of a desperate man, taking advantage of the whole terror frenzy to make people feel sorry for him. Right? Wanna bet?" The other detectives don't want to bet. They agree. "Anyhow, no matter what it is, it's going to keep us at home and from catching any breakfast thieves today. It'll be yet another day at the office, just sitting and waiting", Detective Larsen declares, demonstrating with rolling eyes how annoyed he is. We all get a cup of coffee and the detectives sit down at their respective desks, waiting to see how this possible terror threat plays out. With the threat of terror looming, their workday, as Detective Christensen says before getting yet another cup of coffee, "is suspended until further notice!"

As it turned out, the TFP detectives were right in being skeptical. Later that day, the duct taped man admitted—after many an interrogation and pressure applied—that he had indeed staged the whole thing. For various reasons, his life was in ruins and, instead of a terror threat, it was all a cry for help. A cry for help or not, the detectives did not get any work done that day.

And there were other examples of the Danish detectives' work being halted by the possibility of terror. As I was spending time at TFB, for example, another menacing incident occurred—an incident which was intimidating but also ended up interfering with the investigation the TFB detectives were currently running:

Vignette 23

It was on the front pages of the national Danish news media. Reports of shootings in Denmark's biggest shopping mall, *Fields*, located to the east of Copenhagen, were coming in. Headlines were screaming in bright yellow "BREAKING NEWS". They read: "Three people wounded by gunshots and knife stabbings in a shopping mall". Initially, though, I didn't hear of the alleged attack.

As the incidence plays out, I am in court witnessing a TFB-led prosecution of a group of Romanian defendants. Because of this, I first become aware of the potential terrorist attack as several notifications start to pop up on my smartphone. Sitting in court, reading these, I can see that the Danish media is still trying to establish exactly what is happening, yet without being able to provide any certainty. Only a few moments later, however, I get a group text from TFB Detective Jensen, sent to me and the other detectives from his team:

"Have you seen what has happened in Fields?!", he asks, though instantly calming our nerves as he goes on to explain how it is "just Hussein's group getting back at Abi's group".

When we come in to the office a few hours later, Detective Jensen get us all up to speed.

"Here's the thing", he says, "I was just randomly following the news when they suddenly broke this story. And at the exact same time, I hear through the wire [i.e. the wiretaps they were running] that Abi and his gang are hanging out in that very shopping mall ... And just after that, Abi and his friends start frantically calling each other on their phones, screaming. This was when I knew that this thing was 'just' our burglary suspects doing this shit and not some crazy terrorists—them trying to get at each other ...".

(continued)

> **Vignette 23** (continued)
>
> Detective Jensen went on: "But knowing how this could easily blow up in our faces—like the [police] radio was on fire—and suddenly be seen as some major terror thing, I quickly got Andersen to find out who was the lead investigator on this Fields case and to call him and tell him that we knew who these people were—and of course to tell him that it was *not* terrorism, before he went ahead and suggested anything like that to our colleagues or, worse, to the media. You know, we got really lucky that I was here listening to the wire. If I hadn't been, if I had been somewhere else, this whole thing could've escalated beyond our control. You know how it goes, right? As soon as someone even whispers terrorism these days it all goes completely nuts … The only damned thing now is that instead of us having a good and solid case on some professional burglars, our case will become secondary, not important".

Detective Jensen's take on the situation neatly summed up how the detectives saw this "terrorism issue"—and the trouble it was causing. For over two months they had been running a wiretap, working every day to build a case against a group of young "career criminals", as they called them, living west of Copenhagen—a group suspected of having committed several large-scale burglaries over the past six months or so. TFB not only had a wiretap running; they had conducted several secret house searches, put up hidden cameras and had invested many other surveillance resources or, as they called it, "technical observations" into collecting evidence and securing an arrest. As a result, "a good case" had been built—a case strong enough to get the suspects convicted of being involved in organized crime. A few days before the shootings in the shopping mall, the detectives had even discussed if they in fact had to wait any longer or whether they could go head and make the arrests …

Yet, as described, the case evolved in an unexpected way. The suspects' crimes now included not just organized property crime but attempted murder as well as the unlawful shooting of firearms in a public space. In fact, the process leading to the shootings had already started some weeks before the shootings at the shopping mall. The two groups that ended up shooting at each other had initially been close acquaintances who, it was suspected, had even committed crimes together. Nevertheless, something had happened that had divided them and pitted them against each other. The story I was told was that it had all started because of a romantic conflict between a couple of the young men—a conflict that had then escalated into knife stabbings, an earlier drive-by shooting west of Copenhagen and, now, several discharged firearms in a busy shopping mall alongside a national media and public filled with fears of terrorism. But even though it did look like terrorism, it wasn't. It was not an example of a radicalized ideology but of broken hearts and offended honors, and in the previous case from Copenhagen Central Station it was a matter of a mentally unstable and distressed individual. Still, although in some ways quite ordinary criminal matters, these potential terrorist incidents forced the Danish detectives and pretty much all their adjacent colleagues to put their normal case work aside and prepare for the worst possible scenario. And these weren't the only two times I experienced the police having to pause what they were doing. Though the two examples represent some of the more obvious and dramatic instances of potential terror, there were many other incidents causing similar interruptions. As the detectives were feeling frustrated by these many interruptions to their work, it wasn't unusually for me to hear them think out loud that "we wouldn't have reacted like this before today's terrorism focus, but nowadays it trumps everything".

Terrorizing Practices

It was not only the occasional "might-be-terror" incidents that (negatively) influenced the task forces' work. On a daily basis, the threat of terror, and the subsequent requirements placed on the Danish police to counter it, had the entire police force affected. Police officers were expected to stay alert to react to possible terror attacks. But the ghost of terror also put a lot of additional day-to-day demands on them—things they nowadays had to do, which they didn't have to do before. Here are two examples thereof:

> **Vignette 24**
>
> The day at TFP is just starting. I have come in a bit late, having overslept, only to find Detective Clausen standing at his desk with his uniform in his hand. "Here we go again. I can't believe I have to do this", he tells me, as I watch him dust off and put on his old light blue uniform, preparing, as he tells me, "to go on terror guard duty for the fucking fourth time this month!". "You know, I almost never wear this", he says, pointing to his shirt. "That's the good thing about detective work, right? We get to wear our own normal, civilian clothing not these rags". In saying this, Detective Clausen points to what I have heard many of them say, that is that the detectives tend to prefer their own clothes as well as the professional distinctions that come with such differences in attire.
>
> Nodding my head, I ask him where he is going.
>
> "I'm going to waste my day, standing in front of Jewish Butcher somewhere—or at least I think that's the plan …" "And let me tell you. This is boring as hell, standing outside that tiny Jewish butcher's or wherever the management puts you for so many hours at a time … And it also gets terribly cold. That doesn't help, does it? Even though this is summertime, it gets cold when you just stand there and do nothing. And just think about how it'll be during the winter! No matter how many clothes you wear, when you just stand there without really moving, your body doesn't get any heat. In the end, you're freezing as hell".
>
> "Don't you get any breaks or anything?", I ask.
>
> "Yeah, we do", Detective Clausen admits. "And I guess it does get a bit better when you are on your break and you get to eat some sandwiches and drink some lukewarm coffee and maybe watch a show on the iPad. But, hey, that doesn't really outweigh the fact that it's a shit job!"

The fact that Detective Clausen that day had to spend his entire workday guarding a suspected terror target instead of being able to carry on with his actual work (in his case investigating credit card theft) was something that greatly annoyed him. And he was not alone—neither in having to stand guard because of terrorism fears, nor in being annoyed. Journeying around Copenhagen at the time of my fieldwork, you would be able to see several armed police officers standing in front of designated storefronts, the parliament, the synagogue, embassies and many other targets judged to be at risk of a terrorist attack. At one point, when the risk of terror was estimated to be at its highest level, you would even find heavily armed police officers patrolling railway stations and a number of selected streets in Copenhagen—a rather war-like sight not familiar to the Copenhagener's eye. To be sure, it was also a soldierly display that the detectives found it hard to fully familiarize themselves with. Unfortunately, their being included in such intensified guard work as well as other similarly mundane preventive ways of policing terrorism was becoming increasingly common as a result of the terror threat. As Detective Christensen noted a few days after my conversation with Detective Clausen:

> I know we have a great problem on our hands. But standing out there like simple sentries is really not what I expected I would be doing after becoming a seasoned police investigator and having spent some fifteen years on the force. I get that the job is important, but I think it should be someone other than me, to be honest. On the one hand, I'm overqualified for the job. On the other hand, I'm underqualified as I haven't received any proper training in this kind of security work for many, many years.

At TFB, the detectives echoed their colleagues' frustrations. They were however also thrilled that they were one of the country's very few units that had been exempted from the otherwise obligatory and nation-wide guarding of terrorism targets.

> "We're lucky", TFB Detective Jensen told me. "Politically, there is still too much focus on this big burglary problem we have in Denmark for us to be removed from our daily work. But, trust me, it's just a matter of time before we also get sucked into this frenzy. It's all just a matter of politics—when the focus change, we'll be out there on the streets as well".

His point was even substantiated by his own management, who admitted to me that "these days planning ahead seems rather futile. The best thing to do is take notice of the news if you want to know what the next days are going to be about". (These statements about the pushes and pulls of criminal justice politics form the focus of Chap. 6).

To the best of my knowledge, TFB and its detectives did nevertheless manage to stay clear. But as a Danish police unit, they were the exception to the rule, with police officers from all around Denmark being told to report for duty, and often not in a city or place close to them but far-away in Copenhagen. I will later return to what a long commute from, for example, the western to the eastern parts of Denmark meant to Danish police officers. For now, the above examples should be sufficient to clarify the general perception shared by almost every police officer I came across in my study, namely that standing on guard to protect places and people against terrorism was understood as an important but, nevertheless, a both very boring and bothersome work task.

When it came to other additional practices implemented in the name of fighting terrorism, neither TFP nor TFB detectives remained unaffected. Recalling the earlier mentioned militarization of policing thesis, the following is an example of something all Danish police officers were all forced to do, and increasingly so. To be fully prepared and ready to forcefully answer any eventual attacks, all officers employed in the Danish police were ordered to visit the shooting range to further develop their firearm and combat skills, often with a specific focus on mastering machine guns:

> **Vignette 25**
>
> Driving back to the station from the local shooting range, after having fired an assortment of both handguns and assault rifles, Detectives Larsen and Clausen start to make several negative comments to each other about this specific time expenditure. As we reach the station, punch in the code and unlock the station's front gate, Detective Clausen's frustrations burst out:
> "Yes, and there we have it. The day is almost over—and the only thing we've fucking managed to do was to shoot some stupid holes in a piece of cardboard". "I hear you", Detective Larsen says, "this is why I've been trying to avoid going to the shooting range for quite a while now. It takes up the whole day. Gone it is! And", now looking at me, "even though it can be fun and while it's definitely important these days that we're not complete idiots when it comes to using our weapons, it still feels like a waste of time". Detective Clausen agrees by looking at the both of us with a like-minded, fatigued expression.
> Finally, back at the office, we pass Detective Mikkelsen who is himself on his way to the shooting range. "Gotta get this shit out of the way!" he says grinning as he walks toward the elevator. With Detective Mikkelsen gone, the office is empty besides Detective Larsen, Detective Clausen and me. We all walk out on the balcony to have a smoke and, before going home for the day, Detective Larsen remarks dryly,
> "So, at least now we're ready to shoot up the terrorists when they come. But let's be honest", he continues, "this was also another good day for the cross-border criminals out there. I for instance had planned to follow up on what our good Swedish contact had told us, but I guess I'll do that tomorrow instead. Tomorrow is a new day, you know. Or, come to think of it, maybe it'll be just same, right? Yet another day of us not doing our job".

On this particular day, the TFP detectives could not postpone their shooting practice, which every officer in the force was required to do because of the threat level. Had they been able to choose for themselves, they would have tried *not* to go, probably until they could not avoid doing so. And at TFB they were similarly annoyed about having to spend the day at the shooting range. Detective Jensen, for example, flat out announced that, "personally, I don't really care [about weapons]", since he never wore his gun or intended to use it. Others said the same. "I'm a detective. That's not what I do, you know", Detective Jensen elaborated. Nevertheless, Detective Jensen and all his TFB colleagues eventually had to spend days at the shooting range away from their normal work.

Being ordered to go to the shooting range constitutes a simple yet suggestive example of the everyday practical consequences that the fear/threat of terror had on the detectives' work. Speaking of being increasingly armed and ready, together with all their colleagues in the Danish Police, the detectives had also been ordered always to carry their service weapons, to wear bullet proof vests when leaving the station as well as to wear their police badges visibly on their bodies when at the station—the weapon and vest to protect and prepare them, the badge to make sure that no outsider intent on causing harm could easily infiltrate them. Such various intensifications/manifestations of the use of police insignia and police equipment may be further understood by recalling Manning's (2010, 2012) contentions that policing always involves a performative or spectacular quality (see also Sausdal & Lohne, 2021)– a spectacular quality that often becomes increasingly visible in moments of societal crisis in which the legitimacy and potential effectiveness of the police are threatened. To the Danish police and the Danish detectives, the war on terror constituted such a crisis, prompting them to bolster themselves both symbolically and substantively—to be and show themselves willing and capable of mobilizing against the terrorist Other.

Nevertheless, as the above examples also illustrate, the Danish detectives did not entirely appreciate these more performative and militarizing aspects of their work. Mostly they were seen as a necessary evil. Add to this the number of other less-than-appreciated practices that the detectives were pushed to participate in and it is obvious that what terror was doing to policing was not always welcomed as a useful addendum to their work. The detectives, who preferred and were normally allowed to dress in their own civilian clothes, now had to carry a weapon, wear bullet proof vests and visible badges, as well as other emblems demonstrating that they were indeed law *enforces,* ready to serve and protect. This obvious parading of themselves as police, sometimes at least, ran counter to how the detectives often preferred to carry and see themselves. It, for example, muddied the difference between patrolling officers and investigators. This was a problem because of how the TFB and TFP detectives, denoting a specific 'detective subculture' (see Bacon, 2017; Manning, 2006; Westmarland, 2008), tended to think of themselves as being different from and, in some ways, more achieved than their patrolling colleagues.

Furthermore, besides being sent to the shooting range and having to buff up their police symbols and practices, the task forces' detectives also had to attend an array of different mandatory training courses to better prepare them in this time of terror. One of these, for example, was a course on "How to spot radicalization". One morning at TFB, having again had their normal plans cancelled, all the detectives were told to report to the downstairs lecture hall for a three-hour long training session. During the lackluster and badly designed PowerPoint-based lecture the detectives were trained in how to, as a commanded add-on to their ordinary work, look for signs of possible radicalization. Among other things, they were told who to look for, what to look for, where to look for it, what to do with the information, and how to engage, if need be. "So", I asked Detective Ibsen as the lecture had finally ended, "what do you think?" "What do I think?" she answered rather strongly, "I think I'd like to get back to my cases!"

Terrorizing Working and Private Conditions

The policing of terrorism, in the form of possible terror attacks and time-consuming and often tedious preventive practices, had increasingly become a part of the detectives' work routine. Although these incidents and practices were generally perceived as frustrating, what perhaps remained the most troublesome aspect to them was what the boosted terrorism policing meant for their overall working conditions and personal lives. To these we now turn.

What followed in the wake of the Copenhagen Shootings was not just a simple reshuffling of the Danish police's daily work. The terror attack, coupled with the so-called European refugee crisis (see Bevelander and

Petersson, 2014; Sausdal, 2014), also affected otherwise long-kept and hard-fought ideals of Danish police professionalism. Following the attack, a demand was put on the Danish police to up their efforts to prevent terrorism, protect Danish citizens and to restore a feeling of societal safety. As we have already seen, this among other things meant posting a lot of officers at believed targets of terrorism as well reinforcing the Danish border. The streets were flocked with armed officers like never before. To accomplish this, more police personnel were needed, and more than at that time employed and available within the Danish police force. This shortage of manpower led to a particular drastic decision. The government and Minister of Justice conferred with the police management and came up with some solutions. One of these were to severely shorten the police education, scaling it back from the otherwise freshly developed three-and-a-half-year university bachelor's degree to only two years' worth of course work mixed with real life experiences. A little later, a half-year "police cadet" education and position within the police were also introduced, breaking with the time-honored Danish tradition of having a unified police force with all officers having completed the same generalist education. These different restructurings of police education and ideals of police professionalism was immediately—and continue to be—criticized not only by pundits (Diderichsen, 2017), but also by many of the police officers I have met. Though police officers are not necessarily known for their delight of school and academic theory, shortening the police education was seen as a move in the wrong direction. The TFB and TFP detectives, for example, knew that more knowledge and education is essentially something the police need in an increasing complex world of crime and police work. And they weren't unaware of the advances made in terms of for example intelligence-led policing and other forms of more analytical-based approaches (Hestehave, 2017). A few of them even admitted that a better education could be a way to reform an otherwise old-fashioned police corps steeped in conventional, conservative "police culture" (see Mikkelsen, 2018).

In this way, the decision to scale back the police education/training was seen as an ill-advised and even a desperate move. And in my conversations with the two task forces' detectives, the decision was frequently mentioned (and it still is) as emblematic of how little Danish politicians think little of the police profession. As Detective Clausen tellingly put it:

"You see, David?" speaking to me. "They don't really take us seriously … Although the education wasn't a bachelor's when I went to the academy, I would have probably liked it to be one. I mean, don't get me wrong, I hated the academic stuff, but looking at it from where I am now, it would've provided a way for me to progress in the police or more easily leave the force. You know, having a bachelor's gives you access to different master's programs and so on. I could have gotten a new life! But now, I'm stuck. And so will the next generation of officers be".

The detectives understood that the downsizing of the education was a quick and effective way to increase the police's manpower. And they even recognized that it was probably the right if not only thing that could be done given the circumstances. Yet, trimming and otherwise diluting their education was also seen as a blow to their professional pride as well as a hindrance to their future career paths and exit strategies.

Something that was even more disliked was how the drastically heightened need for and use of police personnel was forcing pretty much all Danish officers, already on the force, to work overtime. In 2017, this had resulted in Danish police officers together working a total of more than 969,000(!) hours of overtime spread over only 11,000 officers. This represented an around 50 percent increase since 2014, when the number of overtime hours was "only" 633,000 (Dansk_Politi, 2017). The extra workload placed on the Danish police has given rise to a powerful and public criticism of management and politicians by frontline officers, who are otherwise known for keeping their criticisms in-house. Both during and after my fieldwork, police officers from all around the country have been writing critical social media posts that have gone viral. Officers have also written op-eds in national newspapers, books, and the police officers' own union has openly referred to the situation as 'a bomb under the Danish Police', stressing that this "might cost officers both their health and their family life" (Bæksgaard et al., 2015). More recently, the Union even came out against what they see as a growing politicization and attack on the police as a vocation, asking Danish politicians to "remove the pressure on the Danish police" (Politiforbundet, 2020), something also further discussed in Chap. 6.

Speaking to the task forces' detectives, the general view among them was that these new vocational developments were bad. Very bad. In their darkest hours, the detectives would even speak about how the overtaxing of them were causing their jobs and them personally to "disintegrate". They spoke about being "overworked". They spoke about being "stressed out" and how it made them "do a mediocre job", and sometimes worse than that: "Seriously", Detective Mikkelsen said one day, as he had again been drafted to a terror-related assignment, "how do they expect us to do a good job when they just throw us around like that and take advantage of us?!" The same sentiment was something conveyed by a former employee whom I met during my stay at TFP:

Vignette 26

Bumping into an ex-TFP detective in the police station kitchen, him and I have a chat. He tells me that he has recently moved to the countryside with his family in order to "get away from the stressfulness of Copenhagen and the Copenhagen police". He among other things points to the troublesome working conditions that have been the outcome by, as he says it, "the fear of terror", but also to how these have been having a negative effect on his family. Going on a longer rant, he says:

"Listen, it's extremely frustrating not being able to take proper care of our day-to-day work tasks, you know, not living up to the promises we have given to a victim of a crime or, for example, the public, because we're told to not work the cases we have but instead to stand somewhere outside on the streets like political poster boys. We are overworked, our families are falling apart, and the rate of officers calling in sick is increasing dramatically ... Of course, we all gladly help when there's a need for it. That's our duty. That's the job. But one starts to feel fooled when we're asked to do all these extra things without really getting any extra resources to do it.

The former TFP detective pauses for a bit, reflecting.

"But yeah, I know that many, many millions have been allocated to counterterrorism activities, but they all seem to go to the Danish Intelligence Service Agency and not to us. And we do a lot of the work! It makes me extremely angry, to be honest. Like, the other day I had promised my wife that I would pick up the kids and take care of them as she was going away on a work seminar. But then they [the police management] called me in and ordered me to stand guard somewhere and my wife had to cancel her thing. Do you think that kind of thing is good for things at home? Listen, they sometimes suddenly call me early in the morning and tell me to report for duty in Copenhagen, some two hundred kilometres away from where I live, even if it might be my day off. All this is making it impossible for me and my family to plan our daily life. It not only frustrates me, it also frustrates my wife. She's carrying a lot these days".

As this clearly shows, the detective and his family felt weighed down by the pressures placed on him in response to terrorism—and so did many of his colleagues and their families.

A *Blue* Army

In conclusion, let us return to where this chapter started, namely the Copenhagen terrorist shootings of February 2015. This tragic incident apparently differs from other examples presented in this chapter because it actually ended up with people being killed. Prior to the incident, the assailant, El-Hussein, had shown signs of having been radicalized and he openly declared that he was carrying out the attack in the name of Allah. As such, the stage was set for everyone to regard the incident as an act of terror.

Given this official terror labelling, together with the perpetrator's intention and the heartbreaking outcome, this incident diverges both symbolically and substantially from the other examples presented in this article. However, if we allow ourselves to only focus on how the incident was understood by Danish police officers, it does not differ very much. When it comes to the average opinion of police officers I encountered, what was officially called an act of terrorism was, unofficially, not truly understood as such. This was at least the impression I was given when observing how both the TFP and TFB detectives and other colleagues of theirs discussed the issue. Although they readily admitted that the assailant who had carried out the shootings had committed these horrendous acts thinking of himself as a righteous terrorist, the detectives still tended to see him as, for example, 'a stupid young man with serious issues'. Another detective even concluded that "most of all, he was just a loser with some gang affiliations— a loser who was trying to explain away all his senselessness and shortcomings by reinventing and redeeming himself through religion". Phrased differently, the Danish detectives did accept that the acts themselves could/should be seen as terrorism, but felt that the person who carried them out should rather be viewed as a stereotypical misguided criminal.

What this again demonstrates is that the terrorism discourse that has been so forcefully presented, if not promoted, by Danish politicians, the media and often also the police organization itself was not unequivocally echoed by frontline officers—even when incidents were officially labelled as terror and where one could expect officers to readily buy in to such a threat-based framework. Recalling Deflem's earlier words, in the eyes of many Danish frontline officers, terrorists were not necessarily seen as being truly war-like but instead viewed as common criminals. And in this way, their "war on terror" was not always a real war. The Danish detectives did not automatically accept and endorse (counter)terrorism in the way much of the literature suggests, that is, as something that is of great value to their work. As something of valor. As a meaningful martial matter. Danish police officers were not, as Bowling and Sheptycki otherwise ponder in relation to global policing and terrorism policing in particular (2012, p. 217), eagerly buying in to a dualistic and antagonistic worldview in which terrorism acts as an unconditional suitable enemy. In Denmark, terrorism was and is certainly perceived as a threat and as something that requires extra policing and vigilance. But when it comes to its workaday consequences, the spectre of terror often seem to haunts Danish police work more than it helps. Terrorism has become a both symbolic and substantive part of Danish policing, but terrorism is also terrorizing the Danish police.

On this point, we return to Cottee and Hayward's (2011) earlier-mentioned threefold approach to the study of the motivational aspects of terror-related actions, entailing a search for (1) the desire for excitement, (2) the desire for ultimate meaning and (3) the desire for glory that terrorism might offer and satisfy. Seeing the different empirical examples presented in this chapter through this theoretical lens, it seems clear that, to Danish detectives, policing terrorism is precisely often *un*exciting, is *lacking* in any ultimate meaning and that it does *not* bring the detectives any apparent glory. As primary societal combatants of terrorism, they did not experience much of an emotional draw—an emotional draw that much of the literature on counterterrorism however strongly hints at as essential to policing by arguing that the police have become militarized and Orwellian, and that police enjoy this because it fits the stereotypical attractions of "police culture" with its action-based, dualistic and often oppositional norms and values. Therefore, to reuse McCulloch's (2001) figurative phrasing I would agree that the Danish detectives have become part of a "blue army", yet with an emphasis on the sensation evoked by the former rather than the latter part of the concept—i.e. more *blue* than armed. Although the war on terror certainly has put weapons in their hands, donned them with tactical vests and increased their powers, for a number of Danish detectives the policing of terrorism was—and still is—primarily inconvenient and dull. This observation should of course not dissuade policing researchers and criminologists from continuing to criticize how the police as a societal institution has become increasingly militarized, powerful and potentially prejudiced. It does, nonetheless, serve as a reminder that significant differences exist between the police as an institution and its individual officers, as well as between specific counterterrorism units and the wider police force's working day. This is certainly also true, as this chapter has demonstrated from a Danish perspective, when it comes to the conspicuous, composite and in many ways calamitous war on terror—a global policing discourse that has swept across the globe but which hasn't swept local Danish police officers off their feet.

Bibliography

Altheide, D. L. (2006). Terrorism and the politics of fear. *Cultural Studies↔Critical Methodologies, 6*(4), 415–439.
Bæksgaard A, Kildegaard K, and Olsen SM (2015). 'Bombe under dansk politi' – presses af massivt overarbejde. *Berlingske*.
Bacon, M. (2017). *Taking care of business: Police detectives, drug law enforcement and proactive investigation*. Oxford University Press.
Bacon, M., Loftus, B., & Rowe, M. (2020). Ethnography and the evocative world of policing (part I). *Policing and Society, 30*, 1–10.
Bevelander, P., & Petersson, B. (2014). *Crisis and migration: Implications of the eurozone crisis for perceptions, politics, and policies of migration*. Nordic Academic Press.
Bowling, B., & Sheptycki, J. (2012). *Global policing*. Sage.
Bowling, B., & Sheptycki, J. (2015). 11 reflections on legal and political accountability for global policing. In S. Lister & M. Rowe (Eds.), *Accountability of policing*. Routledge.

Brodeur, J.-P. (2007). High and low policing in post-9/11 times. *Policing: A Journal of Policy and Practice, 1*(1), 25–37.
Coleman, R., & McCahill, M. (2010). *Surveillance and crime*. Sage.
Cottee, S., & Hayward, K. (2011). Terrorist (e) motives: The existential attractions of terrorism. *Studies in Conflict & Terrorism, 34*(12), 963–986.
Dansk_Politi. (2017). *Overarbejde: 600 politifolk kan holde fri i et år*. Retrieved November 7, from http://www.dansk-politi.dk/artikler/2017/september/overarbejde-600-politifolk-kan-holde-fri-i-et-aar
Deflem, M. (2004). Social control and the policing of terrorism: Foundations for a sociology of counterterrorism. *The American Sociologist, 35*(2), 75–92.
Deflem, M. (2010). *The policing of terrorism: Organizational and global perspectives*. Routledge.
Diderichsen, A. (2017). Renewal and Retraditionalisation:—The short and not very glorious history of the Danish Bachelor's degree in policing. *Nordisk Politiforskning, 4*(2), 149–169.
Drotbohm, H., & Hasselberg, I. (2015). Deportation, anxiety, justice: New ethnographic perspectives. *Journal of Ethnic and Migration Studies, 41*(4), 551–562.
Ericson, R. V., & Haggerty, K. D. (2006). *The new politics of surveillance and visibility*. University of Toronto Press.
Farber, D. (2021). *The war on drugs: A history*. NYU Press.
Flyghed, J. (2002). Normalising the exceptional: The case of political violence. *Policing and Society, 13*(1), 23–41.
Hansen P. (2011). *Terrorbekæmpelse i Danmark siden 11. september 2001*: DIIS Reports/Danish Institute for International Studies.
Heine, J., & Thakur, R. C. (2011). *The dark side of globalization*. United Nations University Press.
Hestehave, N. K. (2017). Predicting crime?: On challenges to the police in becoming knowledgeable organizations 1. *Moral issues in intelligence-led policing* (pp. 62–80). Routledge.
Højer, L., Kublitz, A., Puri, S. S., et al. (2018). Escalations: Theorizing sudden accelerating change. *Anthropological Theory, 18*(1), 36–58.
Hörnqvist, M., & Flyghed, J. (2012). Exclusion or culture? The rise and the ambiguity of the radicalisation debate. *Critical Studies on Terrorism, 5*(3), 319–334.
Kraska, P. B. (1996). Enjoying militarism: Political/personal dilemmas in studying US police paramilitary units. *Justice Quarterly, 13*(3), 405–429.

Kraska, P. B. (2007). Militarization and policing—Its relevance to 21st century police. *Policing, 1*(4), 501–513.

Kroener, I., & Neyland, D. (2012). New technologies, security and surveillance. In Lyon, D., Ball, K & Haggerty, K (Eds.), *Routledge Handbook of Surveillance Studies* (pp. 141–148). Routledge.

Kublitz, A. (2021). Omar is dead: Aphasia and the escalating anti-radicalization business. *History and Anthropology, 32*(1), 64–77.

Lyon, D. (2003). *Surveillance after September 11*. Polity.

Lyon, D. (2007). *Surveillance studies: An overview*. Polity.

Maguire, M., Frois, C., & Zurawski, N. (2014). *Anthropology of security: Perspectives from the frontline of policing, counter-terrorism and border control*. Pluto Press.

Manning, P. (2006). Detective work/culture. *Encyclopedia of Police Science, 2*, 390–397.

Manning, P. K. (2010). *Policing contingencies*. University of Chicago Press.

Manning, P. K. (2012). Drama, the police and the sacred. *Policing: Politics, Culture and Control: Essays in Honour of Robert Reiner*, 173–193.

Mathiesen, T. (2013). *Towards a surveillant society: The rise of surveillance Systems in Europe*. Waterside Press.

McCulloch, J. (2001). *Blue army: Paramilitary policing in Australia*. Melbourne University Publish.

McCulloch, J. (2004). Blue armies, khaki police and the cavalry on the new American frontier: Critical criminology for the 21st century. *Critical Criminology, 12*(3), 309–326.

McCulloch, J., & Pickering, S. (2009). Pre-crime and counter-terrorism imagining future crime in the 'war on terror'. *British Journal of Criminology, 49*(5), 628–645.

Mikkelsen, L. (2018). Konkret eller abstrakt politiarbejde? *Nordisk Politiforskning, 5*(01), 28–49.

Morgan, G., & Poynting, S. (2016). *Global islamophobia: Muslims and moral panic in the west*. Routledge.

Mueller, J. E., & Stewart, M. G. (2016). *Chasing ghosts: The policing of terrorism*. Oxford University Press.

Murray, J. (2005). Policing terrorism: A threat to community policing or just a shift in priorities? *Police Practice and Research, 6*(4), 347–361.

Mythen, G., & Walklate, S. (2006a). Communicating the terrorist risk: Harnessing a culture of fear? *Crime, Media, Culture, 2*(2), 123–142.

Mythen, G., & Walklate, S. (2006b). Criminology and terrorism. *British Journal of Criminology, 46*(3), 379–398.

Nadelmann, E. A. (2010). *Cops across borders: The internationalization of US criminal law enforcement*. Penn State Press.

Pickering, S. (2004). Border terror: Policing, forced migration and terrorism. *Global Change, Peace & Security, 16*(3), 211–226.

Pickering, S., McCulloch, J., & Wright-Neville, D. (2008). Counter-terrorism policing. In *Counter-terrorism policing* (pp. 91–111). Springer.

Politiforbundet. (2020). *Leder: Fjern det politiske pres på politiet*. Retrieved September 27, from https://politiforbundet.dk/nyheder/leder-fjern-politiske-pres-paa-politiet

Rytter, M., & Pedersen, M. H. (2014). A decade of suspicion: Islam and Muslims in Denmark after 9/11. *Ethnic and Racial Studies, 37*(13), 2303–2321.

Sausdal, D. (2014). Cultural culprits: Police apprehensions of pickpockets in Copenhagen. In B. Petterson & P. Bevelander (Eds.), *Crisis and migration: Implications of the eurozone crisis for perceptions, politics, and policies of migration*. Nordic Academic Press.

Sausdal, D. (2020). Everyday policing: Toward a greater analytical appreciation of the ordinary in police research. *Policing and Society*, 1–14.

Sausdal, D., & Lohne, K. (2021). *Theatrics of transnational criminal justice: Ethnographies of penality in a global age*. SAGE Publications Sage UK.

Sheptycki, J. (2017). *Transnational crime and policing: Selected essays*. Routledge.

Stumpf, J. P. (2006). The crimmigration crisis: Immigrants, crime, and sovereign power. *American University Law Review, 56*, 367.

Stuntz, W. J. (2002). Local policing after the terror. *The Yale Law Journal, 111*(8), 2137–2194.

Van Maanen, J., & Kolb, D. (1982). *The professional apprentice: Observations on fieldwork roles in two organizational settings*. Cambridge, MA: Alfred P Sloan School of Management.

Westmarland, L. (2008). Police cultures. *Handbook of policing, 2*, 253–281.

5

Cynicism

My study has not merely been a study comprised of concerned and complaining police detectives. Of course not. It was also a study including many examples of the detectives discussing how to effectively locate, get a hold on and, eventually, make sure that criminals were punished. Though frustrated with their work, the detectives' drive toward catching and bringing criminals to justice was largely intact. It is therefore important that the narrative presented here is not simply read as an example of utter local police apathy and non-action in a globalizing world. The Danish detectives still did their job and, mostly so, with passion. In the larger scheme of things, the detectives were like most other police detectives and officers orldwide.

As described in many prior studies of what the police find to be "real police work" (i.e. the kind of work that officers see as truly defining of the police as a vocation), police officers like to see themselves as law *enforcers* and crime *fighters* (cf. Manning, 1977; Loftus, 2009; Fassin, 2013). Even

---

This chapter is a reworked version of a previously published article: Sausdal, D. (2019). Policing at a distance and that human thing: An appreciative critique of police surveillance. *Focaal*, *2019*(85), 51–64.

though they acknowledge that the job often contains copious amounts of paperwork as well as the day-to-day keeping of social order, the tracing, catching and conviction of criminals remain essential to their professional identity—fighting crime, in other words, is at the heart of police ideas about what makes up not just *real* but also *rewarding* work. Relatedly, as Chap. 2 also illustrated, the Danish detectives did not only find professional satisfaction in fighting and, ultimately, sentencing of criminals; they also found it essential to experience that the criminals they did catch received a properly harsh kind of punishment—a kind of punishment which both in length as well as emotionally would leave the convicted criminal feeling beaten, imprisoned as well as somewhat miserable. Crime-fighting, in other words, only truly feels like a battle won if the opponent acknowledges it. Unfortunately, as further discussed in Chap. 2 as well as in a forthcoming book chapter of mine (Sausdal, 2023), a contributing reason to the Danish detectives' work frustrations was that many foreign national suspects appeared unfaced when caught and convicted in Denmark. It gave the detectives a sense of their policing powers being fairly impotent in a more global world with new and different kinds of criminals not similarly afraid of the Danish criminal justice system as the average Danish person (see also Aliverti, 2021).

In this chapter, I won't be focusing on the detectives' felt impotence as such. Instead, I wish to take a look at the specific determination if not aggression that underlines it. In other words, though feeling cross, the Danish detectives mostly remained rather conventional cops. They remained deeply interested in putting criminals in front of a judge, hoping to see them suffer the consequences. And feeling that the Danish criminal justice system could not always deliver a punishment that foreign nationals felt like punishment, the detectives would sometimes take matters into their own hands, adding some "street justice" of their own (cf. Klockars, 1980; Sykes, 1986; Jauregui, 2016; Fassin, 2018). In my experience however, such "street justice" never came in the form of extreme violence. Mostly, the police's self-conducted and outside-the-courthouse punishments (see also Harkin, 2015 or Fassin, 2028 for a more thorough discussion thereof) for example involved a slightly rougher approach to the physical handling of some foreign nationals when in police custody as well as what may be termed instances of psychological violence. The detectives may in this way have been seen to be working in what Feldman (2019) has also discussed as the "gray zone" of police power more than them evidently overstepping laws and conventions (see also Feldman, 2016). Bracketing for now the nuances of the detectives' (mis)use of force, the fact that the Danish detectives' felt extra annoyed with and willing to punish foreign nationals is the kind of police antagonism of interest to this chapter. Specifically, this chapter looks at how a particular technological/technocratic aspect of the detectives' work may have added to their cynicism and even aggressiveness. In this way complementing the emphasis of Chap. 3 and its focus on the police's increasing use of various information and surveillance technologies, the following pages discuss how an increasing "distance" between police officers and the people they police may negatively affect the policed as well as the police.

Policing at a Distance

> **Vignette 27**
> "Fucking hell. You see what I mean? What bastards! They don't care about anything, do they? The only way we'll ever catch these god damn foreign, cross-border criminals is by becoming as rootless as them … Look!" Detective Nielsen tells me as he points to the screens in front of us, "from here, from this place, we can see what's happening at every train station. And soon we'll get highway license plate cameras. That'll be a big help … That's the future of policing, us sitting in front of computers and punishing these bastards!"
> Detective Christensen is also there, and he agrees. "Yes", he says. "More and more so, we will be stationed at our desks or in some basement with computers, crunching data and monitoring people from afar. In the old days, they might've seen us coming, but now we can sneak up on them without them even knowing that we're there. Suddenly, it's just 'bang', gotcha you motherfucker!"

As Fassin's recently observed, "the police have become a major controversial figure in the contemporary world, while law and order policies have tended to disseminate globally" (2017b, p. 2). Fassin's focus is, just like other global policing scholars' (cf. Bowling and Sheptycki, 2012), not strictly on changes in the surrounding world per se, but on how the practice and organization of policing itself has (also) significantly changed. As he rightly notes, present-day policing is now increasingly shaped and geared toward global as well as local threats. To be sure, in a globalized world, where crime may be carried out online in the confines of one's home or office, or where would-be criminals may more swiftly travel across national borders and thus potentially escape justice, it is widely documented that police forces around the world focus on developing similar mobile methodologies, often including surveillance systems able to trace and tackle such itinerant issues (Bradford et al., 2016). As Chap. 3 exactly highlighted, this is also very much how the Danish police and its officers see things.

Though understandable (from a law enforcement and wider criminal justice perspective at least), the development of global policing efforts also includes some thorny yet too rarely debated vocational hazards—issues that Fassin's use of the word "controversial" hint at. Among these are the issues famously discussed by Didier Bigo and Elspeth Guild (2005) in their work on the problems of "policing at a distance". In strictly functional terms, it appears sound for the police to expand their Orwellian reach through various procedural and technological developments. Nevertheless, Bigo and Guild's argument is that this particular development of globalizing policing practices also includes the risk of making the work of policing a more cynical and potentially more violent profession (see also Aas, 2012; Bowling & Westenra 2018). As law enforcement officers' real life and more substantial engagements with suspects and citizens are declining and replaced by various proxies, the fear is that this will lead to a form of police work less aware and sympathetic of the moral complexities of human life. Indeed, as both anthropological, sociological as well as psychological studies have all shown, a distance from, and reduction of, the densities of the human condition may be a central ingredient of human callousness, discrimination and even violence (cf. Arendt, 1964; Farmer et al. 2004; Collins, 2009).

With this mind, we may again recall the above impassioned words uttered by Danish Police Detective Nielsen and Christensen—impassioned and aggravated words found throughout this book. As Detective Nielsen told me, an increasing use of surveillance technologies was the only way they would be able to catch "these bastard … these goddamn foreign, cross-border criminals". Indeed, his words appeared as a confirmative echo of how the future of policing is envisaged not only in Denmark but worldwide—a future of more and more sweeping means of surveillance by which people can be followed and policed from afar. In this case, Detective Nielsen and Christensen were sitting in front of a large number of computer screens, monitoring old footage as well as livestreams of public transportation. They were "the eye in the sky", as Detective Christensen also teasingly said it, him not being blind to its Orwellian connotations. Yet, this is not in itself why I have included the opening quote. Though not at all being the worst valuation of foreign nationals I encountered during my studies, the reason this chapter begins as it does is that it efficiently illustrates how such policing at a distance may trigger police antipathy. As the two detectives' aggressive words are meant to show, the Danish detectives quite frequently dressed their daily surveillance work in a language of contempt and castigation. Much in line with Fassin's contention, the detectives did seem to turn more uncaring while carrying out law and order work of a more global sort. While being policed via surveillance technologies such as CCTV, wiretaps and GPS trackers, suspects became not only criminal suspects but "fools", "assholes", "motherfuckers", or "bastards" in need of punishment.

In observing the Danish detectives' policing and surveillance work, my research can thus be said to confirm how an increasing policing at a distance may lead to cruder police attitudes, igniting already existing xenophobic inclinations or perhaps even forming the basis of new negative stereotypes (see also Chap. 2). This much is true. What I however also experienced was that this growing technologizing of police/detective work was not just causing a greater lack of appreciation of the people they policed; it also seemed to be the cause of a declining job appreciation among the detectives. Herein, in the observation of the detectives' dislike of merely being the proverbial "eye in the sky", lies the focus of this chapter. Contrary to much research on the matter, which directly or indirectly implies that police officers tend to appreciate being at a covert and calculating distance from the human lives they police (cf. Loftus et al., 2015), what my fieldwork taught me was that this was in fact often something which the Danish detectives found troubling. Though they did also like how technological developments were making their work easier and more effective (but see Chaps. 2 and 3), they did not always like, as Detective Andersen explained it to me,

> how these technologies remove us from the realities out there [pointing toward the exit] ... We sometimes need to not only see suspects on a screen but to also to get close to them out there on the streets to do good police work ... there are simply things you cannot learn and do through electronics, disregarding how fancy they are becoming.

In the remaining pages of this chapter, I will try to explain what the task forces' detectives meant by this and how this connects to critiques of present-day policing.

The Indifference and Violence of (Policing at a) Distance

Questions of distance versus proximity—or aloofness versus more intimate involvement—are central not only to much present-day police research (Fassin, 2013; Feldman, 2019; Jauregui, 2016; Mutsaers, 2019), but arguably also to social science itself. As one of the world's leading (global) criminologists, Katja Franko Aas reminds us, "distance has a long history of being seen as socially conducive to the infliction of pain" (2012, p. 253). We see this in recalling how founding sociological figures such as Durkheim (2014), Marx and Engels (2011), Simmel (2012), and Weber (2004) were all invested in understanding how changes in physical but also sociocultural distance furthered by the genesis of the modern, industrial era (negatively) affected social and individual life. Weber (2004), for example—and this is especially pertinent to this chapter's focus—took a skeptical view of the growing bureaucratization of modern life, arguing that although a bureaucratization of society had many benefits, it also included the risk of "disenchantment". Bureaucracies, he argued, although a more effective form of society-building and governance, encouraged a distanced form of rational thinking, largely uninterested in the specificities of wider sociocultural circumstances.

Today, the issue of (bureaucratic/governmental) distance is still with us—and arguably even more so (see Rose, 2006). Today, distance comes not only in the form of conventional bureaucratic paperwork and rationales but also through a growing technologizing and digitalization of many spheres of public and private life. As humans, we are even facing a new obscure era of oversight and decision-making growingly hinged on machine-learning rather than the alleged "iron cagey" rationalizing of human admins (Young et al., 2019). Public and private actors are increasingly able/required to engage digitally with one another, often without ever meeting in person, something especially true in Denmark, a country which prides itself on being the worlds' leading and most digitalized society (van Kersbergen & Vis, 2022).

In macro-sociological terms, Zygmunt Bauman is one of the more weighty scholars who has expressed a particular worry in relation to the potential negative human effects of digitally mediated interactions. He famously did this through the concept of "adiaphorization"—a term he used to describe what happens when "systems and processes become split off from any consideration of morality". On other occasions, he conceptualized his concern as a matter of "moral blindness" (Bauman & Lyon 2013, p. 8), particularly looking at issues of surveillance. According to Bauman, the (im)moral flipside of a society in which people increasingly meet each other as simulated representations rather than in physical, real life is that it entails a risk of reducing the human richness of such encounters. Through technological as well as transportational innovations, we are able to see and connect across vast distances. Yet, such connections, Bauman reasoned, are often shallower and less substantial, colder rather than warmer, rid of the wider and complex sensations and sensibilities of human life—and thus potentially more "morally blind".

Though resonating, Bauman's concerns do also appear a bit unrefined, romantic and perhaps even misplaced. Obviously, computers have not only allowed for mediated meetings across space and time, which are purely cold and reductionist. Many people worldwide have meaningful and important interactions online that allow them to work well, keep in touch with friends and family, create new relationships or engage with organizations and institutions in easy and effective ways. That surveillance and information technologies cannot strictly be understood as a blinding and adiaphorizing form of sociality is, for example, key to Mirca Madianou and David Miller's (2013) studies of *Migration and New Media*. What their extensive ethnographic work points out is that social media is not just a lesser form of real life; instead, social media effectively connects people with the thoughts and everyday lives of others, who would otherwise have been beyond reach. Another example of the more positive spread and reach of online technologies is that of Juris (2005) work on activism and how people with similar political ideas/ideologies may more easily find and inspire each other. And looking more specifically at issues of contemporary governance, Richard Rottenburg et al. (2015) present quite similar findings in their book, *The Making of Governmental Knowledge through Quantification*.

What the above anthropological observations remind us of is that the concepts of distance versus proximity don't neatly map on to what surveillance and information technologies actually do (or don't do). Things are more complex than one might suppose. And even though Foucault (1977) couldn't have foreseen the vast growth in optical and digital means of surveillance, it is worth recalling how the concepts of distance versus proximity were in fact part and parcel of Foucault's longstanding argument about the panopticon and disciplinary society. To Foucault, the panopticon was indeed a technology both of distance and of proximity, of control and of care, as it provided not only the governmental means to be all-seeing but also the individual incentives to self-govern (Fox, 2001).

That said, even though differences and nuances exist, available research does recognize that increasingly technologized relations between people have a remarkable effect on how they see themselves and others. And most often, as an average, current research is predominantly looking at this development as having a potentially negative effect, especially when looking at how criminal justice actors are now progressively meeting and "seeing" the public in the form of (big) data rather than (complex) humanity— seeing people as mere "data doubles" rather than singular beings (Haggerty & Ericson 2000).

Consequences of Distanced Means of Policing

In policing literature, the problems of an increasing distance between the police and policed was already a central interest of Gary Marx's (1988) old study of undercover police surveillance in the United States. As was also elaborated on in Chap. 3, Marx was highly critical of what he saw as a "surveillance creep"—that is, a growing tendency for governance in general and policing in particular to turn to covert ways of overseeing the public. Be it a case of audio or video surveillance, stakeouts or infiltrators, Marx thought that this kind of policing was both legally and ethically problematic, as it created an insurmountable and undistinguishable distance between the police and policed (Loftus, 2019). Surveillance as a method became a way of pigeonholing and muting suspects as the clandestineness of this type of policing, and its lack of actual human interaction, could mean that the suspect's individual rights were violated and that suspects weren't given a fair opportunity to explain and represent themselves.

Since Marx's study, his concerns have very frequently and often more powerfully echoed (Haggerty & Ericson, 2000, 2006; Ball & Webster, 2003; Ericson & Haggerty, 2006; Ross, 2007; Aas ., 2008; Mathiesen, 2008; Haggerty et al., 2011; Walby & Monaghan, 2011; Wall & Monahan, 2011; Loftus & Goold, 2012; Joh, 2016; Schuilenburg, 2017; Loftus, 2019). This may indeed be because we no longer live in societies where surveillance and other distanced ways of policing are creeping up on us. Instead, we now live in what Lyon (2007), for example, has described as a "surveillance society"; that is, we live in societies where the need for surveillance is not simply expressed and carried out surreptitiously but, often, done so out in the open (see also Lyon, 2018). As illustrated in this chapter's introduction, politicians, the police, and even large parts of the public openly speak of the need to surveil societal threats such as terrorism, undocumented migration, and cross-border criminality. Here we have an openly admitted turn to surveillance, which is only given further sustenance when also remembering that our personal computers and mobile phones are part of a wider everyday and capitalist culture of surveillance in which we all inevitably take part (Lyon, 2019; Zuboff, 2019).

Unsurprisingly, the turn to surveillance has given rise to many and often critical studies (cf. Molland et al., 2018). More recently, for example, Bethan Loftus and colleagues have pointed out how British "covert police officers … ten[d] to objectify their targets [by] reducing the subject of surveillance to a set of indicators" (2015, p. 636). And in their original work on policing at a distance, Bigo and Guild have a similar way of reasoning when they point to how European migration policing is increasingly managed by officials entirely removed from the world of the applicant. This produces a system, they argue, where the applicant "no longer has any intrinsic value, he/she is apprehended as part of a collective entity, as a disrupting flow, often dehumanised" (2005, p. 253) (see also Feldman, 2011, Andersson 2014).

In sum, what the policing at a distance literature is trying to tell us is that ways of surveilling and controlling people from afar, be it through procedural or technological proxies, entails the risk of problematically objectifying the policed party. It is a problematic process that entails an unsettling

> spiraling effect in that control procedures are then designed to operate independently of the individual's participation, to treat him as an object, to reduce him to nothing but a body and no longer a person capable of dialoguing with the various administrations[,] grant[ing] the state the last word. (Bigo & Guild, 2005, pp. 220–21)

Furthermore, the problem of policing at a distance is not just that it potentially diminishes and disarms those at the receiving end. It also includes the risk of kindling (further) police disregard for the people they regulate. Policing people at a distance, Sheptycki maintains, includes

> an enhanced belief in the efficacy of coercion [which] results in the tendency to lose contact with the complexity of reality and to grow ever more reliant on the exercise of force. The psychological price paid is manifest in defensive cynicism and aggressive moralism. (2007, p. 34)

A Balancing Act

While remembering the learnings of prior policing at a distance research, it is important to again consider how it would also be wrong to simply conclude that distance is always a problem and, for instance, that policing in more proximal ways is always a good thing. In terms of policing and surveillance, many both older and current real-life examples demonstrate that police proximity doesn't necessarily bring about less police misconduct—quite the contrary. In numerous countries and places, the police are notorious for over-policing certain communities, using a daily, interpellating proximity to either symbolically or physically remind certain people of their place in the social order (Fassin, 2013; Hornberger, 2011; Jauregui, 2016; Mutsaers, 2019). Obviously, for the people living under such everyday police pressure, it would be preferable if the police were less close.

And, conversely, it is not hard to find examples of (mental) distance that actually allow for greater reflexivity. This was, as I will also discuss later, exactly what William Muir (1979) argued for in his celebrated quest to home in the makings of an incorruptible, good police officer. In Muir's (1979) analysis, an essential quality of respectable and effective police officers is exactly their ability to both physically and intellectually distance themselves from the hardship that their job inevitably brings them into contact with and, instead of seeing it as mere depravity, seeing it as a depressing yet not outlandish part of human existence—to mentally deal with the dirtiness of their job (Hughes, 1962; Dick, 2005; Jauregui, 2013). When this chapter points to policing at a distance as something of a problem, it is therefore important the reader understands this is more as a sort of Weberian ideal type conceptualization, based on how the available literature on policing at a distance generally perceives and presents it, rather than it being a categorical proposition. An overly assertive and closely involved police officer is surely no antidote to a detached policing at a distance. Rather, as Muir points out, good policing—or street-level bureaucracy, in more general terms (Fassin et al., 2015; Lipsky, 2010)—is something of a balancing act between the right kinds of nearness and distance, kindness and authority.

Danish Policing at a Distance

We now move from the theoretical to the empirical. Below, I will provide some further examples of how policing at a distance affected the Danish detectives—that is, examples of how this sometimes led to sentiments of cynicism and aversion amid the detectives. Although I don't include clear-cut examples of how this ended up in actual acts of misconduct, I did observe what could be interpreted as overly assertive ways of policing (see also Sausdal, 2023). However, mostly these were "gray zone" matters more than evident police violations/violence (Westmarland, 2001; Feldman, 2019). And because of this, and because of how the perceptual more than the practical is also the main focus of previous policing at a distance studies, I have decided to merely focus on the detectives' negative views rather than on their actual (mis)conduct.

Doing What the Data Tells You

At both Task Force Burglary (TFB) and Task Force Pickpocketing (TFP), policing at a distance was at the heart of their daily doings. A banal example of this is that the very first thing the detectives did when reporting for work was to turn on their computers and check their phones. Every day. Always. They went through the previous day's report and checked up on different surveillance programs. They looked at the report in search of individual cases or patterns worth investigating. They opened their different data and surveillance programs to check on the wiretaps they had running, video and audio surveillance they had installed, or the different location trackers they had set up. They sometimes went on to request new or more CCTV footage from both private and public organizations or simply looked through the many hours of footage they already had received. And the detectives checked their emails and other available data programs inform to see if they had received any useful intelligence/information from national or international colleagues. In this way, the task force's detectives easily spent much of their workday at the office looking for and collecting evidence or leads electronically. And if/when these various in-house technological means of policing didn't pay off, or when they demanded additional evidence, they would go on stakeouts, setting up surveillance equipment inside or outside of buildings, doing house searches or otherwise covertly searching for suspects either on foot, sitting in their cars, in a flat, café or in a forest from where they could follow the movements of selected suspects.

Especially at TFB, days, weeks, even months could pass without the detectives coming into any physical contact with their suspects. Just as Fassin (2013) notes how his Parisian police interlocutors' workday resembled that of the much-hailed (and deservingly so) TV series *The Wire*, so did that of the Danish detectives'—and perhaps even more so. Their workday was a long way from the action-packed and close-encounter fictional portrayals of police work. Rather than obtaining their intelligence or evidence through a hollywoodesque, hard-hitting hands-on approach, the detectives typically got insights into their suspects' existence either as they spied on them during stakeouts or through video recordings. Alternatively, the detectives would obtain aural information as they listened in on some of the many hundreds if not thousands of hours of wiretap recordings stored and constantly coming in on their computers. These kinds of distanced observations frequently remained the closest the detectives got to the actual lives and bodies of their suspects before they, potentially, would make an arrest. On other occasions, the task forces' detectives would even make arrests relying solely on computer-based information from national or international colleagues (although not always being very keen, see Chap. 3), which the detectives themselves had no or little personal experience of. "We", TFB detective Gustavsen tellingly told me as he was following the whereabouts of two Romanian suspects by checking the mobile phone masts their phones were connecting to, "often just do what the data tells us to do".

Filthy Criminals!

Though much of the detective work I observed was more of an isolated waiting game than of the confrontational sort, there were still many outbursts of emotion. More than anything, this seemed to happen when the task forces' detectives were observing suspects through different surveillance technologies—be it wiretaps, footage, GPS trackers or intelligence reports.

Vignette 28

"They do it because they don't give a shit!" Detective Larsen tells me, his voice raised and filled with antipathy. Larsen is standing just in front of me, dressed in his own civilian clothes, yet with handcuffs, a radio, a tactical vest and a weapon hidden underneath his attire. He and the other TFP colleagues are about to go on a stakeout. They have just received intelligence from a foreign source, pinpointing the whereabouts of a group of Romanian cross-border criminals. And now is the time to "go get them". "They have no respect for other people", Detective Larsen continues,

"Here's the truth. They [foreign criminal suspects] just see Denmark as a reservoir of richness waiting to be looted. Like, when we eventually catch them, it's obvious how fucking indifferent they are. They have a completely different way of thinking about other people. To them, it's natural to live a life of crime. This you have to understand. I mean", he says to me, pointing to a printed CCTV photo of the Romanian suspects that TFP has hanging on a whiteboard together with other surveillance footage and mug shots. "Look at them. No care in the world. Absolutely none!"

Later that day, the detectives and I return to the office empty-handed. They remove their radios, cuffs, vests and store their weapons. Being somewhat of a ritual when reporting for work or upon returning to the office, the detectives go into the nearby staff kitchen for a cup of coffee and then reassemble in front of the whiteboard and the grainy footage of the suspected Romanians.

"Fucking filth!" Detective Clausen mutters, his face tired and damp from yet another encounter with the rainy Danish summer—"fucking filth" reminding me of similarly degrading words he and his colleagues had been uttering throughout the day as they had spent the last six hours in vain staking out different Copenhagen train stations as well as other public places known for credit cards thefts.

Feeling the tension in the air, I again look toward Detective Clausen. He is now standing only a few inches away from one of the pictures of the suspects on the whiteboard, piercing it with an angry stare. "We'll get them soon enough. Don't worry, partner" Detective Mikkelsen promises him, having noticed his colleagues' irascibility, "just you wait and see. These damn gypsies won't know what hit them. It will be like, *bam!*"

Importantly, I have not chosen to include this example to simply single out these particular detectives' disdainful and punitive viewpoints. The same is true of other empirical examples presented in this chapter or elsewhere in the book. Instead, they have been included as they represent sentiments many if not most of the two task forces' detectives shared. Staring at camera recordings or live feeds, the detectives would often voice (very) negative opinions about suspects—even though they had rarely actually encountered them in the real world and new very little of them. And the detectives would have a similar sour way about them as they listened in on the phone calls of Romanian nationals suspected of committing burglaries, looked at footage of what they thought was organized groups of Moroccan or Polish thieves, went through computer records describing a Chilean case, or when receiving different kinds of electronic intelligence and "early warnings" from the Danish National Police or Europol, warning them of how known Lithuanian criminals were on their way to Denmark. The detectives would listen to and look at all this electronically generated and facilitated criminal intelligence, frequently supplementing their observations with words of contempt. The suspect "encountered" through these various media would be labeled "primitive", "backward", "assholes", "idiots", "degenerates", "animals", or "not human", alongside other distasteful terms. And not just that. The Danish detectives would, like Detective Mikkelsen did here, also often supplement their negative words with outspoken punitive wishes.

Before and After Romania

Damaging judgments were also in the air when I, together with TFB Detectives Pallesen and Eriksen, was awaiting permission to board a plane leaving for Romania from Copenhagen Airport. Although most of the task force's investigations were carried out in Denmark, they sometimes had to go on international missions to collect evidence or build up partnerships. In this case, as part of a joint investigative team (JIT) between the Danish police and Romanian authorities (made possible through Eurojust), Detective Pallesen and Eriksen and I were going to the city of Botoșani in Romanian Moldavia. The detectives, together with other teams of Danish investigators dispersed across other Romanian cities, were flying down there in the hope of securing evidence in support of a major case they had been running—a case on a group of Romanian citizens who were thought to be part of a large organized criminal group operating in Denmark. However, the detectives weren't particularly optimistic. They didn't really like Romania or Romanians, nor did they trust their Romanian counterparts. Below is a rendering of the conversations we had before boarding the plane to Romanian contrasted with a later conversation we had upon returning.

> **Vignette 29**
>
> "I'm looking forward, I am, but I honestly don't expect to get much out of this. I mean, we know how Romanians are. They're not gonna talk or cooperate in any way". Detective Pallesen concludes as we walk into the plane. "Agreed!" Detective Eriksen responds emphatically. "We're surely gonna be met with nothing but unresponsiveness and lies from *these kind of people*", accentuating the last part of her sentence both verbally and by rolling her eyes". Trust us, David. This is not going to be much more than a nice little vacation time for us". With these not-so-optimistic words, the detectives and I find our seats and wait for the plane to take off.
>
> Fast-forward a week. The detectives and I find ourselves in a similar situation. This time we were waiting in an airport not to leave but to return to Denmark. We are going back to Copenhagen after having spent several days and hours interviewing Romanian suspects, witnesses and victims. The detectives and I had even been on guided trips in and around Botoșani. Local Romanian police had kindly escorted us and shown, among other things, their Danish colleagues the extremely rundown suburban neighborhoods and villages where the supposed suspects as well as many of their victims lived. Although the week had passed quickly, the Danish detectives had been very moved by what they had experienced:
>
> "Damn, these people are poor! Like, really poor. Did you notice how even the horse carriages have license plates? I mean, wow! It's like being transported back in time … And then seeing all these destroyed high-rises with no windows and holes everywhere, and also these village huts with no plumbing or nothing … Damn … Seriously, seeing this has made me much better understand why they do it, why they steal and stuff. It's pure desperation, no?" Detective Eriksen says, reflecting on her experiences after five days spent in Romania.
>
> Detective Pallesen concurs. "Yes, it surely is. Seeing that, listening to our Romanian colleagues and sitting there talking to some of these poor Romanians with their toothless faces and hearing where they come from have definitely provided me with some perspective. I honestly wish we'd done this before. This was very useful".

What may be learned from this example? Although being only one example, and perhaps even a too histrionic one, it does demonstrate some of the key differences between policing at a distance vis-à-vis conventional police work carried out in more or less close proximity with criminal suspects. As I have so far tried to show, when the Danish detectives only/mostly "met" their suspects through various proxies, they would have a tendency to think and speak of them in crude ways. Objectified as a visual, aural, biometrical, or textual representation, the criminal suspect fell more easily prey to the detectives' negative notions. Suspect was unable to speak back, to acquire a voice and thus potentially become more, in the eyes of the detectives, than a delinquent (see also Chap. 2). Yet, as the above example is meant to illustrate, in both physically and socially overcoming (some of) the distance between Denmark and Romania, between themselves and some underprivileged Romanian citizens, Detective Pallesen and Eriksen had come a bit closer to also overcoming their inclination toward negative stereotyping. I agree, the example of the detectives' enlightening visit to Romania is rudimentary, bordering on the banal. One may even think it only demonstrates a surprising general lack of police empathy and insight, only slightly remedied by an expensive trip abroad. Though there may be some truth to this, it was nevertheless my experience that the detectives' negativity toward suspects waned when they got the occasional chance to look at them beyond the secluded lens of surveillance technologies. The above-described trip to Romania is an admittedly caricatured example thereof. But my experience was that even much more minor opportunities to encounter and engage with suspects often had a similar effect. When this happened, suspected people of a certain uniform "kind" had a better chance of becoming people in their own right—people whom the police could not so easily roll their eyes at as they now appeared as people with a more meaningful backstory—or, as in Agamben's famed words, people who had become more than just "bare life" (Agamben, 1998).

Vignette 30

Things are slow and I am alone in the office with Detective Pedersen. He is going through some of the newest recordings from one of the task force's rather few non-foreign national cases, a case on a group of young Danish men suspected of several burglaries. Sitting next to him, I observe how he is meticulously listening to the different lengths of telephone calls that have come in and reading the text messages the suspects have been sending. I can also tell by the way he controls the mouse that he is probably checking the suspects' whereabouts, looking at what telephone masts their phones have been connecting to. Suddenly, Pedersen smiles and looks at me. I ask him what he is smiling about (as I am normally more used to sneers than smiles).

"Nothing really", he says". I mean, I laugh because it's funny to listen to these young guys. Like, this "tough guy" in a conversation with one of his mates just told a story about how he was getting it on with this girl and how on top of the world he was—only to then phone that girl and have her completely reject him. She was toying with him, and he was just taking it as all unconfident, horny youngsters do. She destroyed him. Fully tore him into pieces. It was brutal …. And you know, although we spend many hours listening to suspects talking about fuck all, the whole thing becomes quite nice when you get these insights into who they actually are, into the wider reality of it all. It makes it worthwhile, I think. [pause]. And it is also quite fun, to be honest".

Listening to him explain what he has found of worth when listening to the wire, I decide to again bring up his and Detective Andersen's earlier reluctance to investigate the suspected Romanian burglars. "Why didn't that seem worthwhile?" I asked him.

Of course, it's worthwhile. It's our job to catch all criminals and especially these foreign, cross-border criminals. No doubt. They need to know that we're on to them … That said, I guess the reason we reacted as we did was that it's often a real tiresome task. We don't understand what they say, so we need an interpreter. And the interpreter only translates that which is of direct relevance to the case. You see, the whole thing becomes very detached and boring [pausing]. I told you this already, David. The problem is that when it is some Dane, I have an easier time understanding what he is about. The Romanians, Chileans or whatever assholes, they are more black-boxes to us. I see their names in reports. I see pictures and hear voices. But it's not the same.

Developing Cynicism

These examples of Danish policing at a distance include another important aspect. Besides demonstrating how (some) police officers become more considerate when actually engaging with criminal suspects in real life, they also show how this emotive turn personally affected the Danish detectives more widely. From often being sour, cynical and mean when observing blurry CCTV footage, listening to wiretaps, or reading intelligence reports of their suspected criminal counterparts, the detectives seemed happier and more content when allowed to experience their criminal suspects as more than simple digital representations. Not only did the detectives' appreciation of the people they policed increase, so did their appreciation of their work (and perhaps even of their own persons).

In Chap. 2 as well as in other published works (Sausdal, 2020, 2021b), I have discussed how the (Danish) police find professional satisfaction in having a more comprehensive understanding of their suspects' backgrounds and motivations—a finding that reaches beyond the particularities of Danish detective work, as it is echoed in other studies from different parts of the world (Björk, 2008; Feldman, 2016; Muir, 1979). Specifically, we may here recall how Detective Pedersen (in Chap. 2) readily admitted that there was a risk of the detectives becoming more cynical and thinking less of their suspects when the detectives were not able to understand what the foreign national suspects were saying on the wire. And this was not just a more distanced kind of police work that made for more cynicism, it was also a "less fun" and less engaging kind of work.

In Chap. 2, however, I primarily focused on how foreign suspects made for more frustrating and superficial work tasks—and how this made for xenophobic sentiments. Obviously, this chapter and its focus on how distanced forms of work foster negative attitudes is much related thereto. Yet, to further underline this point, it is worth spending a bit more time focusing on the greater joys of policing the foreign nationals believed opposite, namely a Danish (speaking) suspect. A few weeks after Detective Pedersen confessed that he often had a greater disregard of foreign suspects an opportunity arose for him and I to discuss it further.

Cynical Police

The before-discussed different ways Danish detectives experience working with either Danes or foreign nationals—or Danish criminal suspects versus cross-border criminal suspects—both accentuate and nuance the problem of how distance plays into professional perceptions. It is noticeable that both work tasks make use of surveillance technologies. In both cases, the task force detectives rarely if ever encounter the suspects in real life before an eventual arrest. And, as such, both cases ostensibly fall under the umbrella of what may be termed policing at a distance. Nevertheless, a vital difference is at play. As the above example illustrates, when wiretapping Danish suspects, the detectives felt better able to minimize the believed distance which the wiretap otherwise created between them and their suspects. Danish suspects had a better chance of becoming "more than just criminals" as the detectives were able to listen in not only on their criminal enterprises but also on the wider circumstances of their lives. These circumstances provided a context. They made it easier for the detectives to situate and understand not only the crime but the criminal. But when the detectives were wiretapping non-Danish speaking national foreigners, contextualizing became harder. In the case of wiretaps, the detectives had to get an interpreter, and the interpreter would normally translate only that deemed directly relevant to the criminal investigation. And, as also covered in Chap. 2, in addition to having an easier time bridging distance by means of a common language, the task force detectives had other contextualizing tools at their disposal. Browsing various Danish national records, the detectives could read up on Danish suspects, getting to know more about their birthday, birthplace, job situation, residence, economy, taxes, criminal history, family situation, and so on. When they were surveilling a foreign suspect, such information was only rarely available and, if it was, had to be acquired from international partners at a much slower pace.

All this is not to say that the detectives' preconceptions didn't have anything to do with it. They did. Ingrained biases mattered. The point here is that policing at a distance practices and technologies don't help. Quite the contrary. Different technologies made them witness a lot, but the detectives didn't get the sense they truly understood what they were looking at. To the detectives, one could say, the work of surveillance often became a decontextualized, cooler, and thus more cynical affair—and so did the detectives' attitudes toward the watched but also, as this entire book is a testament to, toward their own vocation. Herein lies the central point of the chapter. Yes, prior research has rightly argued that policing at a distance involves a greater risk or making the police crude and cynical. But, no, as examples in this and other of chapter are meant to show, this is *not* an added cynicism police officers necessarily welcome, at least not the detectives I followed. Unlike the explicit or implicit notions in much research on the problems of policing at a distance, which tend to argue that police officers find it not only useful but also agreeable that those they are policing are objectified and stripped of any unnecessary human density (Loftus et al., 2015; Loftus, 2019) the Danish detectives I spent time with most often appreciated when criminal suspects appeared as more than just criminals. A more extensive knowledge of suspects not only gave the detectives, as they themselves emphasized it, "an investigational advantage"; "it's also simply nice as it is nice to have a slightly greater understanding of the people we investigate. It keeps us from becoming completely callous assholes", as Detective Clausen admitted to me, the very same Detective Clausen who had earlier been cynically and bellicosely staring at a grainy footage of Romanian suspects, wishing them hell(!)

That some Danish detectives find solace in at least somewhat understanding the people they police beyond their misconducts is relatable to Micael Björk's (2008) insightful description of how the police in Gothenburg "fight cynicism". As Björk reminds us, while it is true that the police vocation and its involvement with the troubling aspects of human life makes the police increasingly immune to human hardship, it is not automatically the same as the police reveling in their indifference. On the contrary, Björk found the officers who displayed a high amount of both professional capability and satisfaction were often the ones who actively engaged in not becoming too indifferent. And one of the main ways for the Gothenburg police officers to "fight cynicism", Björk argues, was precisely for them to try to contextualize and understand their criminal suspects' motivations beyond mere legal reasoning (see also Feldman, 2016).

Good Police

To be sure, as two foundational figures in policing research, John van Maanen (1978) and William K. Muir (1979), have similarly argued, it is an officer's capacity to contextualize crime that makes them less contemptuous. Furthermore, as Muir goes on to conclude, contextualization is not only what makes a police officer able to carry on being an individual who must continuously face human indecency, tragedy, and (use) violence: it is also a key ingredient in what makes "a good police [officer]". Contextualization is the wider anthropological bolstering needed for dexterous (and friendly) officers, as it allows them to not just keep thoughtlessly to the letter of the law—or even from becoming yet another Dirty Harry (Klockars, 1980)—but also to situate their discretions in the complexities of human life. Contextualization, Muir argues, keeps police officers from being either encumbered by apathy or consumed by aggression—from feeling they are utterly different from or perhaps even pitted against people.

Or as Feldman (2016) has also argued (based on a rather similar ethnographic detective study to that of mine), reflective "thinking" rather than mechanical "cognition" is the fine phenomenological line that separates the ethical from the evil. Though his Southern European police investigators often took the law into their own hands (as all police around the world sometimes do) and thus entered "the gray zone" (Feldman, 2019), what primarily kept them from maliciousness, Feldman argues, was their ability to see similarities between themselves and their suspect—and to reflect on these openly with their colleagues as they negotiated what actions to take. If such room for reflection isn't available, Feldman contends, police officers risk living up to Arendt's much-debated analysis of Eichmann (Arendt & Kroh, 1964; Ezra, 2007). They become "thoughtless" and thereby a mechanic yet greatly consequential expression of a system of potential evilness. That possibilities for police contextualization and reflection exist—for bridging the gap and seeing the other, the suspect, as somewhat similar—of course doesn't guarantee police misconduct won't happen. Police misconduct is a much more complex phenomenon. I would however still go as far as saying that contextualization is an indispensable yet, sadly, too little discussed component in the fight against police discrimination and brutality.

Moreover, the problems of policing at a distance, and its inbuilt potential of cynicism and aversion, don't only concern the police. As Lipsky famously argued, all street-level bureaucrats rely not only on procedures but on actual interactions to best exercise their discretions (2010, p. 14). Police, teachers, social workers, health workers, all public and even private service workers rely on means of contextualization to make the scripted laws and regulations they are employed to follow and enforce fit the compositions of everyday life (cf. Fassin et al., 2015). It is therefore disconcerting to observe how not only the police but many other agents of control are increasingly granted panoptic control mechanisms, allowing them to see and do more from afar, without there being a substantial focus on how to keep them thoroughly aware of, and interested in, the lives they oversee. By and large, this otherwise important debate seems almost completely absent in contemporary discourse. In policing and criminal justice, at least, there is often a very narrow focus on the instrumental end-point—a persistent efficacy emphasis on "catching bad guys", and especially when discussing the notion of "transnational uncivil society" (Heine & Thakur, 2011), as the former UN Secretary-General Kofi Annan once phrased it. This is also a limiting instrumental focus also promoted by the police themselves, as they rarely speak to outsiders or even to themselves about how the means, ends, and appreciations of their job go further and deeper than the question of whether a suspect is caught and convicted (Sausdal, 2021b). Yet, as this chapter has aimed to illustrate, policing actors do—unsurprisingly, I would say—have many more convictions than for example the coarse cliché of "police work culture" allows for. Police, for example, don't necessarily find surveillance 100% meaningful just because it helps them catch criminals. Though putting it to use, they also long for the intimacies and intricacies of close contact—not just to be able to correct and convict people but also as a way of making suspects into more than just suspects and, notably, police work into more than just policing.

An Open Question

This chapter has exemplified how Danish detectives' use of policing at a distance measures include the danger of triggering animosity. In this way, it has confirmed many of the apprehensions already expressed in the policing at a distance literature—a literature that among other things foresees growing levels of police cynicism and even antipathy worldwide as policing actors increasingly carry out their work with little or no actual human interaction involved. Yet, the chapter has also shown how the means and ends of policing at a distance are not that easily appreciated by a group of Danish detectives as one might have expected. Contrary to the dominant idea that the police enjoy the analytical and aloof distance offered by surveillance technologies, Danish detectives seem skeptical about it. Though they tend to agree the growing use and integration of police surveillance systems is necessary and useful in the fight against progressively more mobile and complex forms of crime in a global world, they don't always like the way this development is disconnecting them from the daily lives of their suspects. This, again, is closely related to Gavin Smith's (2009) shrewd observation that more and new surveillance technologies may "empower the [surveillance] watcher" yet are "disempowering the [surveillance] worker". Put differently, the Danish detectives do experience how policing at a distance means are giving them effective Orwellian possibilities. But, sadly, they also feel that this is taking away something they truly appreciate about their job; that is their discretional ability to engage with and, of central focus in this chapter, to understand suspects beyond their sheer criminality. Indeed. Understanding criminals as human beings of a more complex sort, and not just as crooks on a computer screen, not only provides the detectives a perceived investigational edge; it also provides them with a cynicism antidote. Gaining insights beyond the limiting neoclassicist tropes of crime is something the detectives felt to be enriching their profession as it frees them from the binaries of the simplistic police-policed polarization. To be sure, as I have also discussed elsewhere (Sausdal, 2021a, 2021b), if asked directly, the Danish detectives will probably often insist on how they don't really care, presenting themselves as crime-fighting automatons. Yet, observing and listening more closely to their cares and concerns, a less simple and combative story arise.

This observation brings the chapter to the words on which it will end. In the literature, there is a predisposition toward criticizing the police, their worldviews, and their too often aloof and intrusive means of surveillance and control. As the world is witnessing a dramatic and often dangerous growth in policing at a distance, this is understandable. Yet, such critical stances also carry with them a problematic tendency. As I see it, some existing critiques are frequently too far removed from Kevin Karpiak and William Garriott's appropriate call for an anthropology of police that aims not at shedding positive light on the police but at understanding "what makes the police—as both individuals and as an institution—human" (2018, p. 6). As Fassin (2017a) has also argued, we as scholars/ethnographers are indeed obligated to treat our interlocutors as intelligent and intelligible humans with, to them, meaningful and multifaceted appreciations. We might disagree with their reasoning and the results thereof (and I often do when it comes to issues of policing), but we must nevertheless be able to ethnographically demonstrate how such reasoning makes sense to the people we study before we condemn it.

Furthermore, such a" humanizing ethic" is not just the sine qua non of conventional ethnography-cum-anthropology; it also carries with it a critical potential. As studies have established (and as I know from working with the police and from (critically) commenting on policing in the media), the police are more likely to listen and change if the critical scholar can also demonstrate an actual understanding of the world the police inhabit (Wuestewald & Steinheider, 2009; Björk, 2018)—not as a matter of sympathizing but as a matter of showing that one has the ability to grasp the complexity of their work/world.

Bearing this in mind, and returning to the issue of the Danish police, I personally didn't find it particularly difficult to understand the Danish detectives' viewpoints in relation to policing at a distance issues. And here I am of course not talking about their negative and belittling comments about suspects they investigated; nor about their added wish to punish them. Instead, I am talking about the detectives' cynicism concerns and the negative effect they thought it had on their daily work. Similar to arguments found all over the scholarly literature, the detectives too felt policing at a distance to be problematic as it further removed them from the convolutions of everyday life. They too missed non-Orwellian ways of policing that brought them into closer contact with their suspects' existence beyond virtual representations and criminalized actions. The detectives, like many of us qualitative (and not purely digital) social science scholars, increasingly longed for "that human thing". Though surveillance technologies promised to lead the detectives more easily toward closed cases, they still found it more meaningful to actively engage with "'the human' as an open, central question" (Karpiak & Garriott 2018, p. 6). Or, as one of detectives put it, feeling frustrated with having spent yet another day in front of screen: "I didn't join the police just to be a computer extension. I wanted to get involved in the messy human life out there [him looking out the window], to know it and sort it out". Surely, in this sentiment lies both the potential of the iron fist and the velvet glove—of wanting to "apprehend" humans in the word's dual meaning both as in catching and comprehending, punishing and perceiving (see Sausdal, 2014; Vigh, 2018). In essence, this chapter has tried to highlight and endorse the latter, and its relation to police surveillance and a group of Danish detectives' concerns thereof, without forgetting the former.

Bibliography

Aas, K. F. (2012). (in)security-at-a-distance: Rescaling justice, risk and warfare in a transnational age. *Global Crime, 13*(4), 235–253.

Aas, K. F., Gundhus, H. O., & Lomell, H. M. (2008). *Technologies of inSecurity: The surveillance of everyday life*. Routledge.

Agamben, G. (1998). *Homo sacer: Sovereign power and bare life*. Stanford University Press.

Aliverti, A. (2021). *Policing the borders within*. Oxford University Press.

Andersson, R. (2014). *Illegality, Inc.: Clandestine migration and the business of bordering Europe*. University of California Press.

Arendt, H., & Kroh, J. (1964). *Eichmann in Jerusalem*. Viking Press.

Ball, K., & Webster, F. (2003). *The intensification of surveillance: Crime, terrorism and warfare in the information age*. Pluto Press London.

Bauman, Zygmunt, & David Lyon. 2013. Liquid surveillance: A conversation. Cambridge: Polity.

Bigo, D., & Guild, E. (2005). Policing at a distance: Schengen visa policies. In D. Bigo & E. Guild (Eds.), *Controlling frontiers. Free movement into and within Europe* (pp. 233–263). Ashgate.

Björk, M. (2008). Fighting cynicism: Some reflections on self-motivation in police work. *Police Quarterly, 11*(1), 88–101.

Björk, M. (2018). Politistudier—Metodologiske problemer og praktiske råd. In M. H. Jacobsen (Ed.), *Kriminologi: Metoder I* (pp. 453–481). Hans Reitzels Forlag.

Bowling, B., & Sheptycki, J. (2012). *Global policing*. Sage.

Bowling, B., & Westenra, S. (2018). 'A really hostile environment': Adiaphorization, global policing and the crimmigration control system. *Theoretical Criminology*. https://doi.org/10.1177/1362480618774034

Bradford, B., Loader, I., Jauregui, B., et al. (2016). *The SAGE handbook of global policing*. SAGE.

Collins, R. (2009). *Violence: A micro-sociological theory*. Princeton University Press.

Dick, P. (2005). Dirty work designations: How police officers account for their use of coercive force. *Human Relations, 58*(11), 1363–1390.

Durkheim, E. (2014). *The division of labor in society*. Simon and Schuster.

Ericson, R. V., & Haggerty, K. D. (2006). *The new politics of surveillance and visibility*. University of Toronto Press.

Ezra, M. (2007). The Eichmann polemics: Hannah Arendt and her critics. *Democratiya, 9*(3), 141–169.

Farmer, P., Bourgois, P., Fassin, D., et al. (2004). An anthropology of structural violence. *Current Anthropology, 45*(3), 305–325.

Fassin, D. (2013). *Enforcing order: An ethnography of urban policing*. Polity Press.

Fassin, D. (2017a). The endurance of critique. *Anthropological Theory, 17*(1), 4–29.

Fassin, D. (2017b). *Writing the world of policing: The difference ethnography makes*. University of Chicago Press.

Fassin, D. (2018). *The will to punish*. Oxford University Press.

Fassin, D., Bouagga, Y., Coutant, I., et al. (2015). *At the heart of the state*. Pluto Press.

Feldman, G. (2011). *The migration apparatus: Security, labor, and policymaking in the European Union*. Stanford University Press.

Feldman, G. (2016). 'With my head on the pillow': Sovereignty, ethics, and evil among undercover police investigators. *Comparative Studies in Society and History, 58*(02), 491–518.

Feldman, G. (2019). *The gray zone: Sovereignty, human smuggling, and undercover police investigation in Europe*. Stanford University Press.

Foucault, M. (1977). *Discipline and punish: The birth of the prison*. Vintage.

Fox, R. (2001). Someone to watch over us: Back to the panopticon? *Criminology and Criminal Justice, 1*(3), 251–276.

Haggerty, K. D., & Ericson, R. V. (2000). The surveillant assemblage. *The British Journal of Sociology, 51*(4), 605–622.

Haggerty, K. D., & Ericson, R. V. (2006). *The new politics of surveillance and visibility*. University of Toronto Press.

Haggerty, K. D., Wilson, D., & Smith, G. J. (2011). Theorizing surveillance in crime control. *Theoretical Criminology, 15*(3), 231–237.

Harkin, D. M. (2015). The police and punishment: Understanding the pains of policing. *Theoretical Criminology, 19*(1), 43–58.

Heine, J., & Thakur, R. (2011). Introduction: Globalization and transnational uncivil society. In J. Heine & R. Thakur (Eds.), *The dark side of globalization* (pp. 1–16). United Nations University Press.

Hornberger, J. (2011). *Policing and human rights: The meaning of violence and justice in the everyday policing of Johannesburg*. Routledge.

Hughes, E. C. (1962). Good people and dirty work. *Social Problems, 10*(1), 3–11.

Jauregui, B. (2013). Dirty anthropology: Epistemologies of violence and ethical entanglements in police ethnography. In W. Garriott (Ed.), *Policing and contemporary governance* (pp. 125–153). Springer.

Jauregui, B. (2016). *Provisional authority: Police, order, and security in India*. University of Chicago Press.

Joh, E. E. (2016). The new surveillance discretion: Automated suspicion, big data, and policing. *Harvard Law & Policy Review, 10*, 15.

Juris, J. S. (2005). The new digital media and activist networking within anti-corporate globalization movements. *The Annals of the American Academy of Political and Social Science, 597*(1), 189–208.

Karpiak, K. G., & Garriott, W. (2018). *The anthropology of police*. Routledge.

Klockars, C. B. (1980). The dirty Harry problem. *The Annals of the American Academy of Political and Social Science, 452*(1), 33–47.

Lipsky, M. (2010). *Street-level bureaucracy: Dilemmas of the individual in public service*. Russell Sage Foundation.

Loftus, B. (2009). *Police culture in a changing world*. Oxford University Press.

Loftus, B. (2019a). Normalizing covert surveillance: The subterranean world of policing. *The British Journal of Sociology, 70*(5), 2070–2091.

Loftus, B., & Goold, B. (2012). Covert surveillance and the invisibilities of policing. *Criminology & Criminal Justice, 12*(3), 275–288.

Loftus, B., Goold, B., & Mac Giollabhui, S. (2015). From a visible spectacle to an invisible presence: The working culture of covert policing. *British Journal of Criminology, 56*(4), 629–645.

Lyon, D. (2007). *Surveillance studies: An overview*. Polity.

Lyon, D. (2018). *The culture of surveillance: Watching as a way of life*. John Wiley & Sons.

Lyon, D. (2019). Surveillance capitalism, surveillance culture and data politics 1. In *Data politics* (pp. 64–77). Routledge.

Madianou, M., & Miller, D. (2013). *Migration and new media: Transnational families and polymedia*. Routledge.

Manning, P. K. (1977). *Police work: The social organization of policing*. MIT Press.

Marx, G. T. (1988). *Undercover: Police surveillance in America*. Univ of California Press.

Marx K, and Engels F (2011) Capital (volume 1: A critique of political economy). .

Mathiesen, T. (2008). Lex Vigilatoria: Global control without a state? *Surveillance and Governance: Crime Control and Beyond, 10*, 101–127.

Molland, S., Andersson, R., Baas, M., et al. (2018). Coproduction of sedentary and Mobile optics. *Current Anthropology, 59*(2), 115–137.

Muir, W. K. (1979). *Police: Streetcorner politicians*. University of Chicago Press.

Mutsaers, P. (2019). *Police unlimited: Policing, migrants, and the values of bureaucracy*. Oxford University Press.

Rose, N. (2006). Governing 'advanced' liberal democracies. In A. Sharma & A. Gupta (Eds.), *The anthropology of the state: A reader*. Hoboken, New Jersey.

Ross, J. E. (2007). The place of covert surveillance in democratic societies: A comparative study of the United States and Germany. *The American Journal of Comparative Law, 55*(3), 493–579.

Rottenburg, R., Merry, S. E., Park, S.-J., et al. (2015). *The world of indicators: The making of governmental knowledge through quantification*. Cambridge University Press.

Sausdal, D. (2014). Cultural culprits: Police apprehensions of pickpockets in Copenhagen. In Bievelander, Pieter and Petersson, Bo (eds) *Crisis and migration: Implications of the Eurozone crisis for perceptions, politics and policies of migration* (pp. 177–204). Nordic Academic Press.

Sausdal, D. (2020). On the Workaday Origin of Police Callousness. *Exertions*. https://doi.org/10.21428/1d6be30e.8d8aeb1d

Sausdal, D. (2021a). A fighting fetish: On transnational police and their warlike presentation of self. *Theoretical Criminology*. https://doi.org/10.1177/13624806211009487.

Sausdal, D. (2021b). *Looking beyond the police-as-control narrative*. In Katarina Jacobsson & Jaber F. Gubrium (eds). Policy Press.

Sausdal, D. (2023) Dirty Harry gone global?: On globalizing policing and punitive impotence. In Jan Beek, Thomas Bier- schenk, Annalena Kolloch and Bernd Meyer (eds) *Policing Race, Ethnicity and Culture: Ethnographic Perspectives Across Europe*. Manchester University Press.

Schuilenburg, M. (2017). *The securitization of society: Crime, risk, and social order*. New York University Press.

Sheptycki, J. (2007). The constabulary ethic and the transnational condition. In *Crafting transnational policing. Police capacity-building and global policing reform* (pp. 31–71). Hart Publishing.

Simmel, G. (2012) The metropolis and mental life. In *The urban sociology reader* (pp. 37–45). Routledge.

Smith, G. J. D. (2009). Empowered watchers or disempowered workers. In K. F. Aas, H. O. Gundhus, & H. M. Lomell (Eds.), *Technologies of InSecurity: The surveillance of everyday life*. Routledge-Cavendish.

Sykes, G. (1986). Street justice: A moral defense of order maintenance policing. *Justice Quarterly, 3*(4), 497–512.

van Kersbergen, K., & Vis, B. (2022). Digitalization as a policy response to social acceleration: Comparing democratic problem solving in Denmark and the Netherlands. *Government Information Quarterly*, 101707.

Van Maanen, J. (1978). The asshole. In P. K. Manning & J. Van Maanen (Eds.), *Policing: A view from the street* (pp. 221–238). Goodyear Publishing.

Vigh, H. (2018). Lives opposed: Perceptivity and tacticality in conflict and crime. *Social Anthropology, 26*(4), 487–501.

Walby, K., & Monaghan, J. (2011). Private eyes and public order: Policing and surveillance in the suppression of animal rights activists in Canada. *Social Movement Studies, 10*(01), 21–37.

Wall, T., & Monahan, T. (2011). Surveillance and violence from afar: The politics of drones and liminal security-scapes. *Theoretical Criminology, 15*(3), 239–254.

Weber, Max. 2004. *The vocation lectures*. Indianapolis, IN: Hackett Publishing.

Weber, M., Owen, D. S., & Strong, T. B. (2004). *The vocation lectures*. Hackett Publishing.

Westmarland, L. (2001). Blowing the whistle on police violence. Gender, ethnography and ethics. *British Journal of Criminology, 41*(3), 523–535.

Wuestewald, T., & Steinheider, B. (2009). Practitioner–researcher collaboration in policing: A case of close encounters? *Policing: A Journal of Policy and Practice, 4*(2), 104–111.

Young, M. M., Bullock, J. B., & Lecy, J. D. (2019). Artificial discretion as a tool of governance: A framework for understanding the impact of artificial intelligence on public administration. *Perspectives on Public Management and Governance, 2*(4), 301–313.

Zuboff, S. (2019). *The age of surveillance capitalism: The fight for a human future at the new frontier of power*. Profile Books.

6

Politics

"You know what I do? What I do is that I get up every morning and turn on the radio. Then I listen. And then I know what I have to do when I eventually show up for work"
—High-ranking Danish police officer

So far, the book has focused on more straightforwardly work-related issues. I have in different ways discussed how local police-cum-detective work in Denmark is affected by it increasingly being part of a more global world order—a discussion including different examples of how a group of Danish detectives have become growingly frustrated with the present and not least future prospect of their work life. This chapter only adds to the misery. Yet, instead of focusing on concrete on-the-job policing practices and perceptions, we turn toward the wider political context, which, together with legal and organizational strictures, if not defines then heavily guides the Danish police's work life, the task forces' detectives' work included.

More specifically, the chapter homes in on the prevailing and mounting law and order discourse that underlines much present-day criminal justice politics not only in Denmark (Tham, 2001; Balvig, 2005; Shammas,

2016; Elholm, 2020; Houborg et al., 2020) but in most Western countries. In Denmark, politicians from across the political spectrum have been and still are regularly basing their political campaigns and mandates on being "tough on crime". It is not necessarily what wins elections, but it does appear to be a key ingredient. Disregarding whether if it is the Social Democrats who are in government or whether Denmark is ruled by more right-leaning parties, what have defined the last 20 to 30 years of Danish criminal justice politics are the different political parties' shared willingness to introduce harsher sentences, to allow for more control and surveillance, to get more police on the streets, to get more "police visibility" (Holmberg, 2019), to increase external and internal forms of border controls, and so and so forth. As the former conservative Minister of Justice, Søren Pape Poulsen, indeed put it in 2017, speaking about Denmark's problems with gangs and drug-related crimes, "if you choose [t]o turn your back on lawful living, then you will experience us coming down hard on you!"—a tough on crime and control-oriented viewpoint including, among other things, the possibility of doubling prison sentences in respect to certain kinds of criminal activities, attempts to make life in prison much less of a positive experience, allowing the police to stop-and-search as they deem fit in certain residential zones, banning convicted criminals from being and living in certain areas, and in general making it easier to ban non-Danish citizens or people with a dual citizenship from living in Denmark altogether. To be sure, Danish criminal justice and migration/integration politics and policing are heavily intertwined (Rytter & Pedersen, 2014; Christensen & Albrecht, 2020; Kublitz, 2021; Lindberg, 2022). And as many studies on "crimmigration" from other parts of the world have shown (see Franko, 2019 for an overview), in our globalized presence many politicians have no problem combining if not conflating the two.

As already stated, punitive inclinations are not a mere right-wing, national conservative perspective. In many ways, tough on crime politics are a political cornerstone of the Social Democratic government anno 2022. For example, as Denmark's Prime Minister, Mette Frederiksen, recently said it, or perhaps rather forewarned, as her government presented a new "security law bill" to counter increasing criminal threats: "We [have] to take some drastic steps … We are knowingly pushing this quite far, including a massive development and spread of surveillance technologies" (Kildegaard & Dandanell, 2019), thereby mirroring her predecessors similar calls for a surveillance society as also discussed in Chap. 3. The current Danish government has even become (in)famous in journalistic and criminological circles for arguing that "surveillance is freedom" (Hækkerup, 2021)—a perplexing argument about how a limiting of personal freedom and individual rights may in fact lead to more security, safety and liberty as such a self-admitted Orwellianism is believed to prevent more crimes and thus make for a better life. (Listening to this, one does get the sense that George Orwell's book was more prophetic than he probably thought it would be…). Furthermore, in the political arguing for the unavoidable need to up the surveillance in society, and to be more tough on crime, Danish politicians frequently single out global, cross-border issues as a central cause. As already discussed earlier in this book, like many other national and international governmental bodies around the world (cf. UNODC, 2010), Danish politicians point to the growing threat of terrorism, organized and gang-related crime, drug trafficking, weapons smuggling, human smuggling, "illegal" migration, financial crime, cybercrime, as well as various others sorts of wrongdoing where the causes and culprits are often understood to represent the so-called "dark side of globalization" (Heine & Thakur, 2011)

Now, one would presume that Danish law enforcement officers value a rise in Danish law and order politics. The hand fits the glove, so to speak. And as this chapter also shows, the Danish police do in many ways welcome the possibility of tougher approaches. As I was observing and listening to the task forces' detectives' conversations, including their many daily political discussions, it became obvious that they were not much different from other police officers worldwide when it came to their politico-moral leanings (cf. Loftus, 2009; Reiner, 2010). The detectives too seemed to appreciate and endorse criminal justice approaches that focus more on retribution than rehabilitation, on force more than forgiveness. The detectives had limited sympathy for criminals. Or, as a minimum, they thought of control and punitive-oriented measures as a both fair and more effective way to approach crime as well as other societal issues, preferring the proverbial stick to the carrot. For example, as TFB Detective Andersen tellingly put it:

We are way too lenient in Denmark. Way too lenient. The only thing that works is coming at people swift and hard, letting them know that we, the police, are there to catch them and that they'll spend a long time in the pokey if they don't behave. That's for sure … Or, to be honest, even if it doesn't always work, it's still the right thing to do. It sends the right signal—the signal being that people should behave and be nice and that the rest of us don't tolerate people who hurt other people and destroy our society.

To be sure, such Kantian ethics were shared by not only all of the task forces' detectives, but by most police officers I have met in my studies of both the Danish police as well as other European and transnational police organizations (Sausdal, 2021a). This was surely also why the Danish detectives openly expressed their contentment with the fact that Danish politicians had begun to "wake up and smell the coffee", increasingly proposing new and harsher laws and offering the police and other authorities' new and growing means of regulating and monitoring suspects in particular and the public in more general terms. "It's good. It's not good enough. But it's better", TFP detective Christensen said, again showing how the Danish police are similar to most of their international colleagues, believing that the answer is *more* not less policing and punishment. "It does seem like our politicians finally understand that in order to properly protect Denmark and Danish citizens in this [global] day and age, we need to step up our game", he happily concluded.

The Danish detectives thus ostensibly applauded Danish politicians' tough on crime approach. And if I had only interviewed them or spent a shorter amount of time with them, this would probably have been my conclusion, that is, that the detectives were all for it. Yet, another and relatively conflicting reality was unearthed as I was spending nights and days with them—a conflicting reality focused on and discussed in this chapter. Looking at law and order politics through the lens of not just hard-hitting statements but through the police's actual, everyday work, what I witnessed was a quite radical decrease in their appreciation of contemporary criminal justice politics. Rather than purely celebrating how Danish politicians were being tough on crime, the detectives found Danish politicians and their criminal justice approaches to also, as it were, be "tough on policing". The detectives repeatedly complained about how an unremitting influx of new laws, regulations and tasks given to and asked of the police were making it increasingly hard for them to mind their normal work tasks; or indeed "to plan and carry out our work", as formulated by a high-ranking figure in the Danish police whom I also interviewed. This, in a nutshell, is the punitive politics paradox laid out in this chapter. Using different empirical examples, I aim to illustrate the absurdity in how a political if not populistic growth in law and order politics may in fact be doing very little for law and order practitioners. Politically and morally, the Danish detectives concurred. Practically and professionally, they felt strained. Rather than waking up to an exciting new day, the Danish police get up in the morning, turn on the radio, them thinking that a politician will probably be turning that day's bad news into that day's criminal justice politics and, ultimately, that day's police work.

Politics and/of Policing

Later, I will be providing some examples of politics that may be tough on their targeted audience but which also ended up being tough on the Danish police. Yet, before continuing, I want to spend some words describing the current state of the research literature when it comes the question of policing politics, also including the question of a more globalized form of policing and the politics included. Doing so will allow for a greater understanding of the specific case at hand as well as how it relates and potentially adds to scholarly knowledge about this topic. To be sure, in policing research and criminology more broadly, issue of policing and politics have frequently been discussed—both directly and indirectly. Broadly speaking, one may say that interests in this subject matter tend to follow three specific themes—themes that respectively revolve around (a) the kind of politics that the police themselves adhere to, (b) the police's almost ideological opposition to political change and, relatedly, (c) the wider society's criminal justice politics, including its (dis)appreciation of policing and attempts to either bolster or reform it.

Police Politics

What and who do police officers politically support? This is a question that has been mulled over in many studies of police work. Although it has rarely been the central research question (but see Jauregui, 2022), it has been of interest especially in studies of the police's occupational culture (Loader & Mulcahy, 2003; Westmarland, 2008; Loftus, 2009; Martin, 2018; Cockcroft, 2020). Ranking among the most conducted and cited studies of policing, "police culture" studies demonstrate not only that police officers worldwide tend to have much similar views on the world and their vocation, but that they also have remarkably similar politico-moral views. Though a few more recent studies are beginning to shed light on how policing (politics) are done and perceived differently beyond the so-called Global North (see Jauregui, 2016; Beek et al., 2017; Martin, 2019), it has nevertheless been a consisting empirical finding that police officers tend to be conservative-leaning individuals. Explained through Bittner's influential Weberian definition of the role of the police as "a mechanism for the distribution of nonnegotiably coercive force employed in accordance with the dictates of an intuitive grasp of situational exigencies" (Bittner, 1970), it makes good sense for a group of professionals mandated to "mechanically" enforce and, thus, conserve the letter of the law to have conservative worldviews.

In a Danish context, Bittner's words ring true. For example, in a rather recent unpublished report which I have been privy to, the Danish police themselves conducted a (rather unscientific) survey of who their employees would vote for. The survey showed that a vast majority would vote for right-wing parties, and that most of the officers at the time would in fact vote for the at the time quite popular anti-immigration, law and order, national-conservative Danish People's Party. To be sure, the inclination unveiled in the survey is very similar to what I have myself personally experienced. Many of the detectives I followed openly spoke about how they supported or at least sympathized with right wing and even far-right wing parties. That this was the average political orientation is further substantiated by how different Danish police officers have run and been elected to the Danish parliament as well as municipal offices, representing almost exclusively parties belonging to the right of the political continuum. Another clear testimony of the police's political right-leaning tendencies which I myself encountered was the fact that the few Danish officers who were more left leaning were frequently and visibly teased by the colleagues. These officers were—and often directly to their faces—called "naïve", "silly" or even "red mercenaries", the latter label signaling that they were working for the enemy. Here is an example:

> **Vignette 31**
>
> Having planned an interview with a police inspector at the North Zealand Police, this particular inspector being an expert in the problems of cross-border criminality in his police district, I report at his office just after lunch. Knocking on his door and stepping into the office, I instantly notice the big blackboard to the right of me. In the very center of the blackboard, chalk-scribbles are spelling out "This is the home of a red mercenary! Beware!". Noticing that I had noticed it, the inspector smiles and quickly explains that the discrediting words are not his doing. "It's the work of some of the fellas", he says. "They have written it as everyone at the station knows that I am a Social Democrat". "I mean, what can you do?", he asks me, only to answer his own question.
>
> "To be honest, the guys are just making fun, and that's alright. I know what they think, but I also know what I believe in, even though I am a political minority here. They can call me a red mercenary or whatever, I know they don't think I'm a communist or anything. It's just fun and games … But yeah, it does show that most people here prefer politicians who belong to the other end of the aisle—and that many of them are captivated by the politicians who promise the most hard-hitting approaches and anti-immigrant agendas".

That more center or left-wing oriented police officers were heavily outnumbered became palpably clear as the at the time Social Democratic Minister of Justice (who is now the current Prime Minister) was visiting TFB. Having just received the message about her upcoming visit during a morning briefing, the detectives seemed more annoyed than thrilled. "Do we really have to do this?", Detective Gustavsen said. Another of his colleagues defiantly announced that he would "definitely not put much work into this. I'll just find an old presentation somewhere and give her that", he agreed with himself, feeling good about it. In stark contrast to their deprecation of the social democratic minister, a similar languid sentiment was definitely *not* projected when it later that same month was announced that the former and extremely popular leader of the Danish People's Party, Pia Kjærsgaard, was also planning to visit the task force. A number of detectives clapped their hands. There were even some hooting and tooting going on to mark many of the detectives' excitement and support.

Lastly, I could also mention how I myself became a target of the Danish detectives' political manifestations (cf. Fassin, 2013; Aliverti, 2021). The detectives openly assumed that I, as a university academic, did not share their political views—an assumption they were often right in making. Being a most dramatic example of our differences of opinion, one day, our differences of opinion ended up with me almost being thrown out a still moving car as the TFP detectives and I were out on the streets of Copenhagen, searching for a group of so-called "false police officers" or "police imposters" (i.e. international thieves posing as police officers to con and steal from tourists). Driving around and discussing the upcoming Danish election, I admitted to be voting for one of Denmark's more liberal parties, the party probably most-despised by the police. "Get the hell out!", Detective Larsen screamed, stepping on the brakes. He was of course making fun. Nevertheless, his reaction again emphasized what he and many in the Danish police believed in. "There is no room for blind and dumb softies like you, in this car or in the police", he said, laughing, only to eventually drive on, generously allowing me to stay in the car.

Real Policing Versus Phony Politics

Police officers are conservatives more than liberals. More so, what the above also illustrates is the police's often-stark and voiced opposition against other and alternative viewpoints. To be sure, these are rarely views voiced in front of the public directly. The Danish police, like most other police forces around the world, are habitually invested in signaling that they are unpolitical and unbiased, knowing their place in the Montesquieuian order (but see Jauregui, 2022). Though seldom pronounced in public, their political opposition nevertheless shows itself, for example, when police officers discuss politics with each other. It also shows itself in the way in which they usually react against most challenges and changes imposed on their views and ways. A way to appreciate this is to take notice of how officers tend to react in relation to organizational changes presented by the management (Reuss-Ianni, 1993; Fleming & Lafferty, 2000; Loader & Mulcahy, 2003; Terpstra & Trommel, 2009; Balvig et al., 2011; de Maillard & Savage, 2021). Indeed, the police, and especially its frontline officers, often apply the, to them, negative and derogatory label of "politics" to many if not most kinds of proposed transformation or reform coming from outside their ranks. Rather than approaching newfangled policing philosophies or practices suggested or demanded by for example politicians or academic pundits or their own management with any kind of curiosity or understanding, frontline officers tend to automatically suspect foul play—suspecting that politicians and pundits (like myself) are proposing things mostly to help themselves more than actually wanting to improve police work. Not unlike the critical criminologist or policing researcher who argue that much present-day criminal justice politics is becoming more and more "symbolic" (Newburn & Jones, 2005; Miller, 2012), made to win votes and obtain power more than produce actual and societally beneficiary change, frontline police officers frequently see the world in similar conniving, Machiavellian colors—seeing self-serving "moral entrepreneurs" (Becker, 1995) all over more than seeing signs of an actual shared interest. Moreover, as Reuss-Ianni (1993) has eminently showed, the same kind of manipulative innuendo is also often attributed to the police's own management—a management who frontline officers frequently suspect to be either controlled by or pampering to politicians more than taking care of "their own", as they will say.

The above is also true in a Danish context. I for example observed this whenever the management presented to the detectives new organizational or more practice-oriented plans. The detectives immediate thought tended to be that these plans were cases of political maneuvering more than them ever materializing into something of actual vocational worth. Another clear-cut example of the task forces' detectives' skepticism showed itself whenever the detectives were to comment on colleagues who had gone to apply for managerial positions. Rather than commending them for their ambition, they were seen as traitors, as sellouts.

> **Vignette 32**
>
> Management has just left the TFP corner office, after announcing that Detective Henriksen would soon be joining the station management. The TFP detectives didn't give off much of a reaction. They just listened, nodding their heads.
>
> Some few minutes later, I'm standing in the corridor, having a coffee and chat about it with detective Christensen. Having followed him and his colleagues for a while already, I know for a fact that he usually thinks highly of Detective Henriksen as he has often pointed to him as a good and respected colleague.
>
> "He is selling his soul! That's how it is. He is making a pact with the devil!" Detective Christensen declares with a disappointed look in his eyes. "Managers are politicians, David", that's just how it is. You stop being a real police officer as soon as you get those added pins on your shoulder", he says.
>
> "Even the good ones like Detective Henriksen, who think they can do good by becoming managers, eventually lose out. They become politicians more than police officers. That's just the way of it works, sadly".

To Detective Christensen, and most of the other detectives I met, managerial work equaled "politics", and "politics", to them, was by and large both a dirty word and dirty profession—a potentially manipulative and almost anti-policing practice that sullen otherwise "honest police work/ officers". In the daily lives of the Danish detectives, "politics" was therefore not only a word used to talk about what someone votes for or believe in, for example as an individual police officer; nor was something simply used to denote what happens in parliament. Even more so, to the detectives, "politics" was a derogatory label they would use to describe pretty much all that was not the positive and practical reality of everyday, frontline police work. Because of this, odds are that you, as a politician, pundit or manager approaching a group of conventional police officers wanting to discuss possible new ways of doing things, will be met with suspicion if not opposition. Frontline officers, like the Danish detectives, will not always voice their disagreement directly in front of management, respecting the rank. What they will do, however, is that they will speak about their dislike with their peers when the meetings has finished. In frequently observing the task forces' detectives as they received orders or decrees concerning changes to their work practices, I would indeed more than once overhear them talking to one another, evaluating the managements' instructions, saying "that's just politics, isn't it?", "what's their plan, really?", "what's the real intention?", "probably good for their own career, right?", and so and so forth.

Criminal Justice and Policing Politics

One thing is the police's own political persuasions, alongside their persuasion that more or less everything that challenges their current way of working is probably "just politics" (and therefore to be mistrusted), another thing are the wider criminal justice and policing politics in society. Many books and articles have been written on the causes and consequences of criminal justice politics in and beyond Denmark. And describing the finer details and developments thereof is beyond the scope of this chapter and the book itself. Providing a very brief summary of it however, it wouldn't be far from the truth to say that the post WW2 story of criminal justice politics, at least in the Western hemisphere, is a story about a declining welfare-oriented trust in more rehabilitative approaches progressively replaced by an increasing believe in the, if not efficacy, then ethics of more retributive and control-oriented methods (Garland, 2002; Newburn & Jones, 2005; Melossi, 2015; Barker, 2017; Bosworth, 2017; Franko, 2017; Fassin, 2018; Lohne, 2020). This is a development often discussed under headers such as "the punitive turn" or "penal populism", also including a greater focus on the rights and sentiments of victims (Walklate, 2006). The tough on crime as well as more victim-oriented approach has also come to define Danish politics—if not always substantively then symbolically (Balvig, 2005; Elholm, 2020). As already described in the introduction to this chapter, as well as elsewhere in the book, Danish politicians have spent the last twenty some years arguing for and suggesting increasingly harsher sentences alongside other control-oriented measures to prevent and punish criminal and otherwise deemed antisocial and fear-inducing activities. In this way, even though it is still fairly accurate to speak of a "Nordic exceptionalism" (Pratt & Eriksson, 2014), with the Nordic countries' comparatively softer approach to crime and punishment, it would also be accurate to say that Denmark and its Nordic neighbors have experienced a significant upswing of law and order politics and practices (Tham, 2001; Smith, 2012; Shammas, 2016; Barker, 2017).

Of more specific interest to this book, the in Denmark and beyond increased political focus on law and order almost always include more specific political deliberations about the need and use of policing, that is law enforcement, as a central measure to achieve said order. A key criminological contribution here is Reiner's longstanding *The Politics of Policing* (2010)—a book that discusses different changes in the law, policies, organization as well as the historically fluctuating use and appreciation of policing. Recently, the book has even been republished in its 5th edition, updated with the most contemporary examples and now including world-leading global/transnational policing researchers Bowling and Sheptycki as co-editors (Bowling, 2019) (thereby signaling how the politics of policing increasingly involves more global issues) (see also Bradford et al., 2016).

Discussing the political and public appreciation of the police (or lack thereof) as it has changed and cemented itself over time, Reiner and his colleagues' book initially focuses on the so-called "glory days" of the British police during the 1950s and 60s. This was not only when police ethnography/research was born (cf. Banton, 1964; Bittner, 1967; Westley, 1970). This was also a time where the British police and its foot-patrolling bobbies were greatly revered (both nationally but also internationally)—seen as a symbol of a well-functioning police organization as well as that of a well-functioning British welfare society more generally (see Banton, 1964). Having discussed the glory days, the *Politics of Policing* book then goes on to discuss and describe the later demise of the police as a celebrated institution and the following declining trust people nowadays have in the police in and beyond Britain—a declining support which, among other things, has included various attempts of reforming to regain support, make the police better reflect the surrounding society and make the police a more efficient organization (Chan, 1997; Loftus, 2009; Reiner, 2010; Fyfe & Richardson, 2018; Holmberg, 2019, 2021; Ralph, 2020; Terpstra, 2020; Björk, 2021).

Building on and adding to Reiner's work, Loader and Mulcahy (2003) argue how attempts to reform the police, in the UK and beyond, have by and large been inspired by two wider political and societal developments; that is a "bureaucratic" development as well as a "sociocultural" one. The bureaucratic or administrative development concerns the many neoliberal, new public management philosophies that more than anything has controlled political thought and public administration particularly during the 1990s and 2000s, including various attempts to centralize and streamline police forces and make them "police by numbers" (Reiner, 1995). In Denmark, this was the very development that gave way to the much-criticized 2007 reform of the Danish police (Balvig et al., 2011; Diderichsen, 2017, 2020)—a centralizing, neoliberal reform which Danish politicians and police very recently tried to undo by re-opening smaller police stations around the country (Warburg, forthcoming). Indeed, police organizational/institutional politics seem to oscillate back and forth between more centralizing vis-à-vis community-oriented ideas, often mirroring larger tendencies in society and politics. In one specific decade, police work is believed to be best carried out from a more central location. A decade or so later, proximity policing ideas crop up and the local station and community "copper" is back in business.

The second police altering development that Loader and Mulcahy speak of refers to the massive social and cultural changes that most if not all Western societies have gone through since the 1950s. Very few, if any, societies nowadays are monocultures with similarly looking, thinking and living populations. Societies have become globalized, more multicultural and are increasingly incorporating various liberal agendas to acknowledge and promote the rights and wellbeing of women, ethnic minorities, sexual minorities as well as other marginalized groups of society. In and outside of Denmark, politically agreed-upon and/or civic-society promoted politics have indeed tried to push the police to reform and incorporate these wider changes. Yet, as Loftus (2009) exemplified some ten years ago, police forces have failed/resisted to do so, many if not most police forces remaining largely tied to their timeworn and conservative ways. Moreover, in the recent aftermath of the police killing of the Black American, George Floyd, police not just in the US but in many other places have come under increasing accusations of being strongholds of racist outlooks and violence. Calls are being made to politically "defund the police" or even "end" or "abolish" the police as we know it (Vitale, 2017; Alves, 2021). Though these calls haven't been similarly strong in Denmark, comparable critiques have reached Danish shores as well as the Danish police (see Sausdal, 2022), with subsequent large demonstrations against the police as well as on-going discussions/accusations of the existence of ethnic profiling within the Danish police (Birk Haller et al., 2020; Kammersgaard et al., 2021, 2022; Søgaard et al., 2022).

What the above, in brief, illustrates is that there are varying form of policing politics in society, or "policing cultures" as Loader and Mulcahy (2003) have also called it, denoting not the police's own occupational culture but the different sociocultural ideas about the worth and work of the police as they exist in wider society (see also Reiner, 2010; Martin, 2018). One thing is what elected politicians think. Another thing is the at times less enthusiastic views of other, less conservative and law and order focused parts of society. These are the political and societal developments and disagreements that the police have to navigate. That said, in a Danish context, although the Danish police do receive its fair amount of criticism, and perhaps more so these days, it is still more accurate to conclude that the Danish police, both historically and today, enjoy not only a good amount of political but also much public support. The public's trust in the Danish police is among the very highest in the world, with the police being rated as one of the most trusted institutions and professions in Danish society—much more trusted than the politicians that make the laws the police are meant to enforce (Justitsministeriet, 2016).

Returning to the question of tough on crime politics, it is furthermore evident that politicians and governing bodies in not just Denmark but in many of the world's countries are not really turning away but increasingly turning toward the police and similar agents of control as, for them, a viable answer to not only criminal but a lot of deemed risks and threats in society. Policing and control are frequently pointed to and promoted as a reasonable political answers to many global issues such as "illegal" migration, terrorism and other forms of transnational crime (Marmo & Chazal, 2016; Sheptycki, 2017). Or as Ericson and Haggerty (1997) famously argued, conventional police organizations have increasingly become involved in policing "risk society" (or now perhaps "world risk society" (Beck, 2009) as the police are increasingly asked to contribute to the solving of not just the obviously criminal or supposed criminogenic but many other territorial, social, security as well as safety issues. Policing politics nowadays has in many ways become bigger than criminal justice politics. In Denmark, at least, the police have been and are enjoying much political backing—both as an obvious tool for the politicians to deliver on their growing retributive and control-oriented promises but also, borrowing from both Simon and Findlay, as a means of governing through (global) crime (Simon, 2007; Findlay, 2013)—that is the tendency to put issues of (global) crime at the political center while also if not legally then discursively criminalize a range of different societal problems to, first and foremost, control them rather than dealing with them.

Tough on Policing Politics

Although the current "police and politics literature" differs in focus and scope, and though it has been tremendously helpful in offering up understandings of the police's own outlooks as well as the wider organizational and socio-political context in which their practices and perceptions are located, the literature also comes with some ostensible preconceptions/limitations. More often than not, existing research furthers the understanding that the police are conservative-minded people—people and professionals who often disagree with or at least think very little of politicians-cum-politics. Spontaneously, I can only agree. This is the same kind of conservative adherence and (post)modern-day skepticism I have experienced in my ethnographic work in and beyond Denmark (Sausdal, 2021a)—experiences that may again help explain why the police have successfully resisted most attempts of reforming its core practices and perception. And applying the same kind of logic, research that focuses on the wider increase of law and order politics often seem to incorporate the (pre)conception that such punitive and pro-policing politics are of course also greatly appreciated by its law and order practitioners (cf. Kraska, 1996; Loftus, 2009; Fassin, 2013; Loftus et al., 2015; Aliverti, 2021)).

The (pre)conception that police officers always enjoy tough on crime politics is however somewhat problematic. A part of the problem seems to be that most research that studies the societal upsurge of law and order politics rarely if ever investigates how the frontline practitioners actually relate thereto (but see Fassin, 2017; Sausdal, 2020; Jauregui, 2022). Instead, being a recurring methodological point in this book, there seems to be a tendency to conflate a matter of discourse with the police's daily doings. Existing research, in other words, at times has a propensity to teleologically presume—which again is intuitively understandable—that conservative police forces and its conservative officers naturally enjoy conservative politics as such politics mobilize the police against "the dross" and otherwise believed anti-conservative menaces of society (cf. Choongh, 1998). Means and ends seem to meet.

As the remainder of this chapter and its following examples are devoted to showing, this is however a presumption that does not always hold water. Below, I will provide some further examples of how a growing tough on crime political discourse in Denmark was in fact loathed more than lauded by the Danish detectives and many of their colleagues. Spontaneously, the detectives did like the discourse. This much is true. And the task forces' detectives did appear to happily vote for those politicians most eager to present themselves and propose laws as national conservative, Beckerian "moral crusaders" (Becker, 1995). In their workaday lives, however, the detectives' appreciation quickly faded, often turning from the positive toward the negative. Though I experienced many examples thereof, having already provided some in the introduction of this chapter, and having earlier discussed the police's frustration with counterterrorism politics and practices, the following example was possibly the example most referred to by the detectives themselves:

Migrants and the Airport

> **Vignette 33**
>
> "We often feel like tiny balls being thrown around as the politicians see fit", TFB Detective Pallesen explains to me over lunch. As so many times before, he has just been asked to do something he wasn't planning to do—in this case, asked by management to transport a suspect from the local jailhouse to the courthouse and back. "It's not even my case. It's not my suspect. The only reason why this happens is because we're spread thin. We're all over the place. Today it was me. Yesterday, it was someone else. And tomorrow it'll be some other poor sucker", he says.
>
> "And that's just the half of it. I might be able stomach the constant moving around from task to task, having too little time to mind my cases. That comes with the territory, you know, that we have to help when needed", he admits, although not looking entirely convinced of his argument. "But", he continuous, "the worst thing is not just that we're asked to do some senseless transport jobs every now and then, or whatever. What really gets me is the constantly lurking risk of being asked to do an entirely new job, you know? I mean, what I'm gunning at here, David, is that we often can't be bothered truly dedicating ourselves anymore because, deep down, we know that there's a big risk we'll be the next ones asked to clean our desk and go to the airport, being asked to put on the stinking uniform again and man the passport control booth.
>
> [pausing].
>
> Trust me, soon the politicians will come up with some new idea again, some new 'brilliant' law or proposal about what we need to do and then I'll have to leave my current job and work somewhere else in the police, maybe the airport or maybe some other place", Detective Jensen eventually concludes while pointing at his desk and the Tower of Pisa-like pile of case files in the corner of it.

Detective Jensen was not alone in dreading being redeployed to "the airport". Among the detectives, speaking of "the airport" had become a commonly used way to speak of what they experienced as the looming danger of being moved to another job within the Danish police. Though they hadn't fully succumbed to this fear, the detectives did often worry about whether the management would come calling today, tomorrow or some other day, asking them or a close colleague to work at the airport, process old cases instead of investigating them, return to patrol duty, to do community police work, to work vice or whatever the new job would be.

Or as Detective Andersen also quite melodramatically put it, "we just sit here waiting to be moved to whatever the people at *Borgen* come up with"—*Borgen* being the shorthand word for the Danish Parliament as people who have watched the Danish TV series already know.

Indeed, the detectives feeling of not being able to commit themselves to a case or detective work in more general terms was often explained by reference to parliamentary politics more than it (only) being an organizational responsibility. Many strands of contemporary politics frustrated the detectives. One thing they found particularly unsatisfying, however, was Danish politicians' focus on migratory issues. Though the detectives certainly agreed with most politicians in the Danish parliament, most Danish politicians thinking that the number of migrants and refugees coming to Denmark should be limited, and though the detectives therefore also tended to agree with the importance of having more closed and manned borders than a membership of Schengen otherwise entails, the detectives found the increasing focus on *them* having to police and control migration and migrants (and not just customs, migration services, etc.) to be far removed from the kind of work they wanted to do (see also Yakhlef, 2018). As TFB Detective Andersen described it, further airing her irritation about "how politicians make promises on our behalf":

> I didn't become police and, then, a detective to now all of a sudden having to hang out on the Danish border somewhere, checking and chatting to asylum seekers and tourists. Neither was my plan to be running around, knocking on random doors to see if some brown dude is allowed to be here or not … I mean, he probably shouldn't be here. Don't get me wrong. I just don't want to do that kind of work—that's not real police work, is it? The issues of migrants should land on someone else's desk, you know?

Notions about "real" versus "not real" police work were as such often a central part of the conversation when the detectives discussed their dislike of policing migration and border control. As also earlier discussed, police officers' notions of real police work tend to include the stark fondness for action-oriented and preferably crime-fighting activities more than the less eventful, bureaucratic or "peacemaking" undertakings (cf. Holmberg, 2003; Loftus, 2009; Fassin, 2013). And while the ruggedness of Danish migration politics may sound like something that could make for "real" police work, real police work (both in terms of rhetoric and its harsh laws, various control mechanism, detention facilities and, at times, deportation), the task forces' detectives weren't convinced.

> **Vignette 34**
>
> "This new migration policing thing" Detective Jørgensen thought out loud, with her, TFP Detective Mikkelsen and I having spent the entire day roaming around Copenhagen, checking up on migrant beggars, migrant prostitutes as well as shops illegally employing (and exploiting) migrants without the correct papers, "is very rarely about investigating real crimes. We don't really get to kick in doors or throw on some cuffs. Nor do we encounter any real criminals. Rather, this job is about standing somewhere or strolling around, checking papers, telling some Gypsy that they're not allow to beg or live on the streets, maybe tearing down an illegal encampment on the outskirts of town, maybe fining some migrants without documents and maybe booking them; or maybe it is just about transporting some foreigner to the airport, putting the guy on a plane to 'faraway-stan'. It's mindless work, let me tell you".
>
> Detective Mikkelsen nods his head. He agrees. "Entirely true", he says. "But here we are, doing this kind of "police work" [using his fingers to make sure we catch the irony] instead of what we thought we should do—what we are supposed to do. But, hey, the politicians want this, so we deliver. We aim to please".

And deliver they did. More or less, at least. Sometimes, like on that particular day, the TFP detectives were relieved from their normal deeds and were sent out to work together with the migration policing unit, Foreigner Control Section East. And together the different officers would go look for often very poor migrants who had come to Denmark from across the world, the officers looking at their papers, watching if they were actively begging (which is illegal in Denmark) and, even though Detective Jørgensen did say it didn't happen, occasionally put a migrant in handcuffs and in a cell to await further processing. As I followed them and stood next to the detectives, when for example booking and throwing an elderly Roma woman beggar in a tiny holding cell, it was obvious that this was not something the detectives were particularly fond of. It wasn't the kind of police and detective work they preferred—the kind of work "they signed up for", as they themselves would say it.

Danish politicians' attraction to what in criminology is also discussed as "crimmigration" (Stumpf, 2006; Franko, 2019) obviously appeared less popular when seen through the perspective of everyday police work. I am however inclined to argue that the Danish detectives' frustrations had less to do with the believed "un-realness" of the work itself and more to do the vocational volatility the increasing political focus on migration was causing. As the above examples have been illuminating, the detectives did find the work tedious but the tedium of migration policing was worsened by the fact that it was an unpredictable yet recurring activity that many in the Danish police could suddenly be asked to carry out "mostly to", I was told, "satisfy political guarantees and drive up the stats". The same seemed true of other political agendas. Be it terrorism, border control issues, a focus on public safety, problems at social housing estates, gang crime, burglary, pickpocketing or whatever seemed to be dominating the political agenda, the detectives were frustrated with how these many and sudden changes affected their work. As for example one of TFP's newest members, Detective Møller, keenly described this to me, telling the story about how he had now ended up at TFP:

> Two years ago, I was working at another station, working vice, pretty happy all things considered. Then the boss came knocking and told me I was needed elsewhere. I was moved downstairs together with a couple of other colleagues who'd also been "chosen" to spent some months looking through and filing old cases. This apparently had something do with a mounting political pressure to get the numbers up. Or was it down? Can't remember. And who cares, really. But, lo and behold, now I'm here, and actually for many of the same reasons. I don't know if you read the papers, but there has been a big rise in pickpocketing lately and some idiot politician has promised to make us [i.e. the police] deal with the problem ASAP. So, yeah. I guess they thought I had filed enough cases and could come here instead, knowing next to nothing about this kind of work before I started.

The story told by Detective Møller was not an unfamiliar story. It was the old story (true or not but nevertheless felt to be true) about how police work is being organized and controlled through an new public management-oriented focus on numbers with politicians asking the police to deliver results, especially if something have caught the eye of the media/public. Yet, as a leading TFB figure maintained,

> what we're seeing these days is not just a political focus on numbers. What we're seeing is political micro-managing. At least that's how it feels. Instead of just providing a framework for our work, the police are increasingly being told what to do and focus on—in detail(!)—by the politicians and their suit-wearing bureaucrats in the ministries. Though I personally agree with the importance of putting more pressure on gangs, focusing more on cross-border crimes, et cetera, the current political sentiment is to tell us *what* to do, and also often *how*, thereby diminishing police professionalism and our chance to choose and structure our work. There is simply a much smaller room to maneuver, to apply our own focus and knowledge.

Reading the above words, we may also recall the critiques raised in Chap. 4, concerning a felt dilution of police self-governance and professional worth.

Though most of the examples included in this chapter, and in the book itself, stem from personal conversations with the detectives alongside daily observations of mine, it is also worth noticing how Danish police officers' frustrations with their jobs and contemporary politics are nowadays increasingly vented in public. Though known for their *esprit de corps*, and for keeping quiet or and criticisms internally, Danish police officers are now writing books, op-eds and Facebook-posts about their dissatisfactions. In publicly available statements, they are, similar to the already included examples from my fieldwork, complaining about being moved from post to post, from office to office, or from a detective's desk to an airport booth. They are complaining about having to work the kinds of crimes and cases that the politicians choose rather than themselves—to be tough on certain, already pre-defined kinds of crimes. More so, the police are not thrilled about increasingly having to monitor and control conventionally non-criminal matter like migrants. Add to this, as also shown in Chap. 4, the fact that they are forced to work overtime and, thereby, too often find themselves unable to balance their personal and professional lives, feeling stressed out and even increasingly falling sick and we can start to understand the Danish police and its detectives' disliking of contemporary politics. Also, it is not just individual officers who complain. The Danish Police Union itself has started to actively campaign against the police's current working conditions, mental health issues and, especially, the politicians' believed micro-management of the Danish police. As the vice head of the police union (Politiforbundet, 2020) recently formulated their critique, in order to function, Danish politicians need to "remove the political pressure on the police" and instead allow the Danish police the liberty to, at least somewhat, plan themselves and apply their competences without being micro-managed.

In this way, it is slightly ironic that the police, in a time and age largely recognized as involving many more tough on crime politics and policies as well as a great political support for the police, experience themselves as betrayed more than bolstered. It is certainly easy to find outspoken support for the politicians' penal populism in the Danish police. Nevertheless, at the end of the day, as the spirit of punitive politics turns into concrete practice, the police's support dwindles. Or as TFB Detective Gustavsen explained it:

> Today, they [the politicians] want us to take care of migration, taking care of the borders, or stand or prance around in our uniforms—you know, for the sake of "visibility". And then we have to come down hard on gang crime, and tomorrow we should focus on the rowdy football fans and hooligans or whatever, then its burglary, then its terror, then financial crime, and then it's something else. You name it. It's all part of the job, of course. It just seems harder to follow suit these days, you know?

Mink and Mental Health Issues

Tough on crime (and crime only) politics, and the ostensibly volatile ways in which these came bear on the police and their workday, were as described not the only thing that the detectives were critical of. As already more than touched upon, Danish politicians' "toughness" often extend beyond the legally defined criminal, including other perceived political problems. The above-mentioned focus on migration as a policing matter is an example thereof—an example known not just to the Danish police but to many local and international police organizations across the world (cf. Franko, 2019). Yet, migration is not the only non-criminal matter the Danish police have been asked to be tough toward and take care of in recent years.

As another example of how the public police's portfolio has expanded beyond conventional, local crime fighting and prevention to become progressively more oriented toward societal risks more widely (Ericson & Haggerty, 1997; Maguire, 2000; Gundhus, 2005), one of the Danish police's newer jobs includes the monitoring and controlling of people with mental health issues. As funding and proper health care support for mental health issues and psychiatric treatment has decreased, the Danish police have been asked to step in. While certain situations undeniably necessitate the presence of police officers, for instance if a person is endangering others or him/herself, the increased use of the police rather than professional healthcare workers includes certain problems. These problems, for example, were the focus of a recent master's thesis (Laursen & Rasmussen, 2021) in social anthropology from the University of Copenhagen which I was lucky enough to supervise.

In the thesis, the authors show how Danish police officers find the work and encounters with people with mental health issues difficult and also, like with migration, "not real police work" [in Danish "galt politiarbejde"] (ibid.). The Danish officers' lack of professional interest coupled with the perceived strains of the work made for a range of issues, among others the potential for violent conflict (ibid., p. 69ff). Danish police officers are in fact almost never involved in shootings or deadly encounters. But when it does happen, it relatively often occurs in relation to the policing of mental health patients. As the master's thesis convincingly argues, a chief reason thereto may be that the Danish police apply an overly assertive control approach (ibid.). The police see mental health patience as a risk. And, as police officers are trained to do, they largely deal with risks by confronting them and seeking to control them by applying force, if necessary. In relation to mental health patience such a confrontative approach may however risk escalate rather than deescalate the situation as the mentally ill doesn't always react positively to pressure and strong displays of authority. Indeed, similar findings are found in the international research literature—a research literature that also points to how the use of law enforcement rather than health care professionals in relation to mental health patients is not only something that is on the rise in Denmark but in many other countries (cf. Ogloff et al., 2013; White & Weisburd, 2018; Hacker & Horan, 2019; McDaniel, 2019).

In my own studies, I also experienced the Danish detectives expressing concerns about the police having to deal with the mentally ill. Here is an example:

> **Vignette 35**
>
> Sitting around the small-ish conference table, just outside their office, TFP detective Larsen and I are talking about what the newspaper on the table is reporting. On the front page there is a story about how a couple of South Zealand police officers have been involved in a fatal episode as they had end up shooting and killing a purportedly aggressive mental patient.
>
> "I get that they [mental patients] can be dangerous and that the police have to be present if it gets too violent. Of course", he agrees. "But it's also a problem that they [politicians] think that we in the police can easily do this job. First of all, we have a lot on our hands already. Secondly, although criminals are often idiots, they are mostly rational beings. You kinda know what they'll do and how they think—and you do your work in relation thereto, right?" he says to me, again agreeing with himself.
>
> "But", he continues, "when we're speaking about crazy people, then the problem exactly is that they are crazy, irrational. You just don't know how they'll react, right? Knowing that they're irrational therefore demands some experience and knowledge we in the police don't necessarily have. What we do, instead, is that we do what we normally do. We do police work—and sometimes that doesn't really help when you're working with a 'nutter'".[1]
>
> "True, this is why it's a big problem", Detective Larsen's downstairs colleague joins in, having overheard our conversation from the adjacent breakroom. "Nowadays, there seems to be the idea that when there is a problem, the police can take care of it. Give it to the police. They'll do it, they'll say … I mean, it seems like we have become a sort Swizz army knife to the politicians—a multitool to be thrown at every imaginable issue".

---

[1] The exact same line of reasoning is found in the before-mentioned master's thesis (Laursen & Rasmussen, 2021). The officers they interviewed also had many conversations about the perceived irrationality and unpredictability of mental patients versus the rationality of their normal "customers"; that is criminals or otherwise disorderly parts of the public.

Though this particular officer's "multitool notion" was a personal perspective and somewhat of an overstatement (as well as a quite striking metaphor), it was a perspective I frequently came across. Sometimes the detectives even spoke about themselves as "the trash can of society". "What should we do about this issue? I know. Let's make the police take care of it", I often heard them reiterate, annoyed that police work was no longer the proverbial thin blue line but, so to speak, a mere and more random last line of defense against all sorts of societal concerns. On the one hand, the detectives and their colleagues were being positively looked at as a tenable political solution. On the other hand, they were not happy with how this increasing attention was causing them to not be able to focus more on the things they found to be more central to their work—things they both wanted to do and felt capable of doing.

During my fieldwork, I stumbled across many such grievances about how the politicians' growing appreciation of the police were fundamentally agreeable yet, unfortunately, misplaced. Looking more at the global issues of interest to this book, the detectives agreed with the majority of the Danish parliament that Danish borders should be less open, that Danish policing should become more international, that more surveillance was necessary, that prison sentences were in general too lenient causing foreign criminals to come to Denmark, that migration was an issue to be further policed, or, for that matter, that dangerous mental health patients should be further controlled. To the detectives, a more Leviathan or Orwellian society was essentially a better society, and thus the right kind of politics. The problem was not *if* it should be done, but *how* and by *whom*.

Recently, a most curious if not tragic example of the above-described puzzle occurred. During the covid pandemic, the Danish police were, like most of their colleagues worldwide (Jones, 2020; cf. Kyprianides et al., 2022; Sadiq, 2022), asked to drop what they had in their hands. Instead, they were told to patrol the streets and the public, looking for infractions of Covid-19 regulations and securing public order and health. While understanding the importance and inevitability thereof, this kind of work was, yet again, not something the Danish detectives enjoyed. "It's boring. Very boring. And, as always, my cases and reports keep piling up", Detective Clausen explained.

These more routine pandemic policing tasks were however not to become the Danish police's biggest problem. As also reported in international media, in what seemed like a spur of the moment, the Danish government decided to order the extermination of Denmark's entire mink population due to the finding of a new and potentially vaccine resistant Covid-19 strain among some of the Danish minks (Laage-Thomsen & Frandsen, 2022). Though this in itself sound drastic, and extremely costly(!), this was not the end of it. As it later turned out, the government did not have the needed legal foundation to make this order. The order was illegal, and a commission has been looking into the process, making suggestions as to what the potential legal outcomes should be.

Returning to the question of the politicians' increasing use of the police in not just criminal but different kinds of situations, it befell the Danish police to be the ones communicating with and supervising the Danish mink farmers. And as an investigation into the matter has indicated (Minkkommissionen, 2022), the choice of using the police to deal with the situation may have ended up being a big part of the problem. Not unlike how the detectives told me that one of the problems of making them deal with mental patients is that they come at the problem as police officers and not as health care professionals, the Danish police appeared to handle the mink-situation in a much similar way. Even though counterorders had seemingly come down, saying that the law did not allow the police to directly order and enforce the mink killings, but, instead, ordering the police to only talk to and gently incentivize mink farmers to put down their animal stock, the police did what they usually do; they told the mink farmers what to do, leaving little room for negation. The minks had to die. That was the end of it. As I later called and interviewed Detective Larsen about the issue, he explained the process (and outcome) to me in the following words:

> That's what we do, right? That's what we do as police officers. We don't have nice little chats with people about what is right or wrong. We enforce the law. I mean, we can of course be friendly about it. But when shits hit the fan, we tell people what they should do or what they shall not do. So, that's what we did, I guess. We told the farmers how it was going to go down.

Put differently, when politicians task a group of professionals like the police with a job, like communicating with mink farmers about the possibility of killing off their animals, there is a great risk that officers will do so in largely authoritarian way. The police don't tend to enter into big discussions with people about whether what they are doing is legal or not. At the end of the day, the police tell people how things are "going to go down", just as Detective Larsen also told me. And as he therefore also suggested, this could easily explain why his colleagues, who had been asked to cancel their plans for the next couple of weeks and instead call up or visit mink farmers, had "overdone it".

> But", he elaborated, "I also heard the argument, that we should have checked up on the law ourselves. But people who say that, don't understand what we do and who we are. We're a hierarchical organization. If an order comes down, you do it. In rare cases, there may be a cause for pause. But the spirit of police work is to parry orders. We are not academics like you, David, who sit down and think—and then think some more. We do things. We get things done.

Taking care of Covid-infected mink, mental health patients or migrants had become part of Danish policing. So had increased efforts in manning the borders and passport control booths; standing guard at supposed terror targets; chasing numbers more than crimes; surveilling for the sake for surveillance; policing for the sake of appearances; being moved from one office to another, from one job to another with little opportunity to really apply oneself; feeling stressed out, calling in sick as well as having problems at home because of the demands of the job. All these issues—and more—were issues I came across and was told about; issues often believed by Danish police officers to be caused by Danish politicians' excessive eagerness to demonstrate their political commitment and decisiveness.

Moreover, in discussing the Danish police's deprecation of current politics, I could also have gone further into what I already touched upon in Chap. 4, namely the debate surrounding the Danish police education, and how it recently was decreased from 3 ½ years to a 2 years length, also with the introduction a whole new kind of policing education named "the police cadet" only demanding half a year's worth of training. Though the

Danish detectives I spent time with were not overly appreciative of academic learnings and added schooltime, they also did not welcome how Danish politicians—in conversations with the police management—had decided to suddenly shorten and, in their view, reduce the quality of the police education, "doing so simply", as Detective Jensen put it,

> to get more men on the streets. Seriously, it was a too rash decision. The politicians promised the public that they would put more police on the streets because of terror and everything like that. Therefore, they came up with a quick way of doing it, thinking only about the present and their own appearances. Of course, I also think it's good to have more men. We always need more men. There's plenty to do. But there is something laughable about the fact that it takes longer to become a hairdresser in Denmark than it takes to become a police officer. That's insane, right? We've said this before. But this is even truer today.

In Conclusion: Political Hubris and a Broken Dynamic

Though one may argue that "[g]lobalization] has not yet led to the wholesale adoption of the neoliberal form of capitalist political economy, nor the 'punitive turn' that it allegedly (according to Garland or Pratt, for example) generates" (Downes, 2016), it seems fair to say that many societies around the world have turned toward more repressive ways of dealing with both the illegal and the illicit (Van Schendel & Abraham, 2005). At least in a Danish/Nordic context, there is some truth to Garland's early contention that different "measures [a]ppear to signify a punitive turn in contemporary penality" (Garland, 2000). Though Denmark and its sibling countries are criminologically famed for their "penal exceptionalism", all of the countries have experienced a turn toward the punitive. This of course is not in any way comparable with what has been, and still is, happening in a US context for example. Danish criminal justice and its politics are in many ways still exceptionally "soft", humane and include a stronger rehabilitation focus compared to many other countries around the world.

As also touched upon in this chapter, and as richly discussed in recent criminological literature, many countries have also witnessed a turn toward the political and administrative treatment of traditionally non-criminal issues via more punitive and criminalizing approaches. Be it mental health, housing, social, migratory, security or safety issues, these are growingly observed through a criminogenic optic. In the literature, this is spoken of as the downfall of the welfare society to a control society (Garland, 2002), as a "governing through crime" (Simon, 2007; Findlay, 2013), or as the policing of risk rather than criminality (Ericson & Haggerty, 1997; Maguire, 2000; Zedner, 2007; Beck, 2009; Hörnqvist, 2010; Schuilenburg, 2017). We simply seem to live in a society where the margins of error and ideas about what is acceptable in society are becoming narrower—thus allowing for a less favorable and harsher handling of that and those who are on or past the margins of "acceptable" being, seeing their problems in the light of individual culpability more than collective responsibility (especially if the people in question are poor or part of an underprivileged minority, that is).

The above-described politics have been and will probably continue to be at the center of Danish politics for the considerable future. And not just at the center of criminal justice, but of an array of political issues. Now, it is logical to think that law enforcement agencies as well as its individual actors find the politicians' growing appreciation of and believe in the effectiveness and versatility of policing meaningful. Why wouldn't they appreciate being thought of as useful and, consequently, being put to use? In many ways, the group of Danish detectives whom I followed around for many hundreds of hours definitely did appreciate the mounting law and order discourse. They more than agreed with Danish politicians that the solution to criminal activity and other societal problems are harsher approaches rather than the more welfare-oriented ones. They were not in any way "softies" or "social workers", as they often would announce and remind each other (Sausdal, 2021b). They strongly believed not just in the effectiveness but also in the morally appropriateness of being tough on crime and in life.

Nevertheless, their appreciation of political punitive measures seems to have ended up causing a state of hubris. As the many hours I spent with

Danish detectives showed me, and as this chapter has meant to illustrate, the detectives did in reality *not* enjoy how Danish politicians' various tough on crime politics were affecting their work. Importantly, this was a dissatisfaction found not just among the detectives I mostly spent time with, but a dissatisfaction I detected throughout the organization. Danish officers of different kinds and in different places did not like how their workday had become growingly controlled by what they saw as the changing whims of Danish politicians. Instead of officers being able to mind what they saw as their actual jobs, they too often found themselves carrying out different and futile tasks. "This is not why I became police". "This is not what produces nice police work"—"nice police work" signaling both what they thought should be the reality of policing but also being a statement about what they found professionally satisfactory. "Nobody likes not being able to plan anything or not being able to invest time in things. But increasingly so, this is what police work is becoming", TFP detective Christensen concluded, having yet again been told to put a hold on what he was doing and to instead report downstairs for a patrol-related duty.

Whether the Danish detectives and many of their colleagues are right (in strict quantitative terms) in saying their work has become more controlled by political wills and whims is hard for me to say. The appropriate statistics don't exist. However, answering this question was never the point. What has been of interest here is the, from a police perspective, paradoxical backside to the punitive politics seen in many parts of the world— punitive and police-positive politics often forged with a look toward global issues and fears. Differing from the habitual political, popular as well as academic notion that the police certainly value tough on crime politics as it enables them in their work, this chapter has been written to show that, in their workaday lives, this is only a half-truth. Other than simply saluting tough on crime politics, Danish police officers find punitive politics to also be hard on them. Of the many things that concerned them, and which therefore concerns this book, I cannot underestimate the experienced negative effective of what inside the police was also often spoken of as an increased "politicizing of police work" (see also Deuchar et al., 2020). This is true, even though this very "politicizing" was framed within a penal framework otherwise relished by most police officers. With the risk of sounding unnecessarily coy, one might say that the Danish police are finding it hard to enjoy their own medicine. Or, more to the point, they feel overmedicated. Indeed, as TFP detective Mikkelsen explained it to me as we were discussing the upcoming election and who he would be voting for:

> Don't get us wrong, David. We think criminals should have a harder time. We're not against surveillance. We're not against more control—at borders or wherever. Not at all. That's all good. I'll vote for that. That's not the problem. The problem is the way it's currently done. The politicians are making promises. A lot of them. And we, the police, are to make those promises come true. That's the dynamic. But the dynamic doesn't work. It's broken. It's breaking us.

Unfortunately, I never got to ask the detective whether he again decided to vote for the people in charge of the broken dynamic. If asked to make a wager, I bet he did, choosing Kant over Aristotle, principle over profession.

Bibliography

Aliverti, A. (2021). *Policing the borders within*. Oxford University Press.
Alves, J. (2021). F*ck the police: Murderous cops, the myth of police fragility and the case for an insurgent anthropology. *Focaal Blog*.
Balvig, F. (2005). When law and order returned to Denmark. *Journal of Scandinavian Studies in Criminology and Crime Prevention, 5*(2), 167–187.
Balvig, F., Holmberg, L., & Nielsen, M. P. H. (2011). *Verdens bedste politi*. Djøf.
Banton, M. (1964). *The policeman in the community*. Basic Books.
Barker, V. (2017). *Nordic nationalism and penal order: Walling the welfare state*. Routledge.
Beck, U. (2009). *World at risk*. Polity.
Becker, H. S. (1995). Moral entrepreneurs: The creation and enforcement of deviant categories. In N. Herman (Ed.), *Deviance: A symbolic interactionist approach* (pp. 169–178). Lanham, MD.
Beek, J., Göpfert, M., Owen, O., et al. (2017). *Police in Africa: The street level view*. Oxford University Press.
Birk Haller, M., Kolind, T., Hunt, G., et al. (2020). Experiencing police violence and insults: Narratives from ethnic minority men in Denmark. *Nordic Journal of Criminology, 21*(2), 170–185.

Bittner, E. (1967). The police on skid-row: A study of peace keeping. *American Sociological Review, 32*, 699–715.

Bittner, E. (1970). *The functions of the police in modern society: A review of background factors, current practices, and possible role models*. National Institute of Mental Health, Center for Studies of Crime and Delinquency.

Bosworth, M. (2017). *Border criminology and the changing nature of penal power* (pp. 373–390). Oxford University Press.

Bowling, B. (2019). *The politics of the police*. Oxford University Press.

Bradford, B., Loader, I., Jauregui, B., et al. (2016). *The SAGE handbook of global policing*. SAGE.

Chan, J. B. (1997). *Changing police culture: Policing in a multicultural society*. Cambridge University Press.

Choongh, S. (1998). Policing the dross: A social disciplinary model of policing. *The British Journal of Criminology, 38*(4), 623–634.

Christensen, M. M., & Albrecht, P. (2020). *Urban borderwork: Ethnographies of policing* (pp. 385–398). SAGE Publications Sage UK.

Cockcroft, T. (2020). *Police culture: Research and practice*. Policy Press.

de Maillard, J., & Savage, S. P. (2021). Performance mechanisms meet professional autonomy: Performance management and professional discretion within police investigation departments. *Policing and Society, 32*, 1–14.

Deuchar, R., Crichlow, V. J., & Fallik, S. W. (2020). Cops in crisis?: Ethnographic insights on a new era of politicization, activism, accountability, and change in transatlantic policing. *Policing and Society, 30*(1), 47–64.

Diderichsen, A. (2017). Renewal and Retraditionalisation:—The short and not very glorious history of the Danish Bachelor's degree in policing. *Nordisk Politiforskning, 4*(2), 149–169.

Diderichsen, A. (2020). McDonaldiseringen af dansk politi. *Dansk Sociologi, 31*(3), 7–29.

Downes, D. (2016). Comparative criminology, globalization and the 'punitive turn'. In *Comparative criminal justice and globalization* (pp. 37–57). Routledge.

Elholm, T. (2020). Country report Denmark. *Harmonisierung strafrechtlicher Sanktionen in der Europäischen Union, 2*, 97.

Ericson, R. V., & Haggerty, K. D. (1997). *Policing the risk society*. Oxford University Press.

Fassin, D. (2013). *Enforcing order: An ethnography of urban policing*. Polity Press.

Fassin, D. (2017). Boredom: Accounting for the ordinary in the work of policing (France). In D. Fassin (Ed.), *Writing the world of policing: The difference ethnography makes* (pp. 269–292). University of Chicago Press.

Fassin, D. (2018). *The will to punish*. Oxford University Press.

Findlay, M. J. (2013). *Governing through globalised crime: Futures for international criminal justice*. Willan.

Fleming, J., & Lafferty, G. (2000). New management techniques and restructuring for accountability in Australian police organisations. *Policing: An International Journal of Police Strategies & Management*.

Franko, K. (2017). Criminology, punishment, and the state in a globalized society. In A. Liebling et al (Eds.), *The Oxford handbook of criminology* (pp. 353–372).

Franko, K. (2019). *The Crimmigrant other: Migration and penal power*. Routledge.

Fyfe, N., & Richardson, N. (2018). Police reform, research and the uses of 'expert knowledge'. *European Journal of Policing Studies, 5*(3), 147–161.

Garland, D. (2000). The culture of high crime societies. *British Journal of Criminology, 40*(3), 347–375.

Garland, D. (2002). The culture of control. In *Crime and social order in contemporary society*. University of Chicago Press.

Hacker, R. L., & Horan, J. J. (2019). Policing people with mental illness: Experimental evaluation of online training to de-escalate mental health crises. *Journal of Experimental Criminology, 15*(4), 551–567.

Hækkerup, N. (2021). Retrieved September 27, from https://politiken.dk/debat/kroniken/art8325078/Jo-det-er-faktisk-rigtigt-mere-overvågning-giver-mere-frihed

Heine, J., & Thakur, R. C. (2011). *The dark side of globalization*. United Nations University Press.

Holmberg, L. (2003). *Policing stereotypes: A qualitative study of police work in Denmark*. Galda & Wilch.

Holmberg, L. (2019). Continuity and change in Scandinavian police reforms. *International Journal of Police Science & Management, 21*(4), 206–217.

Holmberg, L. (2021). Evaluations of police reforms: Utility or futility? *Policing: A Journal of Policy and Practice, 15*(1), 314–326.

Hörnqvist, M. (2010). *Risk, power and the state: After Foucault*. Routledge.

Houborg, E., Søgaard, T. F., & Mogensen, S. A. I. (2020). Making up a new drug user from depenalization to repenalisation of drug users in Denmark. *International Journal of Drug Policy, 80*, 102660.

Jauregui, B. (2016). *Provisional authority: Police, order, and security in India*. University of Chicago Press.

Jauregui, B. (2022). Police worker politics in India, brasil, and beyond. *Policing and Society, 32*(3), 271–290.

Jones, D. J. (2020). The potential impacts of pandemic policing on police legitimacy: Planning past the COVID-19 crisis. *Policing: A Journal of Policy and Practice, 14*(3), 579–586.

Justitsministeriet. (2016). *Danskerne har stor tillid til politi og domstole*. Retrieved February 1, from http://www.justitsministeriet.dk/nyt-og-presse/pressemeddelelser/2016/danskerne-har-stor-tillid-til-politi-og-domstole

Kammersgaard, T., Søgaard, T. F., Haller, M. B., et al. (2021). Community policing in Danish 'ghetto' areas: Trust and distrust between the police and ethnic minority youth. *Criminology & Criminal Justice*. https://doi.org/10.1177/17488958211017390

Kammersgaard, T., Søgaard, T. F., Kolind, T., et al. (2022). 'Most officers are more or less colorblind': Police officers' reflections on the role of race and ethnicity in policing. *Race and Justice*. https://doi.org/10.1177/21533687221127445

Kildegaard, K., & Dandanell, F. (2019). *Mette Frederiksen bebuder massivt øget overvågning i kampen mod kriminelle: 'Vores samfundsmodel er på spil'*. Retrieved September 27, from https://www.berlingske.dk/politik/mette-frederiksen-bebuder-massivt-oeget-overvaagning-i-kampen-mod

Kraska, P. B. (1996). Enjoying militarism: Political/personal dilemmas in studying US police paramilitary units. *Justice Quarterly, 13*(3), 405–429.

Kublitz, A. (2021). Omar is dead: Aphasia and the escalating anti-radicalization business. *History and Anthropology, 32*(1), 64–77.

Kyprianides, A., Bradford, B., Beale, M., et al. (2022). Policing the COVID-19 pandemic: Police officer well-being and commitment to democratic modes of policing. *Policing and Society, 32*(4), 504–521.

Laage-Thomsen, J., & Frandsen, S. L. (2022). Pandemic preparedness systems and diverging COVID-19 responses within similar public health regimes: A comparative study of expert perceptions of pandemic response in Denmark, Norway, and Sweden. *Globalization and Health, 18*(1), 1–18.

Laursen, R. T., & Rasmussen, A. K. (2021). *Det gale politiarbejde*. University of Copenhagen.

Lindberg, A. (2022). Feeling difference: Race, migration, and the affective infrastructure of a Danish detention camp. *Incarceration, 3*(1). https://doi.org/10.1177/26326663221084590

Loader, I., & Mulcahy, A. (2003). *Policing and the condition of England: Memory, politics and culture.* Oxford University Press.

Loftus, B. (2009). *Police culture in a changing world.* Oxford University Press.

Loftus, B., Goold, B., & Mac Giollabhui, S. (2015). From a visible spectacle to an invisible presence: The working culture of covert policing. *British Journal of Criminology, 56*(4), 629–645.

Lohne, K. (2020). Penal humanitarianism beyond the nation state: An analysis of international criminal justice. *Theoretical Criminology, 24*(2), 145–162.

Maguire, M. (2000). Policing by risks and targets: Some dimensions and implications of intelligence-led crime control. *Policing and Society: An International Journal, 9*(4), 315–336.

Marmo, M., & Chazal, N. (2016). *Transnational crime and criminal justice.* SAGE.

Martin, J. T. (2018). Police culture: What it is, what it does, and what we should do with it. In *The anthropology of police* (pp. 34–53). Taylor and Francis.

Martin, J. T. (2019). *Sentiment, reason, and law: Policing in the republic of China on Taiwan.* Cornell University Press.

McDaniel, J. L. (2019). Reconciling mental health, public policing and police accountability. *The Police Journal, 92*(1), 72–94.

Melossi, D. (2015). *Crime, punishment and migration.* SAGE Publications Ltd.

Miller, H. T. (2012). *Governing narratives: Symbolic politics and policy change.* University of Alabama Press.

Minkkommissionen. (2022). Retrieved September 27, from https://www.minkkommissionen.dk/da/nyheder/2022/06/beretningen

Newburn, T., & Jones, T. (2005). Symbolic politics and penal populism: The long shadow of Willie Horton. *Crime, Media, Culture, 1*(1), 72–87.

Ogloff, J. R., Thomas, S. D., Luebbers, S., et al. (2013). Policing services with mentally ill people: Developing greater understanding and best practice. *Australian Psychologist, 48*(1), 57–68.

Politiforbundet. (2020). *Leder: Fjern det politiske pres på politiet.* Retrieved September 27, from https://politiforbundet.dk/nyheder/leder-fjern-politiske-pres-paa-politiet

Pratt, J., & Eriksson, A. (2014). *Contrasts in punishment: An explanation of anglophone excess and Nordic exceptionalism.* Routledge.

Ralph, L. (2020). To protect and to serve: Global lessons in police reform. *Foreign Affairs, 99,* 196.

Reiner, R. (1995). Policing by numbers: The feel-good fallacy. *Policing Today, 1*(3), 22–24.

Reiner, R. (2010). *The politics of the police.* Oxford University Press.

Reuss-Ianni, E. (1993). *Two cultures of policing: Street cops and management cops.* Transaction Publishers.

Rytter, M., & Pedersen, M. H. (2014). A decade of suspicion: Islam and Muslims in Denmark after 9/11. *Ethnic and Racial Studies, 37*(13), 2303–2321.

Sadiq, M. (2022). Policing in pandemic: Is perception of workload causing work–family conflict, job dissatisfaction and job stress? *Journal of Public Affairs, 22*(2), e2486.

Sausdal, D. (2020). Everyday policing: Toward a greater analytical appreciation of the ordinary in police research. *Policing and Society,* 1–14.

Sausdal, D. (2021a). A fighting fetish: On transnational police and their warlike presentation of self. *Theoretical Criminology.* https://doi.org/10.1177/13624806211009487.

Sausdal, D. (2021b). *Looking beyond the police-as-control narrative.* Policy Press.

Sausdal, D. (2022). Police Prejudice or Logics?: Analyzing the "Bornholm Murder Case". *Conflict and Society, 8*(1), 1–19.

Schuilenburg, M. (2017). *The securitization of society: Crime, risk, and social order.* New York University Press.

Shammas, V. L. (2016). The rise of a more punitive state: On the attenuation of Norwegian penal exceptionalism in an era of welfare state transformation. *Critical Criminology, 24*(1), 57–74.

Sheptycki, J. (2017). *Transnational crime and policing: Selected essays.* Routledge.

Simon, J. (2007). *Governing through crime: How the war on crime transformed American democracy and created a culture of fear.* Oxford University Press.

Smith, P. S. (2012). A critical look at Scandinavian exceptionalism. *Penal Exceptionalism,* pp. 38–57.

Søgaard, T. F., Kolind, T., Haller, M. B., et al. (2022). 'Filming is our only weapon against the police': Ethnic minorities and police encounters in the new visibility era. *The British Journal of Criminology.*

Stumpf, J. P. (2006). The crimmigration crisis: Immigrants, crime, and sovereign power. *American University Law Review, 56,* 367.

Terpstra, J. (2020). Police reform as institutional change: Symbols and dilemmas. *International Journal of Law, Crime and Justice, 60,* 100359.

Terpstra, J., & Trommel, W. (2009). Police, managerialization and presentational strategies. *Policing: An International Journal of Police Strategies & Management.*

Tham, H. (2001). Law and order as a leftist project? The case of Sweden. *Punishment & Society, 3*(3), 409–426.

UNODC. (2010). *The globalization of crime: A transnational organized crime threat assessment.* United Nations Office on Drugs and Crime.

Van Schendel, W., & Abraham, I. (2005). *Illicit flows and criminal things: States, borders, and the other side of globalization.* Indiana University Press.

Vitale, A. S. (2017). *The end of policing.* Verso Books.

Walklate, S. (2006). *Imagining the victim of crime.* Open University Press.

Westley, W. A. (1970). *Violence and the police: A sociological study of law, custom, and morality.* MIT Press.

Westmarland, L. (2008). Police cultures. *Handbook of policing, 2,* 253–281.

White, C., & Weisburd, D. (2018). A co-responder model for policing mental health problems at crime hot spots: Findings from a pilot project. *Policing: A Journal of Policy and Practice, 12*(2), 194–209.

Yakhlef, S. (2018). *United agents: Community of practice within border policing in the Baltic Sea area.* Lund University.

Zedner, L. (2007). Pre-crime and post-criminology? *Theoretical Criminology, 11*(2), 261–281.

7

Nostalgia

Vignette 36

Task Force Pickpocketing (TFP) Detectives Clausen, Detective Lassen and I have just brought in three Polish men suspected of stealing people's credit cards in and around Copenhagen. The detectives spotted them at Nørreport Station, hovering over a potential victim, and just as the Polish men were trying to make a run for it, the detectives grabbed and arrested them. Detective Lassen even had to forcefully tackle and push over one of the Polish men as he was trying to escape, sprinting down the platform.

Now the Polish men are being processed one at a time on the bottom floor of Station City. This means, as always, that their possessions are being searched and accounted for, questions are being asked about their possessions, about who they are and what they are doing in Copenhagen, pictures are being taken and, eventually, the Polish men will be escorted into separate holding cells. Here they will have to wait until the detectives are ready to interrogate them and, perhaps, charge them.

Standing there watching this process—a sight I had become quite accustomed to—I overhear the younger police officer in charge of processing incoming arrestees complaining rather loudly. His objections are directed at a female arrestee who has been shouting obscenities from the inside of one of the station's fifteen-ish holding cells ever since we came in—obscenities which, it should be mentioned, are not at all uncommon in this specific

(continued)

> **Vignette 36** (continued)
>
> work environment. "Shut up you!" the young officer shouts back. "We've heard you already. Several times. And no, you're not dying. And if you do, we'll know soon enough. Then we'll finally get some peace and quiet".
>
> He then turns toward his older colleague who is processing one of the suspects we brought in and says, "Sigh! She's a god damn fool, that one. Hell, people like her are driving me mad. Why do we have to endure this absurdity all day? Why can't people just behave like they did in the good old days? Why can't they just be a bit normal and respect what we say? Is that too much to ask?"
>
> His colleague acknowledges his frustrations as he also seems annoyed by the woman's constant shouting and complaining. But, I sense, the older colleague is also a bit tired of his younger colleague's grumpiness. "I hear you, friend" he says, "Still, there is no need to be so overly pessimistic and negative all the time. You know? You're young but you're complaining almost as much as she is". He has a smile on his face as he says this. "Haha", the younger colleague replies, "That's true. Very true! But hey, I'm only following what they teach us at the police academy and what this job teaches you—you know, to be a backward-looking and bitter old man, like yourself!" "Haha. True!" the older colleague answers with a grin on his face, "That is the stone cold truth of it all".

Are some Danish detectives really "the last real policemen?" Should we plainly and perhaps naively buy into their constant complaining and signs of disillusion? Of course not. The Danish detectives, as they very well know themselves, will not be the last police officers to inhabit this world. Nor is there anything such as an ultimately "real" police officer or "real" police work, for that matter. As we already know, such authenticity statements often say more about the ideational than the actual reality of policing (Manning, 1977), something the Danish detectives were of course not completely unaware of themselves. They knew that they were speaking of a certain policing reality—a reality that they preferred, not reality per se.

This book, and this chapter in particular, is therefore not about saying that we should really feel sorry for the police. Nor is it just about showing how Danish detectives and many of their colleagues feel sorry for themselves. During my field studies, both the task forces' detectives and I, the ethnographer, were by and large conscious to the fact that the police's aired concerns and frustrations were at times overdramatizations—overdramatizations performed in front of colleagues, management and various outsiders, like me, willing to listen and take part in the act. Indeed, as policing research has shown (Mawby, 2013; Manning, 1977, 2001; Walsh, 2020; Mawby, 2014; Reiner, 2000), global/transnational policing research included (Sausdal & Lohne, 2021; Franko, 2021), police officers are accomplished performers-cum-playwrites, more or less consciously staging and representing a certain kind of world order in the hope of if not maintaining then producing a certain kind of reaction and, ultimately, a certain kind of reality. Moreover, as policing scholars we also already know that everyday police work habitually consists in a lot of funny talk, trash talk and otherwise collegial prattle, especially when among themselves (van Hulst, 2013; Waddington, 1999; Fielding, 1994; Sausdal, 2020). The police banter. They make fun. They readily express their scorn and contempt. They tell stories—and often crude and brutal ones. They bullshit. They complain and nag. As such, it is important to not get completely and guilelessly drawn into their theatrics, blindly believing that the police's melodramatic complaining necessarily make up entirely real sentiments and situations.

While knowing this, this final chapter of the book nevertheless attempts to take a further and more thoughtful look at the many police concerns expressed. What, it asks, could we perhaps learn from taking the police's nostalgic sentiments more seriously in analytical terms as not just "mere" subcultural tropes or theatrics but as actual, heartfelt expressions of vocational loss? Are there, in other words, anything to be garnered from us listening more carefully to the Danish detectives' disillusionments? I say there is. And I hope the previous chapters, and the explanations of police concern provided therein, have already helped underline this. Nevertheless, there remains both room and a need for providing a larger perspective. Though each of the book's chapters tell their own unique story about feelings of job-related concern and frustration, they may also be said to tell a larger, united story worth paying attention to for (global) policing researchers and other stakeholders alike—a bigger story which may best be told by relating this specific ethnography of change, concern and nostalgia amid Danish police detectives to already existing ones found throughout the policing literature.

The End of Local Policing?

As mentioned a couple of times already, it is certainly odd to be speaking of problems of police complaining and nostalgia in a period of time where policing and other forms of control are the beneficiary of a generous amount of backing. In pecuniary and political terms, the police are not really going through a rough patch. The police may be increasingly criticized by parts of the public, academics included, who think that the police and its officers are hopelessly lost in a timeworn and intolerant past. Nevertheless, police forces and their officers still tend to enjoy generous funding, political and public appraisal, as well as a growing influx of many new and noteworthy policing technologies and collaborations—an ostensibly positive development which certainly also characterizes the more globally oriented forms of law enforcement of interest here (Manning, 2008; Bowling & Sheptycki, 2012; Bradford et al., 2016). To be sure, this understanding of an increasingly backed and mobilized police also defines much present-day policing research as it takes a scrutinizing look at these different developments and their consequences for the police itself and, more so, the policed (ibid).

In policing literature, there do however exist an alternative narrative more in line with the focus of this book. From the mid-1990s and on, a few policing researchers started to tell less spirited stories, and particularly so in relation to traditional, public police forces such as the Danish police. A quite vivid example thereof is McLaughlin and Levi's paper "The end of public policing? Police reform and the 'new managerialism'" (1995). As the title reveals, McLaughlin and Levi here examine the new public management principles that have become central to the reform and practice of public police forces (and much of public administration in general) in many countries around the world, Denmark included (Balvig et al., 2011; Holmberg, 2019). As the authors argue, neoliberal, actuarial policies may be causing a particular radical change in the organization of police work as well as in the police's possibility to self-govern, "ending" long-established ideas about what public policing is about, replacing a regime of police discretion with that of politically determined digits (Reiner, 1995; Feeley & Simon, 1994; Hough, 2010). This was also what among other things, only one year later, led Bayley and Shearing (1996) to ponder the on-going and future transformations of policing—Bayley and Shearing similarly prophesying a potentially grim looking future for local, public police forces growingly governed by a "policing by numbers" (Reiner, 1995).

Bayley and Shearing's contribution to the police "transformation thesis" (see Jones & Newburn, 2002) did not only include a critical look at the consequences of new public management. It also included a wider discussion of other transformational trends in policing. One of these is that which has become known as the privatization as well as pluralization of policing (Jones & Newburn, 2006; Loader, 2000). No longer can the work of policing be said to be the monopoly of the public police. Private security companies have increasingly been given and taken market shares. And speaking of the globalization of local policing, various international policing bodies have come to light and power (cf. Bowling & Sheptycki, 2012). Add to this Ericson and Haggerty's (1997) eminent reminder that it is not just the structural organization of policing that has changed but also its work focus. More than policing being solely directed at crime per ser, it is growingly directed at believed risks. And in "policing risk society" (ibid.) the police are no longer lone wolfs but part of a wider network consisting of a number of public and private actors, monitoring the supposed criminogenic more than the purely criminal. Looking at these transformations, McLaughlin and Levi thus pondered "the end of public policing" (much apropos the fatalism of the Danish detectives' "last real policemen" notion). And Bayley and Shearing pointed to the growing likelihood of an "identity crisis" (1996) within traditional police forces—a force otherwise used to be in charge, to be the only and defining boys in blue, so to speak.

New managerial concepts alongside a pluralizing of policing are however not only the only threats to the dominance and identity of the public police. As Reiner (2010) has for example discussed, the public police's felt identity crisis should not only be seen in the light of these systemic as well as substantive changes in policing itself, but also in terms of a generally decreasing lack of public trust and appreciation (Goldsmith, 2005). No longer are the police automatically hailed as your friendly and society-upholding bobby or beat cop. Instead, the police and its officers are increasingly mistrusted and even crassly criticized by the public and other advocates of society. Indeed, as Loader and Mulcahy (2003) have excellently explored, the public police's crises and complaining may have much to do with the fact that the police are experiencing a surrounding society that has changed—a society that no longer has the same traditionalist core values as many a conservative police officer, making the ink on the social contract between the police and the public less dry and discernible.

Now, time has proven that Jones and Newburn's (2002) nuancing of the transformation thesis was accurate, them arguing against the certain existence of a potential end-game for the public police. Still, it makes good sense to think that part of the public police's concern and nostalgia presented in this book could have something to do with the fact that they are no longer the automatic sole and trusted center of policing activities. And if we think about the rapidly growing globalizing of policing, where powers and attention are increasingly shifting from the domestic to international institutions in the Hague or yonder, we may indeed have found a contributing reason to why local Danish officers feel wistful and adrift. This may, at least partly, answer the question of why a group of Danish detectives spoke of themselves at "the last real policemen"—words of vanishment signaling the nostalgic reminiscence of a policing past in which local public police officers were believed to have a lot more professional freedom, more sway, were they were more revered, were they were real *men*, and where the organization itself and broader society weren't as affected by anti-conservative and liberal values.

Trivial, Troubling or "True" Nostalgia?

Vignette 37

I jump into the front passenger seat with Task Force Burglary (TFB) Detective Mogensen sitting next to me, his hands already on the steering wheel. Just a second ago I helped him load the trunk of the car with food, beverages and other things needed for the retreat that TFB is going on for the next couple of days. The theme of the retreat is centered around a big case TFB is running on a supposed Romanian ring of cross-border criminals and the major challenges involved in this case—challenges that are new not only to TFB but to the entire Danish police, touching upon questions such as how police work should be carried out in a global and, not least, more digital day and age.

(continued)

Vignette 37 (continued)

To address this issue, TFB have invited an investigative journalist. "He's an expert in how to use the Internet as an investigational tool", Detective Mogensen tells me, as we drive onto the highway, heading northwest toward the resort which is located in a beautiful spot by a lake on the fringes of a forest some 40 minutes from the TFB headquarters. Driving up there and bearing in mind this investigative journalist who is going to give a talk, I ask the detective what he thinks about this development whereby police work is increasingly being carried out in front of the computer, amongst other things. I ask him this question, also knowing that he is retiring at the end of next month.

"So, what do I think about the Internet, computers and all that?" He replies cautiously to my question, "Hmmm… Now, I don't want to sound as old as I am, and like someone who can't see the value of any future developments, but truth be told, I don't like it. One thing is that I don't know how to do all these new things, even though I do understand the importance of them. Another and to me more important thing is that I don't like what all this computer stuff is doing to police work and to the world more generally. Like, before people would go out and meet each other when buying stuff at the butcher's or at the market or wherever. As individuals in society you would have to go out and meet each other and look each other in the eye. Now you can just sit there in front of the computer and with a click or two you can buy stuff or 'talk' to people. There's no human factor there, no relationship. You get what I mean, right? This also concerns police work. We used to have the opportunity to go out there and look people in the eye and listen to them. That gave them the opportunity to explain themselves and us the ability to check whether they were lying. Now, as a citizen you can just file a report online and you can therefore report all sorts of stuff stolen or whatever without us really being able to check whether it's true or not. Like, you get what I mean, right?" he eventually pauses and asks me, only to carry on his monologue:

"For example, we had this case with this famous Danish crime writer who reported that she had a lot of gold and diamond jewelry stolen from her house as well as expensive Danish design furniture. However, when we pulled some surveillance footage of the car used by the burglars and when we later talked to them, the pictures and burglars told a different story. They hadn't stolen that much. It seemed suspicious. She was probably lying. But it was impossible to judge. She had filed the report online. And that was it". Detective Mogensen concludes, though still talking, still driving.

"What I mean is that the computer, this technological distance, relieves people from thinking or, worse, it is something people can hide behind and play dumb. For instance, nobody would think that it's not criminal to buy a

(continued)

> **Vignette 37** (continued)
> television set from some shady guy in a dark alleyway somewhere, but people can easily close their eyes and buy stuff online [and] hide behind the uncertainty that the computer transaction offers. They'll just say, 'If I don't really know, it's not really criminal'. You know what I mean, yeah? To me it seems like there is a greater distance between people these days and that people don't care about each other as much as they used to simply because they don't have to".
> "And", he says, searching for the point he is trying to make, "it's the same with my line of work. It seems to have become more distanced and automated. It seems like they want us to become cogs in some big machine. So, yeah, I'm glad I'm retiring. These new developments are not for me. You get what I'm getting at, right? ... Listen, I respect progress and all that, and I see the use of it, at least in some ways, but in other ways I tend to think that we're losing some of the very essence of what this job is about, you know, losing these real interactions between the police and the people ... Yeah", he says exhaling, "the only thing I know for certain is that I prefer the old days". "And being in my sixties and on my way out, I'm luckily allowed such a backward-looking stance".

How are we to analyze police nostalgia? Are expressions of nostalgia just the self-admitted backward-looking stance of an older and soon to be retired policeman? Are they, as this chapter's introductory example also illustrated, an example of a specific police jargon? Does police nostalgia have something to with aforementioned transformations in conventional public policing—changes that Detective Mogensen also seem to hint at? Is it all of the above? Or are there perhaps other options available to us? In the following section of the chapter, I will take a deeper look at how police nostalgia and related wistful sentiments have usually been dealt with in the policing literature. Doing this, two different yet related strands of thought appear. Below, I describe these two approaches, while subsequently offering a third way and different way of dealing with Detective Mogensen and his colleagues' yearning for yesteryear.

Trivial Nostalgia

> The nostalgic sense of the good old days may or may not be an accurate interpretation of the past, but the street cops believe police work should be organised and carried out that way today. The value of this culture, operationalized in maxims guiding day-to-day behaviour and performance, form the reference for precinct level officers, and socialize officers to the job at the precinct ... precinct level cops believ[e] that a number of social and political forces have weakened the character and performance of police work and that the policing function is under strong attack as a result. (Reuss-Ianni, 1993, p. 3)

In the literature, a most conventional way for policing researchers to consider the existence of complaining and past glorifications is to see these as a traditional yet also somewhat trivial part of the profession. This, for example, is what is reflected in the above quotation, stemming from Reuss-Ianni's (1993) study of US frontline police officer's work culture vis-à-vis managerial philosophies. As Reuss-Ianni shows, rather than speaking of one united work culture, we should rather be speaking of two separate ones (and perhaps even more than that), discussing the vocational differences between the management and the rank and file (Gundhus et al., 2021; de Maillard & Savage, 2021; Terpstra & Trommel, 2009; Westmarland, 2008). Specifically, Reuss-Ianni's study helps us to appreciate how "the nostalgic sense of the good old days" is an integral part of frontline officers' work and worldview. Largely disregarding what the proposed changes are, and no matter what outside "social or political force" it is, frontline officers certainly have an ingrown tendency toward greeting these with skepticism. A socialized intuition tells them that rather than proposed changes being of any real assistance, they are probably more of an attack on the officers' vocational function and thinking.

In this way, the policing researcher's noticing of police nostalgia becomes an expected finding. It reminds us again of Bittner's (1970) definition of policing and how policing essentially has to do with the conservative enforcing and maintaining of the law, of the status quo. Knowing that frontline officers are vocationally tied to the keeping of the present, and that the present inevitably turns into the past, it would in other words be more surprising if we as researchers were to find willing reformist or even revolutionaries among the rank and file instead of these usual reactionary tendencies. And not just that. What Reuss-Ianni also tells us is to treat police nostalgia not simply as a conventional part of frontline police work culture (see cf. Loftus, 2009; Fassin, 2013); we are also reminded that police officers' yearnings for yesteryear shouldn't be taken too seriously as truth statements in their own right. "The nostalgic sense of the good old days *may or may not be an accurate interpretation of the past*" (Reuss-Ianni, 1993, p. 3, emphasis added), she writes, thereby again prompting fellow researchers and other interested parties to remember that police nostalgia is first and foremost an automated reaction against any outside pressure and, importantly, not necessarily a factual representation of what was/is.

Troubling Nostalgia

> There is [s]imply no turning back the clock. [T]his is exactly what [police officers] who actively bemoan the "decline" of "the Job" and "the force" at least implicitly envisage or yearn for—often in tones suggesting some realization that the outlooks they cleave to are no longer culturally or politically dominant. [This happens] not only in warm reconstructions of how "bobbying" used to be done, but in often angry, emotive denunciations of such things as the declining status of beat officers; political correctness; women police; the eclipse of unfettered, unquestioned authority; civilians; [and] the end of the devotion denoted by a willingness to work long, unpaid hours. [I]t is an outlook symbolically condensed in the felt demise of the attribute that all police forces qua police forces demand—"discipline" … This [nostalgic] worldview—which looks forward to a past that it mobilizes to assess and condemn the present—today forms a residual element of English policing culture. (Loader & Mulcahy, 2003, pp. 224–225)

While it is common for research to simply take notice of the triviality of police nostalgia (also noticing how it is integral to police jargon and "canteen talk/culture" (van Hulst, 2013; Waddington, 1999; Fielding, 1994), policing research is also growingly pointing to the worrying and potentially antagonistic aspects of such triviality. This, for example, is what Loader and Mulcahy do in their outstanding study on *Policing and the Condition of England* (2003) with the, in terms of police nostalgia, telling subtitle *Memory, Politics and Culture*. Picking up from Reuss-Ianni, Reiner (2010) and others, they show police officers' reactions against believed changes shouldn't be treated as a mere mechanic reaction nor as the insignificant figment of police imagination. As the above quotation reveals, it is important to also take stock of how police nostalgia furthers a *real* societal struggle—a struggle between police officers who revel in a traditionalist past versus (parts of) society which has or at least wants to leave this past behind. In its most dire form, the constant and perhaps even growing existence of police nostalgia should therefore not only be gauged "in warm reconstructions of how 'bobbying' used to be done", "but", Loader and Mulcahy argue, by the "often angry, emotive denunciations of such things as the declining status of beat officers; political correctness; women police; [and] the eclipse of unfettered, unquestioned authority" (2003, pp. 224–225). In this perspective, petulance in the form of announcing oneself "the last real policemen" should thus not only be assessed as a banal, sarcastic statement, but ultimately also as a potential call for arms—as indeed a "mobiliz[ing] to asses and condemn the present" (ibid.). The perpetual existence of police nostalgia, in other words, may be trivial but it is also very troubling.

In recent times, the potential troubling aspects of police nostalgia have indeed come to light in policing studies. As many a policing researcher around the world is arguing (Vitale, 2017; Fassin, 2013; Ralph, 2020; Alves, 2021), it is exactly the police's adherence to national conservative, patriarchal, martial and often also racist outlooks that are driving them to mistreat and even be violent against certain groups in society. Indeed. Be it in an American, European, African, Asian or Australian context, several scholarly publications are pointing to how police misconduct could be seen as a sad example of a kind of Huntingtonian cultural war with people of the past on one side and progressives or otherwise good-hearted people on the other (Hornberger, 2011; Linnemann et al., 2014; Diphoorn, 2015; Fassin, 2017; Karpiak & Garriott, 2018; Ralph, 2020; Alves, 2021).

"True" Nostalgia

> [P]olice nostalgia [r]eflects an increasing alienation among officers about perceived anti-police sentiment as well as disruptive reforms and management, simultaneously serving to collectively bind together the officers who talk about, listen to, and share it. Nostalgia [i]s a fundamental buffer against the existential anxieties many officers express… It is deployed as a means of fortifying meaning in the daily work that police undertake, work that has changed and continues changing with the pluralisation of policing and more immediate organisational reform, and which officers believe no longer receives the same level of public support it once did. Such threats to meaning are a key factor in the emergence and expression of nostalgia. (Wadds, 2019)

There is much that supports how nostalgia is both a trivial and troubling aspect of policing. There is no denying this. As my time with the Danish task forces' detectives also showed me, they too aired their wistfulness in relation to pretty much any kind of proposed change, and the detectives by and large preferred and felt compelled to preserve more traditional values—and sometimes not only verbally but with force. The Danish detectives were, in other words, not in any way "woke". Quite the contrary. More than having been awaken from their slumber, the kept dreaming of past glories. In one of the most recent studies on police nostalgia, these are also the conclusions that Wadds offer. "Nostalgia is a fundamental buffer", he writes. "[P]olice nostalgia [r]eflects an increasing alienation among officers about perceived anti-police sentiment as well as disruptive reforms and management", he further argues, also pointing to how nostalgia is a key ingredient in the necessary forming of an *esprit de corps*.

While I agree, what I find particularly interesting in Wadds' reading of police nostalgia is however his added focus on meaning-making and other-wise existential aspects thereof. As he argues, we as researchers should also remember to appreciate and analyze police nostalgia as an existential and everyday cognitive tool that officers (un)consciously apply to make sense of their world, their work and, for that matter, of themselves. Therefore, instead of immediately judging nostalgia as a mere run-of-the-mill and/or larger reactionary sentiment, there may be something to be garnered from further examining how nostalgia also reflects a both more daily and in-depth struggle—a struggle wherein officers simply try to figure out what they are doing and why. More than just being the melodramatic window to a faux past or a past the police are willing to fight for, police nostalgia in this perspective becomes a window to the multiple efforts police officers (and other professions, for that matter) make in interpreting and appreciating the value of their work.

In a search of an alternative and more encompassing, everyday approach to police nostalgia, we may go on and allow ourselves to be inspired by wider sociological and anthropological studies on nostalgia—studies which have long had a more appreciative understanding of this common human sentiment (Angé & Berliner, 2014; Boym, 2008; Davis, 2011). We may for example take a page from what anthropologist Battaglia (1995) has discussed as a "practical" understanding of nostalgia. As she defines it, a study of practical nostalgia is a way of approaching nostalgia as

> less fused to nativism and a lack of critical distance on self and the sources of cultural identity than is often presumed. Nostalgia may in fact be a vehicle of knowledge, rather than only a yearning for something lost. It may be *practiced* in diverse ways, where the issue *for users* becomes, on the one hand, the attachment of appropriate feelings towards their own histories, products and capabilities, and on the other hand, their detachment from—and active resistance to—disempowering conditions… (Battaglia, 1995, p. 77, emphasis added)

Contrary to the trivial understanding—or what Battaglia calls an uncritical "nativist" perspective where users/utterers of nostalgia with little reflection "yearn for something lost"—her practice-oriented approach entails a conceptualization of nostalgia as a mindful and consequential activity. In this framework, nostalgia becomes something more than just a daydreaming pastime or a political battle cry. It becomes a "vehicle of knowledge" (ibid.) which people use to make sense of their present surroundings and situations—a sort of quotidian cognitive work, a type of everyday hermeneutics (see also Davis, 2011; Angé & Berliner, 2014).

Importantly, applying Battaglia's anthropological take is not an abandoning of a critical perspective. As she also argues, an anthropological study of nostalgia is both a study of the wistful's ideas about his own "histories, products and capabilities" as well as the study of his felt detachment therefrom, including the potential of defiance. Yet, herein also lies its greater potential. First, conceptualizing nostalgia as a daily meaning-making practice divided between positive *and* negative thoughts, between feelings of meaningfulness *and* loss, allows for the ethnographic study thereof. It reminds the policing ethnographer to bracket her preconceptions about the means and ends of police nostalgia and, instead, studying them *in situ* as these sentiments play out in and become comments on the (dis)satisfactions of everyday policing. And not just that. What to me distinguishes Battaglia's "practical nostalgia" from the more conventional approaches found in policing research is its insistence on not studying just the critical but also constructive aspects of nostalgia. We, in other words, here find an approach that doesn't only dwell on how wistfulness relates to felt forfeiture, and thus the potential of fighting back. It is also an approach which reminds us to take more seriously how nostalgia too is a way for people to address the central qualities of their lives. What, indeed, are people trying to tell us about the present while hiding behind their romanticized melancholy? What are they afraid of losing? And why? And how does this relate not just to the ideological but, as Wadds also argues, to day-to-day police work?

Because, speaking of day-to-day work, isn't it true that most people don't show up for work, driven by creeds and climaxes? We may tell ourselves so, but the truth probably is that most people of the world show up for work (here bracketing pecuniary and other obvious needs), hoping that a given workday is going to be "alright"—that they will do a decent job and that the workday will be decent and perhaps even provide some minor satisfactions. Though we are too often led to believe that police officers' are singularly driven by a call to serve and to protect, to fight crime, this, I believe, is a fetishized narrative more than an actual truth—a part of a police cult more than actual work culture (see Sausdal, 2022). Police officers might indeed say that they "live to serve and protect" when asked—especially when interviewing for the academy, for a job or being asked by a journalist or even a researcher (Manning, 1978; Van Maanen, 1978; Sausdal, 2021). But, in my experience, police officers go to work for much the same reasons as most others, i.e. to get some work done and go home (Sausdal, 2018). That they, the police, are allowed to see and speak of their work as a calling of course helps. It does motivate them. Nevertheless, a calling is not worth much if the mundane workaday reality doesn't deliver. This is important to remember. And this, in a nutshell, further explains why a more everyday approach to police nostalgia is of importance.

Danish Police Nostalgia

The Danish detectives frequently spoke of the "good old days". They announced themselves to be the last of their kind. They complained about a number of things and changes, frequently thinking that these had to do with how conventional police and detective work are increasingly subjugated to range of global pulls and pushes. At lot of the time, they were on autopilot, more or less knowingly and jokingly speaking out against the novel because "that's what we do as police officers, right? You quickly learn to be skeptical toward any kind of proposed change? Old is better!", as Detective Gustavsen suggestively put it. The detectives were also mostly men. And they were white, ethnically Danish men. They were often from the suburbs or countryside. Most had a lower middle-class background, nicely matching with their lower-middle-class salary as a police officer. Some were old, some were younger. Most of them worried about losing and sharing their policing powers, including their capacity to choose according to their individual discretion. And almost all of them favored traditionalist, political values, feeling an apprehension if not antagonistic toward more liberal agendas both on and off the job. In short, the Danish detectives' complaining about the present and preference for the past were in many ways on a par with the existing explanations of police nostalgia in the literature. This much is true. Yet, using the above-described more everyday approach to the analyses of nostalgia, I will end this chapter by pondering an auxiliary cause. If we indeed try to appreciate the task forces' detectives' constant complaining and longing for the past as a "practice"—as a daily sense-making activity by which they seek to communicate a sense of loss but, simultaneously, also a message about what they appreciate about their current, workaday lives—what, then, will we be able to see? What are their practical "existential anxieties", to use Wadds' term, beyond the purely ideological or, for that matter, beyond the simple in-group mentality that comes with (self-)victimization?

In looking at and across the individual chapters of the book, an answer does seem to show itself. And as perhaps already revealed, this is an answer that has to do with the Danish detectives' feeling that their everyday work isn't what it used to be—or, at least, that it soon won't be. A focus on the felt worsening of their work lives very much runs through all the chapters—a worsening, again, which is not solely a matter of a felt decrease in local police power and authority in a growingly globalized world of policing, nor just an issue of a decreasing public appreciation of the beforehand prized *boys* in blue. What more so seemed to trouble the Danish detectives were simply the sentiment that their work had become less fun and less giving. Showing up for work, didn't give them the same professional nor personal satisfaction. And, in their eyes, globalizing forces were one of the main culprits.

How were globalizing forces to blame? If we consider what each of the chapters tell us, this is the question that ties the knot. In Chap. 2, we saw how normally gratifying work tasks suddenly felt less fulfilling and even frustrating when involving foreign nationals. Foreign nationals didn't receive their punishment in the right kind of way, and the detectives' encounters with them didn't make for the usual tete-a-tete enjoyed by the detectives. At its worse, the detectives even admitted that these more superficial encounters with foreign suspects were making them think less of their new and more global suspect pool. This was a growing police deprecation and cynicism, which Chap. 5 also touched upon as it discussed the drawbacks of police and detective work increasingly involving surveillance and information technologies. More distanced kinds of work made the detectives more cynical and careless, and they didn't like it.

The problem of technologies as well as the demand for growing police collaboration was also part of the problems mentioned in Chap. 3. These developments often clashed with conventional police work culture preferences for the more personal and experienced-based. By and large, the detectives' liked to apply their own "noses", their "guts", themselves essentially, and they felt that new technologies, internationalism and more intelligence-led/academic approaches were getting in the way. Also, the detectives also frequently experienced themselves overwhelmed by the continuous introduction of new concepts and technologies—new work installments which they felt badly equipped to deal with. And there were other quotidian work problems as well which ultimately led the detectives to be less appreciative of the globalization of their work—a globalization, in the form of better cross-border partnerships and surveillance technologies, they otherwise openly spoke of as necessary.

In Chap. 4 we saw how a growing fear and threat of terrorism wasn't particularly conducive to everyday detective work. Rather than being able to focus on their case work, the detectives were instead drawn into various terrorism policing activities and manifestations—activities and manifestations which they often experienced as futile and sometimes even in conflict with their professional identities as police detectives. The detectives also openly spoke about how they felt overtaxed, and how such overtaxing was having negative effects in terms of their personal lives. And, lastly, in Chap. 6, we saw a much similar vocational frustration. While applauding the mounting law and order political discourse in Denmark, the detectives inevitably faced and feared the consequences. They knew and commended that Danish politics were growing harsher and more punitive in order to combat the darker sides of globalization, among other things. But they also hated how the politicians' tough on crime promises were making their daily work more volatile as well as increasingly involving more "not real police work".

In my experience it was all of these different, daily complications of their work life and, more so, the impression that their work was becoming not more but less gratifying, that was at the heart of the detectives' nostalgia. They weren't so much wincing about the larger scope of things as the existing literature seem to suggest, although this also was a cause of concern. It wasn't so much about greater existential losses as such. It was about them finding it harder and harder to enjoy putting in the hours—a sought-after vocational joy of course formed by certain ideas about the joyful vis-à-vis the less joyful.

With that said, I nevertheless wish to end this chapter on a less quotidian note. Recently, a number of works has been published discussing the end or otherwise abolishment of policing as we know it (cf. Vitale, 2017). Spurred by returning examples of police violence and misconduct, scholars and activist alike have been raising their sound criticism of law enforcement agencies, also proposing new ways of rethinking and restructuring police work. Looking at the global policing literature, similar worries may be found. As particularly discussed in Chap. 5, scholars here worry for example about how unhinged and unaccountable forms of transnational/cross-border/post-colonial policing may be the cause of more violence and oppression (Bowling & Westenra, 2018; Bowling & Sheptycki, 2015; Sheptycki, 2004). Where, for example, is the social (and legal) contract that normally binds the public to its designated overseers—a contract by which we the public agree and allow police forces to control the borders and boundaries of our mutual society, and a contract which we in turn can make the police accountable to? As policing proliferates from the local toward the global, from the analogue to the digital, these are questions we need answers to. Yet, sadly, as global policing research has shown, there a much that points to a severe lack of transparency and answerability in transnational and international policing. And not just that. There are also signs of the more global policing actor being more repressive and violent, seemingly not caring much about the people they police (cf. Bowling & Westenra, 2018; Franko, 2021).

In this darkness, this is also where I find a silver lining. If asked to point to something positive and constructive about the Danish detectives' nostalgia, it would be the following: Besides complaining about a work life turned sour, the losses they spoke about most often concerned a growing distance between them and the people at the end of their toils. If we go back and revisit Detective Mogensen's long monologue, we find what I want to talk about. For various reasons, Detective Mogensen misses the closer physicality and interaction of "old" police work. And although he was part the self-proclaimed old guard, he was not in any way alone in thinking this way. What indeed ties most of the chapters together is the recurring sentiment that police and detective work is more giving when it involves not only real but also substantial encounters with actual people. Data doubles in data programs are not enough. Nor are slightly incomprehensible voices spoken or texted on the wire or, for that matter, grainy CCTV footage or incoming emails or phone calls. All such dissociated and digitalized information may be enough to solve the case, but it doesn't necessarily allow for a more gratifying kind of policing. As the Danish detectives indeed said themselves, these new policing techniques may be given them the criminal more easily, but they don't truly reveal the human hiding behind the crime.

Certainly, the Danish detectives' appreciation of deeper and closer relationships with the people they police shouldn't be misunderstood. This is not police officers saying that they yearn after more profound social scientific or humanist understandings. They don't. Nor is it to be confused with them harboring a deep-seated humanitarian wish. They are not there to help in the most noble sense of the word. They are there to make arrests and secure convictions. In this way, the detectives' concerns about the increasing distance and otherwise obfuscation between them and the people the police is perhaps a more egoistic than altruistic story. It is the simple yet significant story about a group of Danish detectives who are missing the joys and, indeed, also perspective that come with policing real people and not just proxies. Yet, therein also lies a common ground. Although the detectives may be said to mostly miss actual interactions for their own good—as a defense against tedium and complete pessimism—it is a kind of nostalgia largely recognizable to many policing researchers as well as criminologists more broadly. Though we are not dreaming of more proxime kind of policing that involves recurrent physical or symbolic violence, many of us do dream of a kind of policing that isn't fully detached from and indifferent to the people investigated and controlled. We too want a less cynical police, professionally focused on the criminal, though not blind to the hardships of the human condition.

Now, what I am arguing for here is of course not to turn global policing into community/proximity policing. That is neither doable nor desirable. Transnational crimes and threats need a different medicine than the one usually applied in community policing practices. What I am pondering, however, is how we may turn global policing on its head in order to make it less a callous practice. Rather than the global purely affecting the local, it is worth thinking about how to make more global forms of policing embody the spirit of the local police, of the community police officer or the dedicated detective who pride themselves in knowing their citizens and suspects. All this indeed reminds me of how Bittner described the true and appropriate vocational essence of policing as "commensurate with the extent to which they "know the people"—that is not a quasi-theoretical understanding of human nature but rather the common practice of individualized and reciprocal recognition (Bittner, 1967, p. 707). Bittner of course wrote this before there was such a thing as a widespread Internet and when both globalization and the globalization of policing were in their mere infancy. In all its banality, it is however what the Danish detectives' nostalgia was very much about. They wanted to know people, to have more than a quasi-theoretical understanding of people, to recognize and be recognized, to punish and perceive, for better *and* worse.

To be sure, the story I have essentially been telling here is an old story—a story of the potential problems of a growingly globalized and technology-driven world told several times before in other studies of other people and professionals. And now I have told it too with the help of a group of Danish police detectives. Though they have probably never heard of nor read Anthony Giddens, they would surely agree with his argument that even though we thought that the progress of science and technology would make life

> more certain and predictable for us, [it] often [has] quite the opposite effect. [R]ather than being more and more under our control, it seems out of our control—a runaway world. (Giddens, 2011, pp. 1–2)

In a policing world of unprecedented possibilities in reach and control, a group of Danish detectives did indeed feel more at a loss than ever.

Bibliography

Alves, J. (2021). F*ck the police: Murderous cops, the myth of police fragility and the case for an insurgent anthropology. *Focaal Blog*.
Angé, O., & Berliner, D. (2014). *Anthropology and nostalgia*. Berghahn Books.
Balvig, F., Holmberg, L., & Nielsen, M. P. H. (2011). *Verdens bedste politi*. Djøf.
Battaglia, D. (1995). On practical nostalgia: Self-prospecting among urban Trobrianders. In D. Battaglia (Ed.), *Rhetorics of self-making* (pp. 77–96). University of California Press.
Bayley, D. H., & Shearing, C. D. (1996). The future of policing. *Law and Society Review*, 585–606.

Bittner, E. (1967). The police on skid-row: A study of peace keeping. *American Sociological Review, 32*, 699–715.

Bittner, E. (1970). *The functions of the police in modern society: A review of background factors, current practices, and possible role models*. National Institute of Mental Health, Center for Studies of Crime and Delinquency.

Bowling, B., & Sheptycki, J. (2012). *Global policing*. Sage.

Bowling, B., & Sheptycki, J. (2015). 11 reflections on legal and political accountability for global policing. In S. Lister & M. Rowe (Eds.), *Accountability of policing*. Routledge.

Bowling, B., & Westenra, S. (2018). 'A really hostile environment': Adiaphorization, global policing and the crimmigration control system. *Theoretical Criminology*. https://doi.org/10.1177/1362480618774034

Boym, S. (2008). *The future of nostalgia*. Basic books.

Bradford, B., Loader, I., Jauregui, B., et al. (2016). *The SAGE handbook of global policing*. SAGE.

Davis, F. (2011). Yearning for yesterday: A sociology of nostalgia. *The Collective Memory Reader, 5*, 446–451.

de Maillard, J., & Savage, S. P. (2021). Performance mechanisms meet professional autonomy: Performance management and professional discretion within police investigation departments. *Policing and Society, 32*, 1–14.

Diphoorn, T. G. (2015). *Twilight policing: Private security and violence in urban South Africa*. University of California Press.

Ericson, R. V., & Haggerty, K. D. (1997). *Policing the risk society*. Oxford University Press.

Fassin, D. (2013). *Enforcing order: An ethnography of urban policing*. Polity Press.

Fassin, D. (2017). *Writing the world of policing: The difference ethnography makes*. University of Chicago Press.

Feeley, M., & Simon, J. (1994). Actuarial justice: The emerging new criminal law. *The Futures of Criminology, 173*, 174.

Fielding, N. (1994). Cop canteen culture. In T. Newburn & E. Stanko (Eds.), *Just boys doing business* (pp. 46–63). Routledge.

Franko, K. (2021). The two-sided spectacle at the border: Frontex, NGOs and the theatres of sovereignty. *Theoretical Criminology*. https://doi.org/10.1177/13624806211007858.

Giddens, A. (2011). *Runaway world*. Profile books.

Goldsmith, A. (2005). Police reform and the problem of trust. *Theoretical Criminology, 9*(4), 443–470.

Gundhus, H. O., Talberg, N., & Wathne, C. T. (2021). From discretion to standardization: Digitalization of the police organization. *International Journal of Police Science & Management*. https://doi.org/10.1177/14613557211036554

Holmberg, L. (2019). Continuity and change in Scandinavian police reforms. *International Journal of Police Science & Management, 21*(4), 206–217.

Hornberger, J. (2011). *Policing and human rights: The meaning of violence and justice in the everyday policing of Johannesburg*. Routledge.

Hough, M. (2010). *Policing, new public management and legitimacy. The new public leadership challenge* (pp. 70–84). Springer.

Jones, T., & Newburn, T. (2002). The transformation of policing? Understanding current trends in policing systems. *British Journal of Criminology, 42*(1), 129–146.

Jones, T., & Newburn, T. (2006). *Plural policing: A comparative perspective*. Psychology Press.

Karpiak, K. G., & Garriott, W. (2018). *The anthropology of police*. Routledge.

Linnemann, T., Wall, T., & Green, E. (2014). The walking dead and killing state: Zombification and the normalization of police violence. *Theoretical Criminology, 18*(4), 506–527.

Loader, I. (2000). Plural policing and democratic governance. *Social & Legal Studies, 9*(3), 323–345.

Loader, I., & Mulcahy, A. (2003). *Policing and the condition of England: Memory, politics and culture*. Oxford University Press.

Loftus, B. (2009). *Police culture in a changing world*. Oxford University Press.

Manning, P. K. (1977). *Police work: The social organization of policing*. MIT Press.

Manning, P. K. (1978). The police: Mandate, strategies, and appearances. In P. V. M. J. Manning (Ed.), *Policing: A view from the street* (pp. 7–31). Goodyear Publishing Company.

Manning, P. K. (2001). Theorizing policing: The drama and myth of crime control in the NYPD. *Theoretical Criminology, 5*(3), 315–344.

Manning, P. K. (2008). *The technology of policing: Crime mapping, information technology, and the rationality of crime control*. New York University Press.

Mawby, R. (2013). *Policing images*. Willan.

Mawby, R. C. (2014). The presentation of police in everyday life: Police–press relations, impression management and the Leveson inquiry. *Crime, Media, Culture, 10*(3), 239–257.

McLaughlin, Eugene and Levi, Michael (1995) The end of public policing? Police reform and the 'new managerialism'. In, Noakes, Lesleyand Maguire, Mike (eds.) *Contemporary Issues in Criminology*. Cardiff, GB. Cardiff University Press.

Ralph, L. (2020). *The torture letters: Reckoning with police violence.* University of Chicago Press.
Reiner, R. (1995). Policing by numbers: The feel-good fallacy. *Policing Today, 1*(3), 22–24.
Reiner, R. (2000). Romantic realism: Policing and the media. *Core issues in Policing, 2*, 52–66.
Reiner, R. (2010). *The politics of the police.* Oxford University Press.
Reuss-Ianni, E. (1993). *Two cultures of policing: Street cops and management cops.* Transaction Publishers.
Sausdal, D. (2018). Pleasures of policing: An additional analysis of xenophobia. *Theoretical Criminology, 22*(2), 226–242.
Sausdal, D. (2020). Police bullshit. *Journal of Extreme Anthropology, 4*(1), 94–115.
Sausdal, D. (2021). *Looking beyond the police-as-control narrative.* Policy Press.
Sausdal, D., & Lohne, K. (2021). *Theatrics of transnational criminal justice: Ethnographies of penality in a global age.* SAGE Publications Sage UK.
Sausdal, D. B. (2022). A cult(ure) of intelligence-led policing: On the international campaigning and convictions of Danish policing. In Mikkel Jarle Christensen, Kjersti Lohne & Magnus Hörnqvist (eds) *Nordic Criminal Justice in a Global Context* (pp. 111-127). Routledge
Sheptycki, J. (2004). The accountability of transnational policing institutions: The strange case of Interpol. *Canadian Journal of Law and Society, 19*, 107.
Terpstra, J., & Trommel, W. (2009). Police, managerialization and presentational strategies. *Policing: An International Journal of Police Strategies & Management.*
van Hulst, M. (2013). Storytelling at the Police Station the canteen culture revisited. *British Journal of Criminology, 53*(4), 624–642.
Van Maanen, J. (1978). On watching the watchers. In P. K. Manning & J. Van Maanen (Eds.), *Policing: A view from the street* (pp. 309–309). Goodyear Publishing.
Vitale, A. S. (2017). *The end of policing.* Verso Books.
Waddington, P. A. (1999). Police (canteen) sub-culture. An appreciation. *British Journal of Criminology, 39*(2), 287–309.
Wadds, P. (2019). 'It's not like it used to be': Respect and nostalgia in the policing of nightlife. *Australian & New Zealand Journal of Criminology, 52*(2), 213–230.
Walsh, J. P. (2020). Social media and border security: Twitter use by migration policing agencies. *Policing and Society, 30*(10), 1138–1156.
Westmarland, L. (2008). Police cultures. *Handbook of policing, 2*, 253–281.

8

Conclusion: A Policing Puzzle

What does it mean to local police forces that they have become part of a more globalized world? How, for example, does it affect their work, thoughts and motivations? And how did it specifically relate to a group of Danish police detectives—a group of detectives who not only seemed to complain a lot but who even spoke of themselves as "the last real policemen"? These are the questions asked and answered throughout this book.

As already discussed, it arguably makes little sense to talk about Danish or other police officers being the last of their kind. Looking at the vast number of resources spent on law enforcement and criminal justice worldwide (Farrell & Clark, 2004; Bradford et al., 2016), one notices a rise rather than a decline in financial support for various kinds of policing-related efforts. This is a growing expenditure that doesn't only have to do with increasing investments in different countries' local police forces, such as the Danish police, it also has much to do with the on-going globalization of policing as different international and transnational criminal justice and law enforcement agencies have been either further strengthened or established in recent years. In economic terms, having the police presenting themselves as a vanishing entity therefore seems not just paradoxical but counterfactual. Moreover, the counterfactual aspects of a perceived loss of worth only become greater when looking beyond the purely monetary and toward the wider cultural and political discourse that surrounds present-day policing efforts. Although many an academic and activist are critical of policing practices, it would still be fair to say that the conventional public police, and its officers, are living and working in a period of time where policing is still very much venerated by politicians and broad parts of the public alike.

Knowing how the police are the recipient of not just financial but also political and, to some extent at least, public support, it does appear almost asinine for a group of Danish detectives to present themselves as part of a dying profession. Seen from the outside, rather than talking about a vocational weakening, it would appear more accurate to talk about a possible new "golden (global) age of policing". This, from a police perspective at least, more uplifting conclusion was also what I suspected to find as I in 2012 first decided to study how the Danish police was reacting to becoming part of a more global world order. My assumptions, however, were quickly put to shame as I couple of years later started and carried out an extensive ethnographic fieldwork among the two detective task forces that make up this book's empirical field and focus. Rather than hearing songs of glory, I observed both undertones and even open outbursts of frustration and concern. Rather than the detectives being happy about current developments, and enjoying the still widespread political and public backing that the police enjoy, I encountered dissatisfied detectives, more gloomy than grateful—a gloom that came in many varieties and nuances. To be sure, instead of feeling uplifted by the many changes their profession was going through, the Danish detectives felt that they were slowly but surely losing things fundamental to their profession and, not least, to their professional contentment. Importantly, it was not because the detectives did not see the need for change. They did. Witnessing transformations in the growingly global, mobile and digitalized nature of crime, the detectives readily acknowledged the demand to further develop or even rid themselves off many traditional and timeworn policing efforts and investigational approaches. "We get it", they said. "We know we need to change, that police work needs to change, that we need to update ourselves, if we don't want to lose out against criminals who have already changed their ways". Nevertheless, in a sort of sad catch 22, the Danish detectives felt they were losing out anyhow. In many ways, the whole situation had a "damned if you do, damned if you don't" feeling about it.

In essence, this is the very catch 22 paradox reflected in all of the book's chapters. The Danish police and its Danish detectives did understand the need for present-day policing to adjust—to become less locally oriented and more tuned toward a global reality. The detectives got how a more global world equaled less local and, instead, more global criminals and otherwise societal threats of a foreign origin in need of policing. They understood that this development had to involve wider political and organizational change as well as different practical priorities. They understood that they would need to build partnerships and work together with different external and international actors. And they certainly did realize how various technocratic and technological developments were fundamental to the future policing. All this they understood. But at the same time, the detectives couldn't rid themselves of the feeling that such a globalizing of local policing was interfering with what they perceive to be, if not essential, then at least core gratifying aspects of their "normal" police/detective work.

Looking through the chapters, the question is what these gratifications were? What kind of vocational joys and drives were a stake? Though the chapters differ in their respective empirical focuses and theoretical themes, they also tell a shared story. Indeed, while the detectives were surely also exaggerating when speaking about their concerns and their sense of loss, this book has essentially been trying to tell a story about how Danish detectives prefer a kind of police work that involves real life and more profound interactions with the people the police—interactions-cum-relations made if not more difficult then different because of various contemporary changes related to a believed globalization of their work. Herein also lies the story about how various global and political fears have made it increasingly hard for them to fully dedicate themselves; mobilizing them against different global threats yet essentially affording them much less professional and personal time and independence. The local police may have been further "militarized" (Kraska, 2007), having been offered more resources and opportunities, but in the scope of their daily work, many such ostensibly positive policing developments are, somewhat ironically, felt to be more of a hindrance than of any real use. Now, one may of course think that is a terrific idea to have police officers increasingly controlled by democratically elected politicians, having them removed from the streets and having them base their practices more on technocratic and technologically derived "evidence" rather than gut-feeling. It certainly does seem like viable answer to many of the problems of police misconduct we see worldwide. Minimizing and regulating police presence and choice in relation to the public could undeniably be a productive way to deal with the police's often-noted tendency to turn police discretion into police discrimination and even violence (Mastrofski, 2004; Holmberg, 2000). Also, it is hard to disagree with those who argue that policing practices and perceptions should be based more on thorough analyses of available knowledge and data, allowing for more precise and effective forms of policing (cf. Bullock & Tilley, 2009; Hestehave, 2013; Ratcliffe, 2016)

Still, while I haven't in any way written this book as an opposition to such propositions, I have written it to highlight how such developments are (often negatively) experienced by some local Danish police officers. One may again be inclined to ignore the local police's complaints and concerns. Police officers often complain. This is true. And if what the police are complaining about is a much needed and inevitable progress, then why pay it any attention at all? Though perhaps understandable, such an uninterested approach to police concerns may prove problematic. First, even though we may think little of local police officers' cantankerous ways, it is eventually them who will have to carry out the work. Though new, better and more globally devoted officers may be trained and employed, the brunt of the work still needs to be done by currently active officers. Secondly, and more importantly, the problem itself may not be that easily solved by simply waiting on an upcoming future replacement of timeworn old-timers, as some seem to believe, the police included. In my experience the local Danish detectives' concerns expressed in relation to ongoing developments had little to do with age, or any other kind of demographic for that matter. Young and old, men and women, were equally unhappy. Though seeing and understanding why winds of change were blowing, the Danish police officers also sensed how such changes engendered much more politicized, automated and distanced forms of police work—kinds of police work in which the local officer—i.e. the police as an individual professional as well as human being—was simply becoming less important. Various policing changes may certainly be of worth in terms of sheer police productivity, but in terms of local, individual officers' job satisfaction, the detectives felt more discouraged than uplifted. Thirdly, though research and real-life experience have showed us the problems of an uncontrolled and overly present police, research has similarly pointed to the essential need of having police officers with the ability to understand and react to the wider, human circumstances of crime. This goes to the heart of much research on police discretion where numerous scholars have pointed to how the police—and other street level bureaucrats—need "discretion" in order to not only enact and enforce the strictures of law but also humanize it (cf. Muir, 1979; Lipsky, 2010). And, to reiterate, it was very much these daily discretionary aspects of policing which the task forces' detectives seemed afraid of losing—discretionary aspects the detectives which would, for better or worse, allow the detectives to get closer to the people they police, the detectives thereby being both more able to apply force but also to understand those they policed as more than mere criminals, as humans— "to apprehend" them physically as well as conceptually (Sausdal, 2014; Vigh, 2018).

In all this again lies what seems like an unsolvable puzzle.[1] Local policing is changing because it has to. It is going global. Policy makers, policing scholars as well as the police itself acknowledge this, also including the Danish detectives. Nevertheless, this very development seems synchronously to be killing off or at least disheartening the very people asked to carry out these new kinds of police work. They feel at a loss. Though not in any way an uncomplicated matter, what they essentially feel to be losing is their professional ability to choose for themselves and, more so, to have a working day which involves actual, physical interactions with those they police—to keep policing as an essential "human business". Now, to solve this puzzle, one would need to figure out how to retain a kind of local police work, which allows individual officers to not feel overly detached from the people and places they police, *while* also

---

[1] I am grateful to Ian Loader for pointing this out.

allowing local policing to globalize? How, in other words, may we both have a more peripatetic and technology-driven kind of policing *as well as* a kind of policing that permits local police officers to appreciate their work and to not feel overly estranged from the people they police as well as from police work itself? Certainly, this presents itself as an unsolvable riddle. The (policing) world is moving in one direction, leaving local detectives and their vocational preferences behind. Still, the question is whether it absolutely has to be like this?

More than providing an answer hereto, this book's aspiration has been to allow for the initial posing of the question. Indeed, looking at the current state of the research literature, most policing research and practice seems singularly focused on how to generate more efficient means of policing in a global world and/or what the societal and wider organizational consequences thereof may be. Such focuses are both understandable and necessary. Yet, if asked to make a final recommendation, this would be to include the question of professional gratification into the mix. Put differently, more thoughts (and research) should be put into how to have a more globalized police *while* retaining some of the local and everyday qualities here discussed—to make local policing global while keeping it grounded.

Bibliography

Bradford, B., Loader, I., Jauregui, B., et al. (2016). *The SAGE handbook of global policing*. SAGE.

Bullock, K., & Tilley, N. (2009). Evidence-based policing and crime reduction. *Policing: A Journal of Policy and Practice, 3*(4), 381–387.

Farrell, G., & Clark, K. (2004). What does the world spend on criminal justice? HEUNI Paper No. 20.

Hestehave, N. K. (2013). *Proaktiv kriminalitetsbekæmpelse*. Samfundslitteratur.

Holmberg, L. (2000). Discretionary leniency and typological guilt: Results from a Danish study of police discretion. *Journal of Scandinavian Studies in Criminology and Crime Prevention, 1*(2), 179–194.

Kraska, P. B. (2007). Militarization and policing—Its relevance to 21st century police. *Policing, 1*(4), 501–513.

Lipsky, M. (2010). *Street-level bureaucracy: Dilemmas of the individual in public service*. Russell Sage Foundation.

Mastrofski, S. D. (2004). Controlling street-level police discretion. *The Annals of the American Academy of Political and Social Science, 593*(1), 100–118.

Muir, W. K. (1979). *Police: Streetcorner politicians*. University of Chicago Press.

Ratcliffe, J. (2016a). *Intelligence-led policing*. Routledge.

Sausdal, D. (2014). Cultural culprits: Police apprehensions of pickpockets in Copenhagen. In B. Petterson & P. Bevelander (Eds.), *Crisis and migration: Implications of the eurozone crisis for perceptions, politics, and policies of migration*. Nordic Academic Press.

Vigh, H. (2018). Lives opposed: Perceptivity and tacticality in conflict and crime. *Social Anthropology, 26*(4), 487–501.

Bibliography

Aas, K. F. (2007). Analysing a world in motion: Global flows meet 'the criminology of the other'. *Theoretical Criminology, 11*(2), 283–303.

Aas, K. F. (2012). (in)security-at-a-distance: Rescaling justice, risk and warfare in a transnational age. *Global Crime, 13*(4), 235–253.

Aas, K. F. (2014). Bordered penality: Precarious membership and abnormal justice. *Punishment & Society, 16*(5), 520–541.

Aas, K. F., & Bosworth, M. (2013). *The borders of punishment: Migration, citizenship, and social exclusion*. Oxford University Press.

Aas, K. F., & Gundhus, H. O. (2015). Policing humanitarian borderlands: Frontex, human rights and the precariousness of life. *British Journal of Criminology, 55*(1), 1–18.

Aas, K. F., Gundhus, H. O., & Lomell, H. M. (2008). *Technologies of inSecurity: The surveillance of everyday life*. Routledge.

Abbe, A., & Brandon, S. E. (2014). Building and maintaining rapport in investigative interviews. *Police Practice and Research, 15*(3), 207–220.

Agamben, G. (1998). *Homo sacer: Sovereign power and bare life*. Stanford University Press.

Aliverti, A. (2013). *Crimes of mobility: Criminal law and the regulation of immigration*. Routledge.

Aliverti, A. (2014). Enlisting the public in the policing of immigration. *British Journal of Criminology, 55*(2), 215–230.

Aliverti, A. (2021). *Policing the borders within*. Oxford University Press.
Altheide, D. L. (2006). Terrorism and the politics of fear. *Cultural Studies↔ Critical Methodologies, 6*(4), 415–439.
Alves, J. (2021). F*ck the police: Murderous cops, the myth of police fragility and the case for an insurgent anthropology. *Focaal Blog*.
Anderson, B. (2006). *Imagined communities: Reflections on the origin and spread of nationalism*. Verso Books.
Anderson, M. (1989). *Policing the world: Interpol and the politics of international police co-operation*. Clarendon Press.
Anderson, M., Den Boer, M., Den, M., et al. (1996). *Policing the European Union 'theory, law, and practice'*. Oxford University Press.
Andersson, R. (2014). *Illegality, Inc.: Clandestine migration and the business of bordering Europe*. University of California Press.
Andreas, P., & Nadelmann, E. (2006). *Policing the globe: Criminalization and crime control in international relations*. Oxford University Press.
Angé, O., & Berliner, D. (2014). *Anthropology and nostalgia*. Berghahn Books.
Arendt, H., & Kroh, J. (1964). *Eichmann in Jerusalem*. Viking Press.
Bacon, M. (2017). *Taking care of business: Police detectives, drug law enforcement and proactive investigation*. Oxford University Press.
Bacon, M., Loftus, B., & Rowe, M. (2020). Ethnography and the evocative world of policing (part I). *Policing and Society, 30*, 1–10.
Bæksgaard, A., Kildegaard, K., & Olsen, S. M. (2015). Bombe under dansk politi—Presses af massivt overarbejde. *Berlingske*.
Ball, K., & Webster, F. (2003). *The intensification of surveillance: Crime, terrorism and warfare in the information age*. Pluto Press London.
Balvig, F. (2005). When law and order returned to Denmark. *Journal of Scandinavian Studies in Criminology and Crime Prevention, 5*(2), 167–187.
Balvig, F., Holmberg, L., & Nielsen, M. P. H. (2011). *Verdens bedste politi*. Djøf.
Banton, M. (1964). *The policeman in the community*. Basic Books.
Banton, M. (1994). *Discrimination*. Open University Press.
Banton, M. (1996). The cultural determinants of xenophobia. *Anthropology Today, 12*(2), 8–12.
Banton, M. (2018). The concept of racism. In Banton (ed) *Race and racialism* (pp. 17–34). Routledge.
Barker, V. (2017). *Nordic nationalism and penal order: Walling the welfare state*. Routledge.
Basic, G., & Yakhlef, S. (2022). Anomie and collaboration in intelligence and operational police and border guard work in the Baltic Sea area: In-group mentality and construction of the other. *Policing and Society, 32*(9), 1103–1123.

Battaglia, D. (1995). On practical nostalgia: Self-prospecting among urban Trobrianders. In D. Battaglia (Ed.), *Rhetorics of self-making* (pp. 77–96). University of California Press.

Bauman, Z., & Lyon, D. (2013). *Liquid surveillance: A conversation*. Cambridge: Polity.

Bayley, D. H., & Bittner, E. (1984). Learning the skills of policing. *Law and Contemporary Problems, 47*(4), 35–59.

Bayley, D. H., & Shearing, C. D. (1996). The future of policing. *Law and Society Review, 30*, 585–606.

Beck, U. (2009). *World at risk*. Polity.

Becker, H. S. (1995). Moral entrepreneurs: The creation and enforcement of deviant categories. In N. Herman (Ed.), *Deviance: A symbolic interactionist approach* (pp. 169–178). Lanham, MD.

Beek, J., Göpfert, M., Owen, O., et al. (2017). *Police in Africa: The street level view*. Oxford University Press.

Bevelander, P., & Petersson, B. (2014). *Crisis and migration: Implications of the eurozone crisis for perceptions, politics, and policies of migration*. Nordic Academic Press.

Bigo, D. (2008). Globalized (in)security: The field and the ban-Opticon. In D. Bigo & A. Tsoukala (Eds.), *Terror, insecurity and liberty: Illiberal practices of liberal regimes after* (pp. 10–48). Routledge.

Bigo, D., & Guild, E. (2005). Policing at a distance: Schengen visa policies. In D. Bigo & E. Guild (Eds.), *Controlling frontiers. Free movement into and within Europe* (pp. 233–263). Ashgate.

Birk Haller, M., Kolind, T., Hunt, G., et al. (2020). Experiencing police violence and insults: Narratives from ethnic minority men in Denmark. *Nordic Journal of Criminology, 21*(2), 170–185.

Bittner, E. (1967). The police on skid-row: A study of peace keeping. *American Sociological Review, 32*, 699–715.

Bittner, E. (1970). *The functions of the police in modern society: A review of background factors, current practices, and possible role models*. National Institute of Mental Health, Center for Studies of Crime and Delinquency.

Björk, M. (2005). Between frustration and aggression: Legal framing and the policing of public disorder in Sweden and Denmark. *Policing and Society, 15*(3), 305–326.

Björk, M. (2008). Fighting cynicism: Some reflections on self-motivation in police work. *Police Quarterly, 11*(1), 88–101.

Björk, M. (2018). Politistudier—Metodologiske problemer og praktiske råd. In M. H. Jacobsen (Ed.), *Kriminologi: Metoder I* (pp. 453–481). Hans Reitzels Forlag.

Björk, M. (2021). Muddling through the Swedish police reform: Observations from a neo-classical standpoint on bureaucracy. *Policing: A Journal of Policy and Practice, 15*(1), 327–339.

Blaustein, J., Chodor, T., & Pino, N. W. (2020). Making crime a sustainable development issue: From 'drugs and thugs' to 'peaceful and inclusive societies'. *The British Journal of Criminology, 60*(1), 50–73.

Blaustein, J., Chodor, T., & Pino, N. W. (2021). Development as a historical component of the United Nations' crime policy agenda: From social defence to the millennium development goals. *Criminology & Criminal Justice, 21*(4), 435–454.

Bonnichsen, H. J. (2012). *Tvivl på alt og tro på meget: Jagten på sandhed-Politiets afhøringsmetoder*. Rosinante & Co.

Bosworth, M. (2017). *Border criminology and the changing nature of penal power* (pp. 373–390). Oxford University Press.

Bosworth, M., Bowling, B., & Lee, M. (2008). Globalization, ethnicity and racism: An introduction. *Theoretical Criminology, 12*(3), 263–273.

Bosworth, M., Hasselberg, I., & Turnbull, S. (2016). Punishment, citizenship and identity: An introduction. *Criminology and Criminal Justice, 16*(3), 257–266.

Bowling, B. (2009). Transnational policing: The globalization thesis, a typology and a research agenda. *Policing, 3*(2), 149–160.

Bowling, B. (2019). *The politics of the police*. Oxford University Press.

Bowling, B., & Kopf, C. (2017). Transnational policing in Europe and its local effects. *European Law Enforcement Research Bulletin., 3*, 47–57.

Bowling, B., & Sheptycki, J. (2012). *Global policing*. Sage.

Bowling, B., & Sheptycki, J. (2015). 11 reflections on legal and political accountability for global policing. In S. Lister & M. Rowe (Eds.), *Accountability of policing*. Routledge.

Bowling, B., & Sheptycki, J. (2016). Transnational policing and the end times of human rights. In *The Routledge international handbook of criminology and human rights* (pp. 431–442). Routledge.

Bowling, B., & Westenra, S. (2018). 'A really hostile environment': Adiaphorization, global policing and the crimmigration control system. *Theoretical Criminology*. https://doi.org/10.1177/1362480618774034

Bowling, B., Phillips, C., Campbell, A., et al. (2004). Policing and human rights: Eliminating discrimination, xenophobia, intolerance and the abuse of power from police work. *Identities, Conflict and Cohesion (2000–2005)*,

United Nations Research Institute for Social Development, 3–5 September 2001, Durban, South Africa, 3–26.

Boym, S. (2008). *The future of nostalgia*. Basic books.

Bradford, B., Loader, I., Jauregui, B., et al. (2016). *The SAGE handbook of global policing*. SAGE.

Brodeur, J.-P. (2007). High and low policing in post-9/11 times. *Policing: A Journal of Policy and Practice, 1*(1), 25–37.

Brodeur, J.-P. (2010). *The policing web*. Oxford University Press.

Brown, M. K. (1981). *Working the street: Police discretion and the dilemmas of reform*. The Russell Sage Foundation.

Bruinsma, G. (2015). *Histories of transnational crime*. Springer.

Bullock, K., & Tilley, N. (2009). Evidence-based policing and crime reduction. *Policing: A Journal of Policy and Practice, 3*(4), 381–387.

Burawoy, M. (2001). Manufacturing the global. *Ethnography, 2*(2), 147–159.

Burke, R. J. (1993). Work-family stress, conflict, coping, and burnout in police officers. *Stress and Health, 9*(3), 171–180.

Cain, M. E. (2015). *Society and the Policeman's role*. Routledge.

Casey, C. (1995). *Work, self, and society: After industrialism*. Psychology Press.

Chan, J. (2011). Racial profiling and police subculture. *Canadian Journal of Criminology and Criminal Justice, 53*(1), 75–78.

Chan, J. B. (1997). *Changing police culture: Policing in a multicultural society*. Cambridge University Press.

Charman, S., & Bennett, S. (2022). Voluntary resignations from the police service: The impact of organisational and occupational stressors on organisational commitment. *Policing and Society, 32*(2), 159–178.

Choongh, S. (1998). Policing the dross: A social disciplinary model of policing. *The British Journal of Criminology, 38*(4), 623–634.

Christensen, M. J. (2017). Crafting and promoting international crimes: A controversy among professionals of Core-crimes and anti-corruption. *Leiden Journal of International Law, 30*(2), 501–521.

Christensen, M. J. (2021). Battles to define the Danish police. *Global Perspectives in Policing and Law Enforcement, 61*.

Christensen, M. J. (2021). Battles to define the Danish police. In J. Mbuba (Ed.), *Global perspectives in policing and law enforcement*. Rowman and Littlefield.

Christensen, M. M., & Albrecht, P. (2020). *Urban borderwork: Ethnographies of policing* (pp. 385–398). SAGE Publications Sage UK.

Christie, N., & Bruun, K. (1985). *Den goda fienden: Narkotikapolitik i Norden*. Rabén & Sjögren.

Cockcroft, T. (2020). *Police culture: Research and practice*. Policy Press.
Collins, R. (2009). *Violence: A micro-sociological theory*. Princeton University Press.
Cottee, S., & Hayward, K. (2011). Terrorist (e) motives: The existential attractions of terrorism. *Studies in Conflict & Terrorism, 34*(12), 963–986.
Dansk_Politi. (2017). *Overarbejde: 600 politifolk kan holde fri i et år*. Retrieved November 7, from http://www.dansk-politi.dk/artikler/2017/september/overarbejde-600-politifolk-kan-holde-fri-i-et-aar
Dansk_Politi. (2018). *Redaktionens fokus—DANSK POLIT—flot og fjernt*. Retrieved May 18, from https://dansk-politi.dk/nyheder/redaktionens-fokus-dansk-politi-flot-fjernt
Davis, F. (2011). Yearning for yesterday: A sociology of nostalgia. *The Collective Memory Reader, 5*, 446–451.
Davis, K. C. (1975). *Police discretion*. West Group.
De Bolle, C. (2020). The role of Europol in international interdisciplinary European cooperation. *European Police Science and Research Bulletin, 19*, 17.
De Botton, A. (2010). *The pleasures and sorrows of work*. Knopf Doubleday Publishing Group.
De Genova, N. P. (2010). *The Deportation Regime: Sovereignty, Space, and the Freedom of Movement*. Durham, NC: Duke University Press.
de Maillard, J., & Savage, S. P. (2021). Performance mechanisms meet professional autonomy: Performance management and professional discretion within police investigation departments. *Policing and Society, 32*, 1–14.
Dean, G., Fahsing, I. A., & Gottschalk, P. (2006). Profiling police investigative thinking: A study of police officers in Norway. *International Journal of the Sociology of Law, 34*(4), 221–228.
Deflem, M. (2002). *Policing world society: Historical foundations of international police cooperation*. Oxford University Press.
Deflem, M. (2004). Social control and the policing of terrorism: Foundations for a sociology of counterterrorism. *The American Sociologist, 35*(2), 75–92.
Deflem, M. (2006). Europol and the policing of international terrorism: Counter-terrorism in a global perspective. *Justice Quarterly, 23*(3), 336–359.
Deflem, M. (2010). *The policing of terrorism: Organizational and global perspectives*. Routledge.
Den Boer, M., & Bruggeman, W. (2007). Shifting gear: Europol in the contemporary policing era. *Politique Européenne, 23*, 77–91.
Deuchar, R., Crichlow, V. J., & Fallik, S. W. (2020). Cops in crisis?: Ethnographic insights on a new era of politicization, activism, accountability, and change in transatlantic policing. *Policing and Society, 30*(1), 47–64.

Dick, P. (2005). Dirty work designations: How police officers account for their use of coercive force. *Human Relations, 58*(11), 1363–1390.

Diderichsen, A. (2017). Renewal and Retraditionalisation:—The short and not very glorious history of the Danish Bachelor's degree in policing. *Nordisk Politiforskning, 4*(2), 149–169.

Diderichsen, A. (2020). McDonaldiseringen af dansk politi. *Dansk Sociologi, 31*(3), 7–29.

Diphoorn, T. G. (2015). *Twilight policing: Private security and violence in urban South Africa.* University of California Press.

Downes, D. (2016). Comparative criminology, globalization and the 'punitive turn'. In *Comparative criminal justice and globalization* (pp. 37–57). Routledge.

Drotbohm, H., & Hasselberg, I. (2015). Deportation, anxiety, justice: New ethnographic perspectives. *Journal of Ethnic and Migration Studies, 41*(4), 551–562.

Durkheim, E. (2014). *The division of labor in society.* Simon and Schuster.

Egbert, S., & Leese, M. (2021). *Criminal futures: Predictive policing and everyday police work.* Taylor & Francis.

Elholm, T. (2020). Country report Denmark. *Harmonisierung strafrechtlicher Sanktionen in der Europäischen Union, 2*, 97.

Emerson, R. M., Fretz, R. I., & Shaw, L. L. (2011). *Writing ethnographic fieldnotes.* University of Chicago Press.

Ericson, R. V. (1981). *Making crime: A study of detective work.* Butterworths.

Ericson, R. V., & Haggerty, K. D. (1997). *Policing the risk society.* Oxford University Press.

Ericson, R. V., & Haggerty, K. D. (2006). *The new politics of surveillance and visibility.* University of Toronto Press.

Ezra, M. (2007). The Eichmann polemics: Hannah Arendt and her critics. *Democratiya, 9*(3), 141–169.

Farber, D. (2021). *The war on drugs: A history.* NYU Press.

Farmer, P., Bourgois, P., Fassin, D., et al. (2004). An anthropology of structural violence. *Current Anthropology, 45*(3), 305–325.

Farrell, G., & Clark, K. (2004). What does the world spend on criminal justice? *HEUNI Paper No. 20—The European Institute for Crime Prevention and Control, affiliated with the United Nations.*

Fassin, D. (2013). *Enforcing order: An ethnography of urban policing.* Polity Press.

Fassin, D. (2015). *Instituttseminaret SAI: Didier Fassin 'Boredom: The temporality of policing and the politics of time'.* Retrieved January 29, 2017, from http://www.sv.uio.no/sai/forskning/aktuelt/arrangementer/instituttseminaret/2015/desember-02-fassing.html

Fassin, D. (2017a). Boredom: Accounting for the ordinary in the work of policing (France). In D. Fassin (Ed.), *Writing the world of policing: The difference ethnography makes* (pp. 269–292). University of Chicago Press.
Fassin, D. (2017b). The endurance of critique. *Anthropological Theory, 17*(1), 4–29.
Fassin, D. (2017c). *Writing the world of policing: The difference ethnography makes*. University of Chicago Press.
Fassin, D. (2018). *The will to punish*. Oxford University Press.
Fassin, D., Bouagga, Y., Coutant, I., et al. (2015). *At the heart of the state*. Pluto Press.
Feagin, J. (2013). *Systemic racism: A theory of oppression*. Routledge.
Feeley, M., & Simon, J. (1994). Actuarial justice: The emerging new criminal law. *The Futures of Criminology, 173*, 174.
Feldman, G. (2011). *The migration apparatus: Security, labor, and policymaking in the European Union*. Stanford University Press.
Feldman, G. (2016). 'With my head on the pillow': Sovereignty, ethics, and evil among undercover police investigators. *Comparative Studies in Society and History, 58*(02), 491–518.
Feldman, G. (2019). *The gray zone: Sovereignty, human smuggling, and undercover police investigation in Europe*. Stanford University Press.
Fielding, N. (1994). Cop canteen culture. In T. Newburn & E. Stanko (Eds.), *Just boys doing business* (pp. 46–63). Routledge.
Findlay, M. J. (2013). *Governing through globalised crime: Futures for international criminal justice*. Willan.
Fleming, J. (2018). How do the police respond to evidence-based policing? In R. A. W. Rhodes (Ed.), *Narrative policy analysis* (pp. 221–239). Springer.
Fleming, J., & Lafferty, G. (2000). New management techniques and restructuring for accountability in Australian police organisations. *Policing: An International Journal of Police Strategies & Management, 23*(2), 154–168.
Flyghed, J. (2002). Normalising the exceptional: The case of political violence. *Policing and Society, 13*(1), 23–41.
Foucault, M. (1977). *Discipline and punish: The birth of the prison*. Vintage.
Fox, R. (2001). Someone to watch over us: Back to the panopticon? *Criminology and Criminal Justice, 1*(3), 251–276.
Franko, K. (2017). Criminology, punishment, and the state in a globalized society. In A. Liebling, S. Maruna, & L. Mcara (Eds.), *The Oxford handbook of criminology* (pp. 353–372). Oxford University Press.
Franko, K. (2019a). *The Crimmigrant other: Migration and penal power*. Routledge.

Franko, K. (2019b). *Globalization and crime*. SAGE Publications Limited.

Franko, K. (2021). The two-sided spectacle at the border: Frontex, NGOs and the theatres of sovereignty. *Theoretical Criminology*. https://doi.org/10.1177/13624806211007858.

Franko, K., & Gundhus, H. I. (2015). A divided fraternity: Transnational police cultures, proximity, and loyalty. *European Journal of Policing Studies, 3*(2), 162–184.

Friesen, N., Feenberg, A., & Smith, G. (2009). Phenomenology and surveillance studies: Returning to the things themselves. *The Information Society, 25*(2), 84–90.

Friesen, N., Feenberg, A., Smith, G., et al. (2012). Experiencing surveillance. In A. Feenberg & N. Friesen (eds) *(Re)inventing the Internet* (pp. 73–84). Brill.

Fyfe, N., Gundhus, H. O., & Rønn, K. V. (2017). *Moral issues in intelligence-led policing*. Routledge.

Fyfe, N., & Richardson, N. (2018). Police reform, research and the uses of 'expert knowledge'. *European Journal of Policing Studies, 5*(3), 147–161.

Garbarino, S., Cuomo, G., Chiorri, C., et al. (2013). Association of work-related stress with mental health problems in a special police force unit. *BMJ Open, 3*(7).

Garland, D. (2000). The culture of high crime societies. *British Journal of Criminology, 40*(3), 347–375.

Garland, D. (2002). The culture of control. In *Crime and social order in contemporary society*. University of Chicago Press.

Giddens, A. (2011). *Runaway world*. Profile books.

Gill, M., & Hart, J. (1997). Exploring investigative policing: A study of private detectives in Britain. *The British journal of criminology, 37*(4), 549–567.

Goffman, E. (1957). Alienation from interaction. *Human relations, 10*, 47–60.

Goffman, E. (1961). *Encounters: Two Studies in the Sociology of Interaction*. Indianapolis: Bobbs-Merril.

Goldsmith, A. (2005). Police reform and the problem of trust. *Theoretical Criminology, 9*(4), 443–470.

Gordon, D. R. (1987). The electronic panopticon: A case study of the development of the National Criminal Records System. *Politics and Society, 15*(4), 483–511.

Guild, E., & Bigo, D. (2017). Policing at a distance: Schengen visa policies. *Controlling frontiers* (pp. 233–263). Routledge.

Gundhus, H. O. (2005). 'Catching' and 'targeting': Risk-based policing, local culture and gendered practices. *Journal of Scandinavian Studies in Criminology and Crime Prevention, 6*(2), 128–128.

Gundhus, H. O. (2013). Experience or knowledge? Perspectives on new knowledge regimes and control of police professionalism. *Policing: A Journal of Policy and Practice, 7*, 178–194. https://doi.org/10.1093/police/pas039

Gundhus, H. O., & Franko, K. (2016). Global policing and mobility: Identity, territory, Sovereignty. In B. Bradford, B. Jauregui, I. Loader, et al. (Eds.), *The SAGE handbook of global policing*. SAGE Publications.

Gundhus, H. O., Talberg, N., & Wathne, C. T. (2021). From discretion to standardization: Digitalization of the police organization. *International Journal of Police Science & Management*. https://doi.org/10.1177/14613557211036554

Hacker, R. L., & Horan, J. J. (2019). Policing people with mental illness: Experimental evaluation of online training to de-escalate mental health crises. *Journal of Experimental Criminology, 15*(4), 551–567.

Hækkerup, N. (2021). Retrieved September 27, from https://politiken.dk/debat/kroniken/art8325078/Jo-det-er-faktisk-rigtigt-mere-overvågning-giver-mere-frihed

Haggerty, K. D. (2006). Tear down the walls: On demolishing the panopticon. In D. Lyon (Ed.), *Theorizing surveillance* (pp. 37–59). Willan.

Haggerty, K. D., & Ericson, R. V. (2000). The surveillant assemblage. *The British Journal of Sociology, 51*(4), 605–622.

Haggerty, K. D., Wilson, D., & Smith, G. J. (2011). Theorizing surveillance in crime control. *Theoretical Criminology, 15*(3), 231–237.

Hall, S., Critcher, C., Jefferson, T., et al. (2013). *Policing the crisis: Mugging, the state and law and order*. Palgrave Macmillan.

Harkin, D. M. (2015). The police and punishment: Understanding the pains of policing. *Theoretical Criminology, 19*(1), 43–58.

Hartmann, M. R. K., Hestehave, N. K., Høgh, L., et al. (2018). Knowing from within. *Nordisk Politiforskning, 5*(01), 7–27.

Hartwig, M., Anders Granhag, P., & Vrij, A. (2005). Police interrogation from a social psychology perspective. *Policing and Society, 15*(4), 379–399.

Heine, J., & Thakur, R. (2011a). Introduction: Globalization and transnational uncivil society. In J. Heine & R. Thakur (Eds.), *The dark side of globalization* (pp. 1–16). United Nations University Press.

Heine, J., & Thakur, R. C. (2011b). *The dark side of globalization*. United Nations University Press.

Hestehave, N. K. (2013). *Proaktiv kriminalitetsbekæmpelse*. Samfundslitteratur.

Hestehave, N. K. (2017). Predicting crime?: On challenges to the police in becoming knowledgeable organizations 1. *Moral issues in intelligence-led policing* (pp. 62–80). Routledge.

Hobbs, D. (1988). *Doing the business: Entrepreneurship, the working class, and detectives in the east end of London.* Clarendon Press.

Højer, L., Kublitz, A., Puri, S. S., et al. (2018). Escalations: Theorizing sudden accelerating change. *Anthropological Theory, 18*(1), 36–58.

Holdaway, S., & O'Neill, M. (2006). Institutional racism after Macpherson: An analysis of police views. *Policing and Society, 16*(4), 349–369.

Holmberg, L. (1999). *Inden for lovens rammer.* Gyldendal.

Holmberg, L. (2000). Discretionary leniency and typological guilt: Results from a Danish study of police discretion. *Journal of Scandinavian Studies in Criminology and Crime Prevention, 1*(2), 179–194.

Holmberg, L. (2003). *Policing stereotypes: A qualitative study of police work in Denmark.* Galda & Wilch.

Holmberg, L. (2014). Nordisk politiforskning–udfordringer og muligheder. *Nordisk Politiforskning, 1*(01), 24–40.

Holmberg, L. (2015). Challenges to Nordic police research. In *The past, the present and the future of police research: Proceedings from the fifth Nordic police research seminar* (pp. 43–57). Scandinavian Research Council for Criminology.

Holmberg, L. (2019). Continuity and change in Scandinavian police reforms. *International Journal of Police Science & Management, 21*(4), 206–217.

Holmberg, L. (2021). Evaluations of police reforms: Utility or futility? *Policing: A Journal of Policy and Practice, 15*(1), 314–326.

Hornberger, J. (2011). *Policing and human rights: The meaning of violence and justice in the everyday policing of Johannesburg.* Routledge.

Hörnqvist, M. (2010). *Risk, power and the state: After Foucault.* Routledge.

Hörnqvist, M., & Flyghed, J. (2012). Exclusion or culture? The rise and the ambiguity of the radicalisation debate. *Critical Studies on Terrorism, 5*(3), 319–334.

Houborg, E., Søgaard, T. F., & Mogensen, S. A. I. (2020). Making up a new drug user from depenalization to repenalisation of drug users in Denmark. *International Journal of Drug Policy, 80,* 102660.

Hough, M. (2010). *Policing, new public management and legitimacy. The new public leadership challenge* (pp. 70–84). Springer.

Hughes, E. C. (1962). Good people and dirty work. *Social Problems, 10*(1), 3–11.

Hunt, J. (1984). The development of rapport through the negotiation of gender in field work among police. *Human Organization, 43*(4), 283–296.

Innes, M. (2003). *Investigating murder: Detective work and the police response to criminal homicide.* Oxford University Press.

Jauregui, B. (2013). Dirty anthropology: Epistemologies of violence and ethical entanglements in police ethnography. In W. Garriott (Ed.), *Policing and contemporary governance* (pp. 125–153). Springer.

Jauregui, B. (2016). *Provisional authority: Police, order, and security in India.* University of Chicago Press.

Jauregui, B. (2022). Police worker politics in India, brasil, and beyond. *Policing and Society, 32*(3), 271–290.

Joh, E. E. (2016). The new surveillance discretion: Automated suspicion, big data, and policing. *Harvard Law & Policy Review, 10*, 15.

Jones, D. J. (2020). The potential impacts of pandemic policing on police legitimacy: Planning past the COVID-19 crisis. *Policing: A Journal of Policy and Practice, 14*(3), 579–586.

Jones, T., & Newburn, T. (2002). The transformation of policing? Understanding current trends in policing systems. *British Journal of Criminology, 42*(1), 129–146.

Jones, T., & Newburn, T. (2006). *Plural policing: A comparative perspective.* Psychology Press.

Juris, J. S. (2005). The new digital media and activist networking within anti-corporate globalization movements. *The Annals of the American Academy of Political and Social Science, 597*(1), 189–208.

Justitsministeriet. (2016). *Danskerne har stor tillid til politi og domstole.* Retrieved February 1, from http://www.justitsministeriet.dk/nyt-og-presse/pressemeddelelser/2016/danskerne-har-stor-tillid-til-politi-og-domstole

Kahn, W. A. (1990). Psychological conditions of personal engagement and disengagement at work. *Academy of Management Journal, 33*(4), 692–724.

Kammersgaard, T., Søgaard, T. F., Haller, M. B., et al. (2021). Community policing in Danish 'ghetto' areas: Trust and distrust between the police and ethnic minority youth. *Criminology & Criminal Justice.* https://doi.org/10.1177/17488958211017390

Kammersgaard, T., Søgaard, T. F., Kolind, T., et al. (2022). 'Most officers are more or less colorblind': Police officers' reflections on the role of race and ethnicity in policing. *Race and Justice.* https://doi.org/10.1177/21533687221127445

Karpiak, K. G., & Garriott, W. (2018). *The anthropology of police.* Routledge.

Keith, M. (1993). *Race, riots and policing: Lore and disorder in a multi-racist society.* Ucl Press.

Kildegaard, K., & Dandanell, F. (2019). *Mette Frederiksen bebuder massivt øget overvågning i kampen mod kriminelle: 'Vores samfundsmodel er på spil'.*

Retrieved September 27, from https://www.berlingske.dk/politik/mette-frederiksen-bebuder-massivt-oeget-overvaagning-i-kampen-mod

Kingshott, B., & Prinsloo, J. (2004). The universality of the 'police canteen culture'. *Acta Criminologica, 17*(1), 1–16.

Klockars, C. B. (1980). The dirty Harry problem. *The Annals of the American Academy of Political and Social Science, 452*(1), 33–47.

Kraska, P. B. (1996). Enjoying militarism: Political/personal dilemmas in studying US police paramilitary units. *Justice Quarterly, 13*(3), 405–429.

Kraska, P. B. (2007). Militarization and policing—Its relevance to 21st century police. *Policing, 1*(4), 501–513.

Kruger, E., & Haggerty, K. D. (2006). Review essay: Intelligence exchange in policing and security. *Policing and Society, 16*(1), 86–91.

Kruize, P. (2016). *Omrejsende kriminelle i Danmark*. Det Juridiske Fakultet, Københavns Universitet.

Kruize, P., & Sorensen, D. W. M. (2017). *Det danske indbrudsniveau*. Det Kriminalpræventive Råd.

Kublitz, A. (2021). Omar is dead: Aphasia and the escalating anti-radicalization business. *History and Anthropology, 32*(1), 64–77.

Kyprianides, A., Bradford, B., Beale, M., et al. (2022). Policing the COVID-19 pandemic: Police officer well-being and commitment to democratic modes of policing. *Policing and Society, 32*(4), 504–521.

Laage-Thomsen, J., & Frandsen, S. L. (2022). Pandemic preparedness systems and diverging COVID-19 responses within similar public health regimes: A comparative study of expert perceptions of pandemic response in Denmark, Norway, and Sweden. *Globalization and Health, 18*(1), 1–18.

Larsson, P. (2006). International police co-operation: A Norwegian perspective. *Journal of Financial Crime, 13*(4), 456–466.

Laursen, R. T., & Rasmussen, A. K. (2021). *Det gale politiarbejde*. University of Copenhagen.

Lemieux, F. (2013). *International police cooperation: Emerging issues, theory and practice*. Routledge.

Lindberg, A. (2022). Feeling difference: Race, migration, and the affective infrastructure of a Danish detention camp. *Incarceration, 3*(1). https://doi.org/10.1177/26326663221084590

Linnemann, T., Wall, T., & Green, E. (2014). The walking dead and killing state: Zombification and the normalization of police violence. *Theoretical Criminology, 18*(4), 506–527.

Lipsky, M. (2010). *Street-level bureaucracy: Dilemmas of the individual in public service*. Russell Sage Foundation.

Loader, I. (2000). Plural policing and democratic governance. *Social & Legal Studies, 9*(3), 323–345.

Loader, I., & Mulcahy, A. (2003). *Policing and the condition of England: Memory, politics and culture.* Oxford University Press.

Loftus, B. (2009). *Police culture in a changing world.* Oxford University Press.

Loftus, B. (2010). Police occupational culture: Classic themes, altered times. *Policing and Society, 20*(1), 1–20.

Loftus, B. (2019a). Normalizing covert surveillance: The subterranean world of policing. *The British Journal of Sociology, 70*(5), 2070–2091.

Loftus, B., & Goold, B. (2012). Covert surveillance and the invisibilities of policing. *Criminology & Criminal Justice, 12*(3), 275–288.

Loftus, B., Goold, B., & Mac Giollabhui, S. (2015). From a visible spectacle to an invisible presence: The working culture of covert policing. *British Journal of Criminology, 56*(4), 629–645.

Lohne, K. (2020). Penal humanitarianism beyond the nation state: An analysis of international criminal justice. *Theoretical Criminology, 24*(2), 145–162.

Lyon, D. (1994). *The electronic eye: The rise of surveillance society.* University of Minnesota Press.

Lyon, D. (2003). *Surveillance after September 11.* Polity.

Lyon, D. (2007). *Surveillance studies: An overview.* Polity.

Lyon, D. (2018). *The culture of surveillance: Watching as a way of life.* John Wiley & Sons.

Lyon, D. (2019). Surveillance capitalism, surveillance culture and data politics 1. In *Data politics* (pp. 64–77). Routledge.

Madianou, M., & Miller, D. (2013). *Migration and new media: Transnational families and polymedia.* Routledge.

Maguire, M. (2000). Policing by risks and targets: Some dimensions and implications of intelligence-led crime control. *Policing and Society: An International Journal, 9*(4), 315–336.

Maguire, M., Frois, C., & Zurawski, N. (2014). *Anthropology of security: Perspectives from the frontline of policing, counter-terrorism and border control.* Pluto Press.

Manning, P. (2006). Detective work/culture. *Encyclopedia of Police Science, 2*, 390–397.

Manning, P. K. (1977). *Police work: The social organization of policing.* MIT Press.

Manning, P. K. (1978). The police: Mandate, strategies, and appearances. In P. Manning (Ed.), *Policing: A view from the street* (pp. 7–31). Goodyear Publishing Company.

Manning, P. K. (2001). Theorizing policing: The drama and myth of crime control in the NYPD. *Theoretical Criminology, 5*(3), 315–344.

Manning, P. K. (2008). *The technology of policing: Crime mapping, information technology, and the rationality of crime control.* New York University Press.

Manning, P. K. (2010). *Policing contingencies.* University of Chicago Press.

Manning, P. K. (2012). Drama, the police and the sacred. In T. Newburn & J. Peay (Eds.), *Policing: Politics, culture and control: Essays in honour of Robert Reiner* (pp. 173–193). Hart.

Marmo, M., & Chazal, N. (2016). *Transnational crime and criminal justice.* SAGE.

Martin, J. T. (2018). Police culture: What it is, what it does, and what we should do with it. In *The anthropology of police* (pp. 34–53). Taylor and Francis.

Martin, J. T. (2019). *Sentiment, reason, and law: Policing in the republic of China on Taiwan.* Cornell University Press.

Marx, G. T. (1988). *Undercover: Police surveillance in America.* University of California Press.

Marx K, and Engels F (2011) Capital (volume 1: A critique of political economy).

Mastrofski, S. D. (2004). Controlling street-level police discretion. *The Annals of the American Academy of Political and Social Science, 593*(1), 100–118.

Mathiesen, T. (1997). The viewer society Michel Foucault's panopticon' revisited. *Theoretical Criminology, 1*(2), 215–234.

Mathiesen, T. (2008). Lex Vigilatoria: Global control without a state? *Surveillance and Governance: Crime Control and Beyond, 10,* 101–127.

Mathiesen, T. (2013). *Towards a surveillant society: The rise of surveillance Systems in Europe.* Waterside Press.

Mawby, R. (2013). *Policing images.* Willan.

Mawby, R. C. (2014). The presentation of police in everyday life: Police–press relations, impression management and the Leveson inquiry. *Crime, Media, Culture, 10*(3), 239–257.

McCahill, M., & Norris, C. (1999). Watching the workers: Crime, CCTV and the workplace. In *Invisible crimes* (pp. 208–231). Springer.

McCulloch, J. (2001). *Blue army: Paramilitary policing in Australia.* Melbourne University Publish.

McCulloch, J. (2004). Blue armies, khaki police and the cavalry on the new American frontier: Critical criminology for the 21st century. *Critical Criminology, 12*(3), 309–326.

McCulloch, J., & Pickering, S. (2009). Pre-crime and counter-terrorism imagining future crime in the 'war on terror'. *British Journal of Criminology, 49*(5), 628–645.

McDaniel, J. L. (2019). Reconciling mental health, public policing and police accountability. *The Police Journal, 92*(1), 72–94.

McLaughlin, E., & Levi, M. (1995). The end of public policing? Police reform and the 'new managerialism'. In Noakes, Lesleyand Maguire, Mike (Eds.), *Contemporary Issues in Criminology*. Cardiff, GB: Cardiff University Press.

McWilliam, E. (1999). *Pedagogical pleasures*. P. Lang.

Melossi, D. (2015). *Crime, punishment and migration*. SAGE Publications Ltd.

Mikkelsen, L. (2018). Konkret eller abstrakt politiarbejde? *Nordisk Politiforskning, 5*(01), 28–49.

Miller, H. T. (2012). *Governing narratives: Symbolic politics and policy change*. University of Alabama Press.

Minkkommissionen. (2022). Retrieved September 27, from https://www.minkkommissionen.dk/da/nyheder/2022/06/beretningen

Molland, S., Andersson, R., Baas, M., et al. (2018). Coproduction of sedentary and Mobile optics. *Current Anthropology, 59*(2), 115–137.

Monahan, T. (2011). Surveillance as cultural practice. *The Sociological Quarterly, 52*(4), 495–508.

Morgan, G., & Poynting, S. (2016). *Global islamophobia: Muslims and moral panic in the west*. Routledge.

Mueller, J. E., & Stewart, M. G. (2016). *Chasing ghosts: The policing of terrorism*. Oxford University Press.

Muir, W. K. (1979). *Police: Streetcorner politicians*. University of Chicago Press.

Murray, J. (2005). Policing terrorism: A threat to community policing or just a shift in priorities? *Police Practice and Research, 6*(4), 347–361.

Mutsaers, P. (2019). *Police unlimited: Policing, migrants, and the values of bureaucracy*. Oxford University Press.

Mythen, G., & Walklate, S. (2006a). Communicating the terrorist risk: Harnessing a culture of fear? *Crime, Media, Culture, 2*(2), 123–142.

Mythen, G., & Walklate, S. (2006b). Criminology and terrorism. *British Journal of Criminology, 46*(3), 379–398.

Nadelmann, E. A. (2010). *Cops across borders: The internationalization of US criminal law enforcement*. Penn State Press.

Newburn, T., & Jones, T. (2005). Symbolic politics and penal populism: The long shadow of Willie Horton. *Crime, Media, Culture, 1*(1), 72–87.

Newburn, T., & Stanko, E. A. (1994). *Just boys doing business?* Routledge.

Ogloff, J. R., Thomas, S. D., Luebbers, S., et al. (2013). Policing services with mentally ill people: Developing greater understanding and best practice. *Australian Psychologist, 48*(1), 57–68.

Olwig, K. F., Grünenberg, K., Møhl, P., et al. (2019). *The biometric border world: Technology, bodies and identities on the move*. Routledge.

Pakes, F. (2012). *Globalisation and the challenge to criminology*. Routledge.

Pickering, S. (2004). Border terror: Policing, forced migration and terrorism. *Global Change, Peace & Security, 16*(3), 211–226.

Pickering, S., Bosworth, M., & Aas, K. F. (2015). The criminology of mobility. In S. Pickering & J. Ham (Eds.), *The Routledge handbook on crime and international migration*. Routledge.

Pickering, S., McCulloch, J., & Wright-Neville, D. (2008). Counter-terrorism policing. In *Counter-terrorism policing* (pp. 91–111). Springer.

Politiforbundet. (2020). *Leder: Fjern det politiske pres på politiet*. Retrieved September 27, from https://politiforbundet.dk/nyheder/leder-fjern-politiske-pres-paa-politiet

Pratt, J., & Eriksson, A. (2014). *Contrasts in punishment: An explanation of anglophone excess and Nordic exceptionalism*. Routledge.

Punch, M. (1979). Observation and the police: The research experience. In *Policing the inner city* (pp. 1–18). Springer.

Punch, M. (1989). Researching police deviance: A personal encounter with the limitations and liabilities of field-work. *The British Journal of Sociology, 40*(2), 177–204.

Queirós, C., Passos, F., Bártolo, A., et al. (2020). Burnout and stress measurement in police officers: Literature review and a study with the operational police stress questionnaire. *Frontiers in Psychology, 11*, 587.

Ralph, L. (2020a). To protect and to serve: Global lessons in police reform. *Foreign Affairs, 99*, 196.

Ralph, L. (2020b). *The torture letters: Reckoning with police violence*. University of Chicago Press.

Ratcliffe, J. (2016a). *Intelligence-led policing*. Routledge.

Reiner, R. (1995). Policing by numbers: The feel-good fallacy. *Policing Today, 1*(3), 22–24.

Reiner, R. (2000). Romantic realism: Policing and the media. *Core issues in Policing, 2*, 52–66.

Reiner, R. (2010). *The politics of the police*. Oxford University Press.

Reiner, R., & Newburn, R. (2007). Police research. In R. King & E. Wincup (Eds.), *Doing research on crime and justice*. Oxford University Press.

Reuss-Ianni, E. (1993). *Two cultures of policing: Street cops and management cops*. Transaction Publishers.

Robinson, W. I. (2020). *The global police state*. JSTOR.

Rose, N. (2006). Governing 'advanced' liberal democracies. In A. Sharma & A. Gupta (Eds.), *The anthropology of the state: A reader*. Hoboken, New Jersey.

Ross, J. E. (2004). Impediments to transnational cooperation in undercover policing: A comparative study of the United States and Italy. *The American Journal of Comparative Law, 52*(3), 569–623.

Ross, J. E. (2007). The place of covert surveillance in democratic societies: A comparative study of the United States and Germany. *The American Journal of Comparative Law, 55*(3), 493–579.

Rottenburg, R., Merry, S. E., Park, S.-J., et al. (2015). *The world of indicators: The making of governmental knowledge through quantification*. Cambridge University Press.

Rowe, M. (2012). *Policing, race and racism*. Routledge.

Ruggiero, V. (2013). Organised and transnational crime in Europe. In S. Body-Gendrot, M. Hough, K. Kerezsi, R. Lévy, & S. Snacken (Eds.), *The Routledge handbook of European criminology* (pp. 154–168). Routledge.

Rytter, M., & Pedersen, M. H. (2014). A decade of suspicion: Islam and Muslims in Denmark after 9/11. *Ethnic and Racial Studies, 37*(13), 2303–2321.

Sadiq, M. (2022). Policing in pandemic: Is perception of workload causing work–family conflict, job dissatisfaction and job stress? *Journal of Public Affairs, 22*(2), e2486.

Safjański, T., & James, A. (2020). Europol's crime analysis system—Practical determinants of its success. *Policing: A Journal of Policy and Practice, 14*(2), 469–478.

San, S. (2022). Transnational policing between national political regimes and human rights norms: The case of the Interpol red notice system. *Theoretical Criminology*. https://doi.org/10.1177/13624806221105280

Sausdal, D. (2014a). Cultural Culprits. *Crisis and Migration: Implications of the Eurozone crisis for perceptions, politics, and policies of migration*. 177.

Sausdal, D. (2014b). Cultural culprits: Police apprehensions of pickpockets in Copenhagen. In B. Petterson & P. Bevelander (Eds.), *Crisis and migration: Implications of the eurozone crisis for perceptions, politics, and policies of migration*. Nordic Academic Press.

Sausdal, D. (2018). Pleasures of policing: An additional analysis of xenophobia. *Theoretical Criminology, 22*(2), 226–242.

Sausdal, D. (2020a). Everyday policing: Toward a greater analytical appreciation of the ordinary in police research. *Policing and Society, 31*, 1–14. https://doi.org/10.1080/10439463.2020.1798955

Sausdal, D. (2020b). On the Workaday Origin of Police Callousness. *Exertions*. https://doi.org/10.21428/1d6be30e.8d8aeb1d

Sausdal, D. (2020c). Police bullshit. *Journal of Extreme Anthropology*, 4(1), 94–115.

Sausdal, D. (2021a). A fighting fetish: On transnational police and their warlike presentation of self. *Theoretical Criminology*. https://doi.org/10.1177/13624806211009487

Sausdal, D. (2021b). *Looking beyond the police-as-control narrative*. In Katarina Jacobsson & Jaber F. Gubrium (eds). Policy Press.

Sausdal, D. B. (2022). A cult(ure) of intelligence-led policing: On the international campaigning and convictions of Danish policing. In Mikkel Jarle Christensen, Kjersti Lohne & Magnus Hörnqvist (Eds.), *Nordic Criminal Justice in a Global Context* (pp. 111–127). Routledge.

Sausdal, D. (2023). A collaborator? Ethnographic issues of police and peer suspicion. In Fleming, J & Charman. S (Eds.), *Routledge International Handbook of Police Ethnography*. Abingdon, Oxon: Routledge.

Sausdal, D. (2023). Dirty Harry gone global? On globalizing policing and punitive impotence. In J. Beek, T. Bierschenk, A. Kolloch, & B. Meyer (Eds.), *Policing race, ethnicity and culture: Ethnographic perspectives across Europe*. Manchester University Press.

Sausdal, D., & Lohne, K. (2021). *Theatrics of transnational criminal justice: Ethnographies of penality in a global age*. SAGE Publications Sage UK.

Schinkel, W. (2011). Prepression: The actuarial archive and new technologies of security. *Theoretical criminology*, 15, 365–380. https://doi.org/10.1177/1362480610395366

Schuilenburg, M. (2017). *The securitization of society: Crime, risk, and social order*. New York University Press.

Shammas, V. L. (2016). The rise of a more punitive state: On the attenuation of Norwegian penal exceptionalism in an era of welfare state transformation. *Critical Criminology*, 24(1), 57–74.

Sheptycki, J. (2000). *Issues in transnational policing*. Routledge.

Sheptycki, J. (2002). *In search of transnational policing: Towards a sociology of global policing*. Ashgate.

Sheptycki, J. (2004a). The accountability of transnational policing institutions: The strange case of Interpol. *Canadian Journal of Law and Society*, 19, 107.

Sheptycki, J. (2004b). Organizational pathologies in police intelligence systems: Some contributions to the lexicon of intelligence-led policing. *European journal of criminology*, 1(3), 307–332.

Sheptycki, J. (2005). Transnational policing. *The Canadian Review of Policing Research*. https://crpr.icaap.org/index.php/crpr/article/view/31/48

Sheptycki, J. (2007). The constabulary ethic and the transnational condition. In *Crafting transnational policing. Police capacity-building and global policing reform* (pp. 31–71). Hart Publishing.

Sheptycki, J. (2017). *Transnational crime and policing: Selected essays*. Routledge.

Sheptycki, J. (2018). Transnational organization, transnational law and the ambiguity of Interpol in a world ruled with law. In M. J. Christensen & N. Boister (Eds.), *New perspectives on the structure of transnational criminal justice* (pp. 65–86). Leiden.

Siegel, D. (2014). *Mobile banditry: East and central European itinerant criminal groups in the Netherlands*. Eleven International Publishing.

Simmel, G. (2012). The metropolis and mental life. In *The urban sociology reader* (pp. 37–45). Routledge.

Simon, J. (2007). *Governing through crime: How the war on crime transformed American democracy and created a culture of fear*. Oxford University Press.

Skogan, W. G., & Antunes, G. E. (1979). Information, apprehension, and deterrence: Exploring the limits of police productivity. *Journal of Criminal Justice, 7*(3), 217–241.

Skolnick, J. H. (1982). Deception by police. *Criminal Justice Ethics, 1*(2), 40–54.

Smith, G. J. D. (2009). Empowered watchers or disempowered workers. In K. F. Aas, H. O. Gundhus, & H. M. Lomell (Eds.), *Technologies of InSecurity: The surveillance of everyday life*. Routledge-Cavendish.

Smith, P. S. (2012). A critical look at Scandinavian exceptionalism. In T. Ugelvik & J. Dullum (Eds.), *Penal exceptionalism* (pp. 38–57). Routledge.

Søgaard, T. F., Kolind, T., Haller, M. B., Kammersgaard, T., & Hunt, G. (2022). 'Filming is our only weapon against the police': Ethnic minorities and police encounters in the new visibility era. *The British Journal of Criminology*, azac056. https://doi.org/10.1093/bjc/azac056

Solhjell, R., Saarikkomäki, E., Haller, M. B., et al. (2019). 'We are seen as a threat': Police stops of young ethnic minorities in the Nordic countries. *Critical Criminology, 27*(2), 347–361.

Sollund, R. (2007). Canteen banter or racism: Is there a relationship between Oslo Police's use of derogatory terms and their attitudes and conduct towards ethnic minorities? *Journal of Scandinavian Studies in Criminology and Crime Prevention, 8*(1), 77–96.

Stalcup, M. (2013). Interpol and the emergence of global policing. In W. Garriott (Ed.), *Policing and contemporary governance* (pp. 231–261). New York, NY.

Stumpf, J. P. (2006). The crimmigration crisis: Immigrants, crime, and sovereign power. *American University Law Review, 56*, 367.

Stuntz, W. J. (2002). Local policing after the terror. *The Yale Law Journal, 111*(8), 2137–2194.

Sykes, G. (1986). Street justice: A moral defense of order maintenance policing. *Justice Quarterly, 3*(4), 497–512.

Terpstra, J. (2020). Police reform as institutional change: Symbols and dilemmas. *International Journal of Law, Crime and Justice, 60*, 100359.

Terpstra, J., & Trommel, W. (2009). Police, managerialization and presentational strategies. *Policing: An International Journal, 32*(1), 128–143. https://doi.org/10.1108/13639510910937157

Tham, H. (1995). Drug control as a national project: The case of Sweden. *Journal of Drug Issues, 25*(1), 113–128.

Tham, H. (2001). Law and order as a leftist project? The case of Sweden. *Punishment & Society, 3*(3), 409–426.

UNODC. (2010). *The globalization of crime: A transnational organized crime threat assessment*. United Nations Office on Drugs and Crime.

van Hulst, M. (2013). Storytelling at the Police Station the canteen culture revisited. *British Journal of Criminology, 53*(4), 624–642.

van Kersbergen, K., & Vis, B. (2022). Digitalization as a policy response to social acceleration: Comparing democratic problem solving in Denmark and the Netherlands. *Government Information Quarterly, 39*(3), 101707.

Van Maanen, J. (1973). Working the street; a developmental view of police behavior. *Working paper. Sloan Working Papers*. Sloan School of Management, MIT.

Van Maanen, J. (1978a). The asshole. In P. K. Manning & J. Van Maanen (Eds.), *Policing: A view from the street* (pp. 221–238). Goodyear Publishing.

Van Maanen, J. (1978b). On watching the watchers. In P. K. Manning & J. Van Maanen (Eds.), *Policing: A view from the street* (pp. 309–309). Goodyear Publishing.

Van Maanen, J., & Kolb, D. (1982). *The professional apprentice: Observations on fieldwork roles in two organizational settings*. MIT. https://dspace.mit.edu/bitstream/handle/1721.1/2015/SWP-1323-15473323.pdf?sequence=1&isAllowed=y

Van Schendel, W., & Abraham, I. (2005). *Illicit flows and criminal things: States, borders, and the other side of globalization*. Indiana University Press.

Vigh, H. (2018). Lives opposed: Perceptivity and tacticality in conflict and crime. *Social Anthropology, 26*(4), 487–501.

Vigh, H., & Sausdal, D. (2021). *Global crime ethnographies: Three suggestions for a criminology that truly travels* (p. 171). Oxford University Press.

Vitale, A. S. (2017). *The end of policing*. Verso Books.

Von Lampe, K. (2012). Transnational organized crime challenges for future research. *Crime, Law and Social Change, 58*(2), 179–194.

Wacquant, L. (1999). Suitable enemies. *Punishment and Society, 1*(2), 215–222.

Waddington, P. A. J. (1999). Discretion, 'respectability' and institutional police racism. *Sociological Research Online, 4*(1), 175–183. https://doi.org/10.5153/sro.243

Waddington, P. A. (1999b). Police (canteen) sub-culture. An appreciation. *British Journal of Criminology, 39*(2), 287–309.

Wadds, P. (2019). 'It's not like it used to be': Respect and nostalgia in the policing of nightlife. *Australian & New Zealand Journal of Criminology, 52*(2), 213–230.

Walby, K., & Monaghan, J. (2011). Private eyes and public order: Policing and surveillance in the suppression of animal rights activists in Canada. *Social Movement Studies, 10*(01), 21–37.

Walklate, S. (2006). *Imagining the victim of crime*. Open University Press.

Wall, T., & Monahan, T. (2011). Surveillance and violence from afar: The politics of drones and liminal security-scapes. *Theoretical Criminology, 15*(3), 239–254.

Walsh, J. P. (2020). Social media and border security: Twitter use by migration policing agencies. *Policing and Society, 30*(10), 1138–1156.

Weber, L. (2013). *Policing non-citizens*. Routledge.

Weber, L., & Bowling, B. (2013). *Stop and search: Police power in global context*. Routledge.

Weber, M., Owen, D. S., & Strong, T. B. (2004). *The vocation lectures*. Hackett Publishing.

Westley, W. A. (1970). *Violence and the police: A sociological study of law, custom, and morality*. MIT Press.

Westmarland, L. (2001). Blowing the whistle on police violence. Gender, ethnography and ethics. *British Journal of Criminology, 41*(3), 523–535.

Westmarland, L. (2008). Police cultures. *Handbook of policing, 2*, 253–281.

Westmarland, L. (2015). Outsiders inside: Ethnography and police culture. In *Introduction to policing research* (pp. 163–173). Routledge.

White, C., & Weisburd, D. (2018). A co-responder model for policing mental health problems at crime hot spots: Findings from a pilot project. *Policing: A Journal of Policy and Practice, 12*(2), 194–209.

Wilson, D., & Sutton, A. (2003). *Open-street CCTV in Australia*. Australian Institute of Criminology Canberra.

Wuestewald, T., & Steinheider, B. (2009). Practitioner–researcher collaboration in policing: A case of close encounters? *Policing: A Journal of Policy and Practice, 4*(2), 104–111.

Yakhlef, S. (2018). *United agents: Community of practice within border policing in the Baltic Sea area*. Lund University.

Young, M. M., Bullock, J. B., & Lecy, J. D. (2019). Artificial discretion as a tool of governance: A framework for understanding the impact of artificial intelligence on public administration. *Perspectives on Public Management and Governance, 2*(4), 301–313.

Zedner, L. (2007). Pre-crime and post-criminology? *Theoretical Criminology, 11*(2), 261–281.

Zuboff, S. (2019). *The age of surveillance capitalism: The fight for a human future at the new frontier of power*. Profile Books.

Index

A
Aas, K. Franko, 3, 32, 128, 130
Academia, 4, 9, 10, 115, 162, 163, 181, 182, 184, 196, 208, 218
Accountability, 16, 102, 210
Adiaphorization, 131, 132
Aliverti, A., 3, 27, 32, 65, 126, 162, 170
Anthropology, 51, 54, 128, 132, 146, 149, 177, 205
Arendt, H., 128, 146
Assemblage, 64, 65
Assholes, 46, 88, 129, 139, 142

B
Bacon, M., 8, 10, 80, 114
Balvig, F., 155, 163, 165, 167, 196
Banter, 10, 12, 51, 195
Banton, M., 30, 33, 55, 166
Bauman, Z., 131

Bayley, D., 17, 44, 197
Beck, U., 169, 183
Becker, H., 32, 163, 170
Bigo, D., 16, 64, 128, 134
Bittner, E., 44, 160, 166, 201, 212
Björk, M., 4, 50, 51, 145, 149, 166
Blaustein, J., 3
Borders, 1, 4, 5, 7, 8, 13, 15, 52, 53, 61–64, 67, 70, 75, 76, 79, 84–86, 89, 90, 96, 100, 101, 112, 115, 127–129, 133, 138, 142, 144, 156, 157, 161, 172, 174–176, 179, 181, 185, 198, 209, 210
Bosworth, M., 30, 32, 165
Bowling, B., 2, 3, 8, 11, 14, 26, 27, 30, 32, 62, 97, 100, 102, 119, 128, 166, 196, 197, 210
Brodeur, J.-P., 64, 101, 103
Burglary, 5, 7, 27, 53, 107, 111, 174, 176

C

Canteen culture, 8, 51, 202
Chan, J., 11, 25, 166
Charman, S., 12
Christie, N., 32
Collins, R., 16, 128
Complaining, 11–13, 29, 33, 37, 74, 91, 125, 159, 175, 193–196, 198, 201, 207, 210, 217, 220
Concern, 2, 8, 11–14, 16, 17, 28, 63, 65, 82, 96, 125, 131, 133, 148, 150, 178, 179, 184, 195, 198, 209, 211, 218–220
Conservative, 11, 12, 17, 25, 81, 115, 156, 160, 162, 167–170, 198, 201, 203
Control, 4, 7, 28, 47, 64, 65, 67, 77, 101, 108, 132, 134, 147, 149, 156, 157, 165, 168, 169, 171–175, 177, 179, 181, 183–185, 196, 210–212, 221
Covert, 5, 65, 101, 129, 133, 134, 137
Criminology, 2, 16, 17, 32, 64, 90, 99–101, 104, 120, 130, 157, 159, 163, 166, 174, 183, 211
Crimmigration, 32, 156, 174
Crisis, 17, 31, 113, 114, 197
Cross-border crime, 4, 6, 13, 15, 52, 75, 80, 84, 85, 96
Cynicism, 16–18, 31, 50, 51, 125–150, 208, 211

D

Data double, 65, 132, 210
Deflem, M., 3, 14, 96, 104, 105, 119
Detective culture, 80, 110, 209
Diderichsen, A., 115, 167

Discourse, 18, 53, 63, 66, 67, 89, 100, 104, 119, 120, 147, 155, 170, 183, 209, 218
Discretion, 6, 15, 31, 69, 81, 90, 146–148, 196, 207, 220, 221
Discrimination, 25, 30, 31, 66, 101, 105, 128, 147, 220
Disillusion, 10, 11, 18, 194, 195
Displeasure, 14, 34, 36, 41, 62
Distance, 16, 127–136, 141, 143–145, 147–149, 199, 200, 205, 208, 210, 211, 221
Distrust/mistrust, 7, 68, 72, 73, 77, 165, 197
Durkheim, E., 130

E

Ericson, R., 8, 64–66, 80, 101, 102, 132, 133, 183
Ethnicity, 6, 30–32, 46, 53, 100, 167, 168, 207
Ethnography, 9, 15, 88, 96, 97, 149, 166, 195
Eurojust, 7, 63, 76, 139
Europol, 3, 7, 61, 63, 72–74, 76–78, 139
Everyday life, 10–14, 17, 18, 30, 34, 50, 51, 61, 63, 67, 69, 72, 74, 86, 89, 90, 96, 97, 104, 105, 113, 132, 133, 147, 149, 158, 164, 174, 195, 204–209, 222

F

Fassin, D., 18, 25, 33, 34, 125–130, 135, 137, 147, 149, 162, 165, 170, 172, 202, 203

Fear, 17, 31, 32, 38, 39, 71, 97, 99–101, 105, 109, 113, 117, 128, 165, 171, 184, 209, 219
Feldman, G., 3, 8, 14, 26, 67, 80, 127, 130, 134, 136, 143, 145, 146
Fleming, J., 69, 163
Flyghed, J., 32, 99, 101
Foreigners, 4, 6, 7, 11, 15, 25, 27, 28, 30, 31, 33, 36–41, 44–47, 50, 51, 53–55, 62, 72, 81, 86, 100, 126, 127, 129, 138, 143, 144, 173, 179, 208, 219
Foucault, M., 132
Franko, K., 3, 32, 65, 67–69, 130, 156, 165, 174, 177, 195, 210
Friesen, N., 63, 67
Frontex, 3, 7, 67
Frustration, 11, 13, 15, 17, 28, 33, 36–38, 42, 43, 54, 73, 85, 88, 109, 111, 112, 114, 117, 125, 126, 143, 150, 155, 170, 172, 174, 175, 194, 195, 208, 209, 218
Fun, 2, 13, 27, 28, 33, 35, 40, 52–54, 112, 142, 143, 161, 162, 195, 208
Future policing, 5, 65, 70, 71, 85, 127, 129, 155, 197, 199, 219, 220

Garland, D., 165, 182
Giddens, A., 212
Globalization, 2, 11, 14, 18, 28, 62, 68, 90, 96, 100, 157, 197, 209, 212, 217, 219

Globalization of local policing, 2, 3, 5, 7, 11, 13–15, 17, 18, 25, 28, 55, 61, 63, 69, 81, 86, 90, 104, 120, 125, 128, 155, 176, 197, 198, 208, 210, 211, 217, 219–222
Gratification, 15, 33–36, 39, 47, 54, 81, 208–210, 219, 222
Gundhus, H. O., 3, 32, 67–69, 80, 81, 177

Haggerty, K., 64–66, 69, 101, 102, 132, 133, 177, 183, 197
Hayward, K., 98, 105, 119
Holmberg, L., 4, 11, 15, 25, 31, 156, 166, 172, 196, 220
Hörnqvist, M., 183
Human condition, 50, 128, 211

Identity, 17, 126, 197, 205
Information technology, 5, 40, 65, 69, 70, 72, 81, 131, 132, 136, 208
Intelligence-led policing, 52, 62, 65, 69, 70, 73, 74, 79, 82–84, 89, 115, 136–139, 143, 208
International collaboration/cooperation, 3, 5, 16, 62, 64, 68, 76, 87, 90, 96, 196, 208
Interpol, 3, 7, 63
Interpreter, 6, 29, 42, 44, 46, 47, 50, 104, 142, 144
Interrogations, 29, 35, 40–43, 45, 46, 80, 107, 193

J

Jargon, 12, 200, 202
Jauregui, B., 126, 130, 135, 160, 162, 170

K

Kammersgaard, T., 25, 168
Karpiak, K., 149, 150, 203
Klockars, C. B., 126, 146
Kraska, P., 16, 96, 104, 170, 219

L

Law and order, 17, 18, 99, 127, 129, 155–160, 166, 168–171, 173, 183, 209
Legitimacy, 31, 35, 97, 101, 113
Lipsky, M., 30, 135, 147, 221
Loader, I., 160, 163, 166–168, 197, 202
Loftus, B., 8, 11, 25, 30, 33, 50, 67, 69, 91, 125, 133, 145, 157, 160, 166, 167, 170, 172, 202
Lohne, K., 113, 165, 195
Loss, 2, 12, 15, 17, 195, 206, 207, 209, 210, 212, 218, 219, 221
Lyon, D., 64, 66, 100, 101, 131, 133

M

Management, 4, 5, 8, 9, 15, 28, 62, 63, 71, 73, 76, 77, 79, 83–88, 110, 111, 115–117, 163–165, 167, 171, 175, 176, 182, 195–197, 201, 204
Manning, P., 11, 33, 66, 69, 70, 80, 85, 86, 113, 114, 125, 194, 196, 206
Marx, G., 8, 64, 66, 133
Marx, K., 130
Mathiesen, T., 64, 101, 103, 133
McCulloch, J., 16, 96, 104, 120
Melancholy, 206
Method/methodology, 3–10, 18, 66, 67, 170
Migration, 32, 65, 103, 132, 133, 156, 157, 160, 161, 168, 171–177, 179, 181, 183
Militarization, 16, 18, 96, 103–104, 112, 113, 119, 120, 219
Misconduct, 135, 136, 145, 146, 203, 209, 220
Mobile, 63
Mobility, 32, 128, 148, 218
    itinerant, 65
Monahan, T., 66, 133
Muir, 44, 135, 143, 146, 221
Mutsaers, P., 11, 130, 135
Mythen, G., 99

N

Nadelmann, E., 14, 32, 103
Neoliberal, 167, 196
Newburn, T., 4, 9, 10, 33, 64, 163, 165, 197, 198
New public management, 167, 197
Nostalgia, 13, 17
    wistful, 13, 17, 198, 200, 204, 205

O

Ordinary and banal, 34, 63, 67, 71, 88, 89, 101, 104, 109, 114, 136, 141, 203, 212
Overtime/overworked, 27, 89, 116, 117, 175

P

Panoptic, 64, 71, 100, 102, 132, 147
Paperwork, 33, 126, 131
Partnerships, 5, 16, 62, 65, 68, 69, 72, 77, 90, 139, 144, 209, 219
Peacemaking, 172
Performance, 2, 12, 162, 172, 195, 201, 205
Pickering, S., 99, 103–105
Pickpocketing, 7, 36, 47, 62, 79, 88, 89, 164, 174
Pleasure, 35, 36, 40, 48
Plural policing, 197, 204
Police nose/gut, 77–81, 208
Police occupational culture, 11, 12, 17, 30, 31, 33, 68, 72, 80, 97, 115, 119, 147, 160, 168, 201, 202, 206, 208
Policing at a distance, 16, 17, 127–130, 133–136, 143, 144, 147–149, 199, 208, 210, 220
Policing risk, 69, 71, 104, 110, 169, 177, 183, 197
Politics, 18, 31, 32, 53, 99, 100, 103, 111, 203, 209
Power, 6, 15, 16, 30, 39, 81, 91, 100, 102, 120, 126, 127, 148, 163, 197, 198, 205, 207, 208
Prejudice, 25, 30, 31, 33, 43, 55, 77, 101, 120
Professionalism, 11, 13, 27, 34, 39, 47, 51, 53, 62, 68, 77, 81, 91, 98, 110, 115, 116, 126, 143–145, 159, 160, 169, 175, 177, 181, 184, 198, 208, 209, 212, 219, 221
Punch, M., 4, 9, 80

Punishment, 17, 37–39, 125–127, 129, 139, 149, 150, 156–159, 166, 169, 176, 182–184, 208, 209, 212

R

Racism, 25, 29, 30, 32, 33, 167, 203
Ratcliffe, J., 62, 69, 220
Real police work, 14, 33, 34, 39, 63, 80, 86, 104, 125, 126, 162–165, 172–174, 177, 184, 194, 200, 209–211, 219
Reform, 115, 159, 163, 166, 167, 169, 196, 202, 204
Reiner, R., 4, 9, 10, 157, 166, 168, 195–197, 203
Resignations, 12
Reuss-Ianni, E., 163, 201–203
Risk society, 169, 197

S

Satisfaction, 10–14, 33–52, 54, 71, 90–91, 98, 119, 126, 145, 184, 206, 208, 221
Schengen, 172
Schuilenburg, M., 67, 133, 183
Sheptycki, J., 3, 8, 13, 14, 26, 32, 52, 62, 66, 68–70, 83, 97, 100, 102, 104, 119, 128, 134, 166, 168, 196, 197, 210
Simmel, G., 130
Skepticism, 4, 10–12, 25, 55, 68, 75, 81, 130, 148, 163, 169, 201, 207
Skogan, W. G., 50

Skolnick, J. H., 35
Smith, G., 65, 67, 81, 90, 148
Smith, P. S., 166
Social contract, 198, 210
Sociology, 16, 34, 128, 130, 131, 205
Stakeouts, 5, 8, 78, 133, 136, 138
Street justice, 126
Street-level bureaucracy, 135, 147, 221
Stress, 87, 117, 175, 181
Surveillance, 5, 8, 16, 18, 40, 49, 61–69, 71, 72, 78, 79, 81, 83, 84, 86, 88–91, 100, 101, 108, 127–129, 131–137, 141, 144, 145, 147, 148, 150, 156, 157, 160, 179, 181, 185, 199, 208
Suspicion, 68, 72, 76, 80, 81, 106, 164, 199
Symbolism, 33, 36, 99, 100, 113, 114, 118, 119, 135, 163, 165, 166, 202, 211

Technology, 5, 8, 16, 40, 61, 65, 66, 69, 71, 72, 77, 78, 80–87, 90, 96, 101, 127–129, 131, 132, 136, 137, 141, 144, 148, 150, 157, 196, 199, 209, 212, 219, 220, 222
Terror, 16, 32, 118–120, 133, 157, 168, 174, 176, 181, 182, 209
Tham, H., 32, 155, 166
Tough on crime, 156–159, 165, 168, 170, 175, 176, 183, 184
Transformation thesis, 17, 197, 198, 200
Transnational crime, 101, 168, 211

Transnational policing, 3, 12, 14, 158, 166, 195
Transparency, 16, 102, 210
Trust in the police, 166, 168

Union/police union, 116, 176
UNODC, 3, 7, 13, 157

Van Maanen, J., 10, 34, 46, 51, 97, 146, 206
Vigh, H., 3, 13, 150, 221
Violence, 16, 18, 127, 128, 130–132, 136, 146, 167, 210, 211, 220

Waddington, P. A., 12, 30, 51, 195, 202
Weber, L., 26, 27, 32, 65
Weber, M., 130, 135, 160
Westmarland, L., 11, 114, 136, 160, 201
Wiretaps, 8, 26, 35, 38, 48–51, 54, 89, 108, 129, 136, 137, 142–144, 210

Xenophobia, 32

Zedner, L., 183

GPSR Compliance

The European Union's (EU) General Product Safety Regulation (GPSR) is a set of rules that requires consumer products to be safe and our obligations to ensure this.

If you have any concerns about our products, you can contact us on

ProductSafety@springernature.com

In case Publisher is established outside the EU, the EU authorized representative is:

Springer Nature Customer Service Center GmbH
Europaplatz 3
69115 Heidelberg, Germany

www.ingramcontent.com/pod-product-compliance
Lightning Source LLC
LaVergne TN
LVHW021336080526
838202LV00004B/190